Anne T. Ritchie

The Story of Elizabeth

Two hours, and From an island

Anne T. Ritchie

The Story of Elizabeth
Two hours, and From an island

ISBN/EAN: 9783337850098

Printed in Europe, USA, Canada, Australia, Japan

Cover: Foto ©Andreas Hilbeck / pixelio.de

More available books at **www.hansebooks.com**

THE
STORY OF ELIZABETH,

TWO HOURS,

AND

FROM AN ISLAND

BY

MISS THACKERAY

LONDON
SMITH, ELDER, & CO., 15 WATERLOO PLACE
1890

To

JULIA MARGARET CAMERON

CONTENTS.

	PAGE
THE STORY OF ELIZABETH .	1
TWO HOURS	197
FROM AN ISLAND	252

THE
STORY OF ELIZABETH.

CHAPTER I.

> If singing breath, or echoing chord,
> To every hidden pang were given,
> What endless melodies were poured
> As sad as earth, as sweet as heaven!

THIS is the story of a foolish woman, who, through her own folly, learnt wisdom at last; whose troubles—they were not very great, they might have made the happiness of some less eager spirit—were more than she knew how to bear. The lesson of life was a hard lesson to her. She would not learn, she revolted against the wholesome doctrine. And while she was crying out that she would not learn, and turning away and railing and complaining against her fate; days, hours, fate, went on their course. And they passed unmoved; and it was she who gave way, she who was altered, she who was touched and torn by her own complaints and regrets.

Elizabeth had great soft eyes and pretty yellow hair, and a sweet flitting smile, which came out like sunlight over her face, and lit up yours and mine, and any other it might chance to fall upon. She used to smile at herself in the glass, as many a girl has done before her; she used to dance about the room, and think, 'Come life, come life, mine is going to be a happy one. Here I am awaiting, and I was made handsome to be admired, and to be loved, and to be hated by a few, and worshipped by a few, and envied by all. I am handsomer than Lætitia a thousand times. I am glad I have no money as she has, and that I shall be loved for myself, for my *beaux yeux*. One person turns pale when they look at him. Tra la la, tra la la!' and she danced along the room singing. There was no carpet, only a smooth polished floor. Three tall windows looked out into a busy Paris street paved with stones, over which carriages, and cabs, and hand-trucks were jolting. There was a clock, and artificial flowers in china vases on the chimney, a red velvet sofa, a sort of *étagère* with ornaments, and a great double-door wide open, through which you could see a dining-room, also bare, polished, with a round table and an oilcloth cover, and a white china stove, and some wax-work fruit on the sideboard, and a maid in a white cap at work in the window.

Presently there came a ring at the bell. Elizabeth stopped short in her dance, and the maid rose, put down her work, and went to open the door; and then a voice, which made Elizabeth smile and look handsomer than ever, asked if Mrs. and Miss Gilmour were at home?

Elizabeth stood listening, with her fair head a little bent, while the maid said, '*No, sare*,' and then Miss Gilmour flushed up quite angrily in the inner room, and would have run out. She hesitated only for a minute, and then it was too late; the door was shut, and Clementine sat down again to her work.

'Clementine, how dare you say I was not at home?' cried Elizabeth, suddenly standing before her.

'Madame desired me to let no one in in her absence,' said Clementine, primly. 'I only obeyed my orders. There is the gentleman's card.'

'Sir John Dampier' was on the card, and then, in pencil, 'I hope you will be at home in Chester Street next week. Can I be your *avant-courier* in any way's I cross to-night.'

Elizabeth smiled again, shrugged her shoulders, and said to herself, 'Next week; I can afford to wait better than he can, perhaps. Poor man! After all, *il y en a bien d'autres*;' and she went to the window, and, by leaning out, she just caught a glimpse of the Madeleine and of Sir John Dampier walking away; and then presently she saw her mother on the opposite side of the street, passing the stall of the old apple-woman, turning in under the archway of the house.

Elizabeth's mother was like her daughter, only she had black eyes and black hair, and where her daughter was wayward and yielding, the elder woman was wayward and determined. They did not care much for one another, these two. They had not lived together all their lives, or learnt to love one another, as a matter of course; they were too much alike, too much of an age: Elizabeth was eighteen, and her mother thirty-six. If Elizabeth looked twenty, the mother looked thirty, and she was as vain, as foolish, as fond of admiration as her daughter. Mrs. Gilmour did not own it to herself, but she had been used to it all her life—to be first, to be made much of; and here was a little girl who had sprung up somehow, and learnt of herself to be charming—more charming than she had ever been in her best days; and now that they had slid away, those best days, the elder woman had a dull, unconscious discontent in her heart. People whom she had known, and who had admired her but a year or two ago, seemed to neglect her now and to pass her by, in order to pay a certain homage to her daughter's youth and brilliance: John Dampier, among others, whom she had known as a boy, when she was a young woman. Good mothers, tender-hearted women, brighten again and grow young over their children's happiness and success. Caroline Gilmour suddenly became old, somehow, when she first witnessed her daughter's triumphs, and she felt that the wrinkles were growing under her wistful eyes, and that the colour was fading from her cheeks, and she gasped a little sigh and thought, 'Ah! how I suffer! What is it? what can have come to me?' As time passed on, the widow's brows grew darker, her lips set ominously. One day she suddenly declared that she was weary of London and London ways, and that she should go abroad; and Elizabeth, who liked everything that was change, that was more life and more experience—she had not taken into account that there was any other than the experience of pleasure in store for her—Elizabeth clapped her hands and cried, 'Yes, yes, mamma; I am *quite* tired of London and all this excitement. Let us go to Paris for the winter, and lead a quiet life.'

'Paris is just the place to go to for quiet,' said Mrs Gilmour, who was smoothing her shining locks in the glass, and looking intently into her own dark gloomful eyes.

'The Dampiers are going to Paris,' Elizabeth went on; 'Lady Dampier and Sir John, and old Miss Dampier and Lætitia. He was saying how he wished you would go. We could have such fun! *Do* go, dear, pretty mamma!'

As Elizabeth spoke, Mrs. Gilmour's dark eyes brightened, and suddenly her hard face melted; and, still looking at herself in the glass, she said, 'We will go if you wish it, Elly. I thought you had had enough of balls.'

But the end of the Paris winter came, and even then Elly had not had enough: not enough admiration, not enough happiness, not enough new dresses, not enough of herself, not enough time to suffice her eager, longing desires, not enough delights to fill up the swift flying days. I cannot tell you—she could not have told you herself—what she wanted, what perfection of happiness, what wonderful thing. She danced, she wore beautiful dresses, she flirted, she chattered nonsense and sentiment, she listened to music; her pretty little head was in a whirl. John Dampier followed her from place to place; and so, indeed, did one or two others. Though she was in love with them all, I believe she would have married this Dampier if he had asked her, but he never did. He saw that she did not really care for him; opportunity did not befriend him. His mother was against it; and then, her mother was there, looking at him with her dark reproachful eyes—those eyes which had once fascinated and then repelled him, and that he mistrusted so and almost hated now. And this is the secret of my story; but for this it would never have been written. He hated, and she did not hate, poor woman! It would have been better, a thousand times, for herself and for her daughter, had she done so. Ah me! what cruel perversion was it, that the best of all good gifts should have turned to trouble, to jealousy and wicked rancour; that this sacred power of faithful devotion, by which she might have saved herself and ennobled a mean and earthly spirit, should have turned to a curse instead of a blessing!

There was a placid, pretty niece of Lady Dampier, called Lætitia, who had been long destined for Sir John. Lætitia and Elizabeth had been at school together for a good many dreary years, and were very old friends. Elizabeth all her life used to triumph over her friend, and to bewilder her with her careless, gleeful ways, and yet win her over to her own side, for she was irresistible, and she knew it. Perhaps it was because she knew it so well that she was so confident and so charming. Lætitia, although she was sincerely fond of her cousin, used to wonder that her aunt could be against such a wife for her son.

'She is a sort of princess,' the girl used to say; 'and John *ought* to have a beautiful wife for the credit of the family.'

'Your fifty thousand pounds would go a great deal further to promote the credit of the family my dear,' said old Miss Dampier, who was a fat, plain-spoken, kindly old lady. 'I like the girl, though my sister-in-law does not; and I hope that some day she will find a very good husband. I confess that I had rather it were not John.'

And so one day John was informed by his mother, who was getting alarmed, that she was going home, and that she could not think of crossing without him. And Dampier, who was careful, as men are mostly, and wanted to think about his decision, and who was anxious to do the very best for himself in every respect—as is the way with just, and good, and respectable gentlemen—was not at all loth to obey her summons.

Here was Lætitia, who was very fond of him—there was no doubt of that—with a house in the country and money at her bankers'; there was a wayward, charming, beautiful girl, who didn't care for him very much, who had little or no money, but whom he certainly cared for. He talked it all over dispassionately with his aunt—so dispassionately that the old woman got angry.

'You are a model young man, John. It quite affects me, and makes me forget my years to see the admirable way in which you young people conduct yourselves. You have got such well-regulated hearts, it's quite a marvel. You are quite right; Tishy has got 50,000*l*., which will all go into your pocket, and respectable connections, who will come to your wedding, and Elly Gilmour has not a penny except what her mother will leave her—a mother with a bad temper, and who is sure to marry again; and though the girl is the prettiest young creature I ever set eyes on, and though you care for her as you never cared for any other woman before, men don't marry wives for such absurd reasons as that. You are quite right to have nothing to do with her; and I respect you for your noble self-denial.' And the old lady began to knit away at a great long red comforter she had always on hand for her other nephew the clergyman.

'But, my dear aunt Jean, what is it you want me to do?' cried John.

'Drop one, knit two together,' said the old lady, cliquetting her needles.

She really wanted John to marry his cousin, but she was a spinster still and sentimental; and she could not help being sorry for pretty Elizabeth; and now she was afraid that she had said too much, for her nephew frowned, put his hands in his pockets, and walked out of the room.

He walked downstairs, and out of the door into the Rue Royale, the street where they were lodging; then he strolled across the Place de la Concorde, and in at the gates of the Tuileries, where the soldiers were pacing, and so along the broad path, to where he heard a sound of music, and saw a glitter of people. Tum te tum, bom, bom, bom, went the military music; twittering busy little birds were chirping up in the branches; buds were bursting; colours glimmering; tinted sunshine flooding the garden, and the music, and the people; old gentlemen were reading newspapers on the benches; children were playing at hide-and-seek behind the statues; nurses gossiping, and nodding their white caps, and dandling their white babies; and there on chairs, listening to the music, the mammas were sitting in grand bonnets and parasols, working, and gossiping too, and ladies and gentlemen went walking up and down before them. All the windows of the Tuileries were ablaze with the sun; the terraces were beginning to gleam with crocuses and spring flowers.

As John Dampier was walking along, scarcely noting all this, he heard his name softly called, and turning round he saw two ladies sitting under a budding horse-chestnut tree. One of them he thought looked like a fresh spring flower herself smiling pleasantly, all dressed in crisp light grey, with a white bonnet, and a quantity of bright yellow crocus hair. She held out a little grey hand and said,

'Won't you come and talk to us? Mamma and I are tired of listening to music. We want to hear somebody talk.'

And then mamma, who was Mrs Gilmour, held out a straw-coloured hand, and said, 'Do you think sensible people have nothing better to do than to listen to your chatter, Elly? Here is your particular friend, M. de Vaux, coming to us. You can talk to him.'

Elizabeth looked up quickly at her mother, then glanced at Dampier, then greeted M. de Vaux as pleasantly almost as she had greeted him.

'I am afraid I cannot stay now,' said Sir John to Elizabeth. I have several things to do. Do you know that we are going away immediately?'

Mrs. Gilmour's black eyes seemed to flash into his face as he spoke. He felt them, though he was looking at Elizabeth, and he could not help turning away with an impatient movement of dislike.

'Going away! Oh, how sorry I am!' said Elly. 'But, mamma, I forgot—you said we were going home, too, in a few days; so I don't mind so much. You will come and say good-by, won't you?' Elizabeth went on, while M. de Vaux, who had been waiting to be spoken to, turned away rather provoked, and made some remark to Mrs. Gilmour. And then Elizabeth seeing her opportunity, and looking up frank, fair, and smiling, said quickly, 'To-morrow at *three*, mind—and give my love to Lætitia,' she went on, much more deliberately, ' and my best love to Miss Dampier! and oh, dear! why does one ever have to say good-by to one's friends? Are you sure you are all really going?'

'Alas!' said Dampier, looking down at the kind young face with strange emotion and tenderness, and holding out his hand. He had not meant it as good-by yet, but so Elly and her mother understood it.

'Good-by, Sir John; we shall meet again in London,' said Mrs. Gilmour.

'Good-by,' said Elly, wistfully raising her sweet eyes.

As he walked away, he carried with him a bright picture of the woman he loved, looking at him kindly, happy, surrounded with sunshine and budding green leaves, smiling and holding out her hand; and so he saw her in his dreams sometimes; and so she would appear to him now and then in the course of his life; so he sometimes sees her now, in spring-time, generally when the trees are coming out, and some little chirp of a sparrow or some little glistening green bud conjures up all these old bygone days again.

Mrs. Gilmour did not sleep very sound all that night. While Elizabeth lay dreaming in her dark room, her mother, with wild-falling black hair, and wrapped in a long red dressing-gown, was wandering restlessly up and down, or flinging herself on the bed or the sofa, and trying at her bedside desperately to sleep, or falling on her knees with clasped outstretched hands. Was she asking for her own happiness at the expense of poor Elly's? I don't like to think so—it seems so cruel, so wicked, so unnatural. But remember, here was a passionate selfish woman, who for long years had had one dream, one idea; who knew that she loved this man twenty times—twenty years— more than did Elizabeth, who was but a child when this mad fancy began.

'She does not care for him a bit,' the poor wretch said to herself over and over again. 'He likes her, and he would marry her, if—if I chose to give him the chance. She will be as happy with anybody else. I could not bear this—it would kill me. I never suffered such horrible torture in all my life. He hates me. It is hopeless; and I—I do not know whether I hate him or I love him most. How dare she tell him to come to-morrow, when she knew I would be out. She shall not see him. We will neither of us see him again; never—oh! never. But I shall suffer, and she will forget. Oh! if I could forget!' And then she would fall down on her knees again; and because she prayed, she blinded herself to her own wrong-doings, and thought that heaven was on her side.

And so the night went on. John Dampier was haunted with strange dreams, and saw Caroline Gilmour more than once coming and going in a red gown and talking to him, though he could not understand what she was saying; sometimes she was in his house at Guildford; sometimes in Paris; sometimes sitting with Elly up in a chestnut-tree, and chattering like a monkey; sometimes gliding down interminable rooms and opening door after door. He disliked her worse than ever when he woke in the morning. Is this strange? It would have seemed to me stranger had it not been so. We are not blocks of wax and putty with glass eyes, like the people at Madame Tussaud's; we have souls, and we feel and we guess at more than we see round about us, and we influence one another for good or for evil from the moment we come into the world. Let us be humbly thankful if the day comes for us to leave it before we have done any great harm to those who live their lives alongside with ours. And so the next morning Caroline asked her daughter if she would come with her to M. le Pasteur Tourneur's at two. 'I am sure you would be the better for listening to a good man's exhortation,' said Mrs. Gilmour.

'I don't want to go, mamma. I hate exhortations,' said Elizabeth, pettishly; 'and you know how ill it made me last Tuesday. How can you like it—such dreary, sleepy talk? It gave me the most dreadful headache.'

'Poor child,' said Mrs. Gilmour, 'perhaps the day may come when you will find out that a headache is not the most terrible calamity. But you understand that if you do not choose to come with me, you must stay at home. I will not have you going about by yourself, or with any chance friends—it is not respectable.'

Elly shrugged her shoulders, but resigned herself with wonderful good grace. Mrs. Gilmour prepared herself for her expedition: she put on a black silk gown, a plain bonnet, a black cloak. I cannot exactly tell you what change came over her. It was not the lady of the Tuileries the day before; it was not the woman in the red dressing-gown. It was a respectable, quiet personage enough, who went off primly with her prayer-book in her hand, and who desired Clementine on no account to let anybody in until her return.

'Miss Elizabeth is so little to be trusted,' so she explained quite unnecessarily to the maid, 'that I cannot allow her to receive visits when I am from home.'

And Clementine, who was a stiff, ill-humoured woman, pinched her lips and said, 'Bien, madame.

And so when Elizabeth's best chance for happiness came to the door, Clementine closed it again with great alacrity, and shut out the good fortune, and sent it away. I am sure that if Dampier had come in that day and seen Elly once more, he could not have helped speaking to her and making her and making himself happy in so doing. I am sure that Elly, with all her vanities and faults, would have made him a good wife, and brightened his dismal old house; but I am not sure that happiness is the best portion after all, and that there is not something better to be found in life than mere worldly prosperity.

Dampier walked away, almost relieved, and yet disappointed too. 'Well, they will be back in town in ten days,' he thought, 'and we will see then. But why the deuce did the girl tell me three o'clock, and then not be at home to see me?' And as ill-luck would have it, at this moment, up came Mrs. Gilmour. 'I have just been to see you, to say good-by,' said Dampier. 'I was very sorry to miss you and your daughter.'

'I have been attending a meeting at the house of my friend the Pasteur Tourneur,' said Mrs. Gilmour; 'but Elizabeth was at home—would not she see you?' She blushed up very red as she spoke, and so did John Dampier; her face glowed with shame, and his with vexation.

'No; she would not see me,' cried he. 'Good-by, Mrs. Gilmour.'

'Good-by,' she said, and looked up with her black eyes;

but ne was staring vacantly beyond her, busy with his own reflections, and then she felt it was good-by for ever.

He turned down a wide street, and she crossed mechanically and came along the other side of the road, as I have said; past the stall of the old apple-woman; advancing demurely, turning in under the archway of the house.

She had no time for remorse. 'He does not care for me,' was all she could think; 'he scorns me——he has behaved as no gentleman would behave.' (Poor John!— in justice to him I must say that this was quite an assumption on her part.) And at the same time John Dampier, at the other end of the street, was walking away in a huff, and saying to himself that 'Elly is a little heartless flirt; she cares for no one but herself. I will have no more to do with her. Lætitia would not have served me so.'

Elly met her mother at the door. 'Mamma, how *could* you be so horrid and disagreeable?—*why* did you tell Clementine to let no one in?' She shook back her curly locks, and stamped her little foot, as she spoke, in her childish anger.

'You should not give people appointments when I am out of the way,' said Mrs. Gilmour, primly. 'Why did you not come with me? Dear M. Tourneur's exposition was quite beautiful.'

'I hate Monsieur Tourneur!' cried Elizabeth; 'and I should not do such things if you were kind, mamma, and liked me to amuse myself and to be happy; but you sit there, prim and frowning, and thinking everything wrong that is harmless; and you spoil all my pleasure; and it is a shame—and a shame—and you will make me hate you too;' and she ran into her own room, banged the door, and locked it.

I suppose it was by way of compensation to Elly that Mrs. Gilmour sat down and wrote a little note, asking Monsieur de Vaux to tea that evening to meet M le Pasteur Tourneur and his son.

Elizabeth sat sulking in her room all the afternoon, the door shut; the hum of a busy city came in at her open window; then the glass panes blazed with light, and she remembered how the windows of the Tuileries had shone at that time the day before, and she thought how kind and how handsome Dampier looked, as he came walking along, and how he was worth ten Messieurs de Vaux and twenty foolish boys like Anthony Tourneur. The dusky shadows came creeping round the room, dimming a pretty picture.

It was a commonplace little *tableau de genre* enough— that of a girl sitting at a window, with clasped hands, dreaming dreams more or less silly, with the light falling on her hair, and on the folds of her dress, and on the blazing petals of the flowers on the balcony outside, and then overhead a quivering green summer sky. But it is a little picture that nature is never tired of reproducing; and,

C

besides nature, every year, in the Royal Academy, I see half-a-dozen such representations.

In a quiet unconscious sort of way, Elly made up her mind, this summer afternoon—made up her mind, knowing not that perhaps it was too late, that the future she was accepting, half glad, half reluctant, was, maybe, already hers no more, to take or to leave. Only a little stream, apparently easy to cross, lay, as yet, between her and the figure she seemed to see advancing towards her. She did not know that every day this little stream would widen and widen, until in time it would be a great ocean lying between them. Ah! take care, my poor Elizabeth, that you don't tumble into the waters, and go sinking down, down, down, while the waves close over your curly yellow locks.

'Will you come to dinner, mademoiselle?' said Clementine, rapping at the door with the finger of fate which had shut out Sir John Dampier only a few hours ago

'Go away!' cries Elizabeth.

'Elizabeth! dinner is ready,' says her mother, from outside, with unusual gentleness.

'I don't want any dinner,' says Elly; and then feels very sorry and very hungry the minute she has spoken. The door was locked, but she had forgotten the window, and Mrs. Gilmour, in a minute, came along the balcony, with her silk dress rustling against the iron bars.

'You silly girl! come and eat,' said her mother, still

strangely kind and forbearing. 'The Vicomte de Vaux is coming to tea, and Monsieur Tourneur and Anthony; you must come and have your dinner, and then let Clementine dress you; you will catch cold if you sit here any longer;' and she took the girl's hand gently and led her away.

For the first time in her life, Elizabeth almost felt as if she really loved her mother; and, touched by her kindness, and with a sudden impulse, and melting, and blushing, and all ashamed of herself, she said, almost before she knew what she had spoken, 'Mamma, I am very silly, and I've behaved very badly, but I did so want to see him again.'

Mrs. Gilmour just dropped the girl's hand. 'Nonsense, Elizabeth; your head is full of silly school-girl notions. I wish I had had you brought up at home instead of at Mrs. Straightboard's.'

'I wish you had, mamma,' said Elly, speaking coldly and quietly; 'Lætitia and I were both very miserable there.' And then she sat down at the round table to break bread with her mother, hurt, wounded, and angry. Her face looked hard and stern, like Mrs. Gilmour's; her bread choked her; she drank a glass of water, and it tasted bitter, somehow. Was Caroline more happy? did she eat with better appetite? She ate more, she looked much as usual, she talked a good deal. Clementine was secretly thinking what a good-for-nothing, ill-tempered girl mademoiselle was; what a good woman, what a good mother was madame. Clementine revenged some of madame's wrongs upon Elizabeth, by pulling her hair after dinner, as she was plaiting and pinning it up. Elly lost her temper, and violently pushed Clementine away, and gave her warning to leave.

Clementine, furious, and knowing that some of the company had already arrived, rushed into the drawing-room with her wrongs. 'Mademoiselle m'a poussée, madame; mademoiselle m'a dit des injures; mademoiselle m'a congédiée——' But in the middle of her harangue, the door flew open, and Elizabeth, looking like an empress, bright cheeks flushed, eyes sparkling, hair crisply curling, and all dressed in shining pink silk, stood before them.

CHAPTER II.

*But for his funeral train which the bridegroom sees in the distance,
Would he so joyfully, think you, fall in with the marriage procession?
But for that final discharge, would he dare to enlist in that service?
But for that certain release, ever sign to that perilous contract?*

I DON'T think they had ever seen anybody like her before, those two MM. Tourneurs, who had just arrived; they both rose, a little man and a tall one, father and son; and besides these gentlemen, there was an old lady in a poke bonnet sitting there too, who opened her shrewd eyes and held out her hand. Clementine was crushed, eclipsed, forgotten. Elizabeth advanced, tall, slim, stately, with wide-spread petticoats; but she began to blush very much when she saw Miss Dampier. For a few minutes there was a little confusion of greeting, and voices, and chairs moved about, and then—

'I came to say good-by to you,' said the old lady, 'in case we should not meet again. I am going to Scotland in a month or two—perhaps I may be gone by the time you get back to town.'

'Oh, no, no! I hope not,' said Elizabeth. She was very much excited, the tears almost came into her eyes.

'We shall most likely follow you in a week or ten days,' said Mrs. Gilmour, with a sort of laugh; 'there is no necessity for any sentimental leave-taking.'

'Does that woman mean what she says?' thought the old lady, looking at her; and then turning to Elizabeth again she continued: 'There is no knowing what may happen to any one of us, my dear. There is no harm in saying good-by, is there? Have you any message for Lætitia or Catherine?'

'Give Lætitia my very best love,' said Elly, grateful for the old lady's kindness; 'and—and I was very, very sorry that I could not see Sir John when he came to-day so good-naturedly.'

'He must come and see you in London,' said Miss Dampier, very kindly still. (She was thinking, 'She does care for him, poor child.')

'Oh, yes! in London,' repeated Mrs. Gilmour; so that Elly looked quite pleased, and Miss Dampier again said to herself, 'She is decidedly not coming to London. What can she mean? Can there be anything with that Frenchman, De Vaux? Impossible!' And then she got up, and said aloud, 'Well good-by. I have all my old gowns to pack up, and my knitting, Elly. Write to me, child, sometimes!'

'Oh, yes, yes!' cried Elizabeth, flinging her arms round the old lady's neck, kissing her, and whispering, 'Good-by, dear, dear Miss Dampier.'

At the door of the apartment, Clementine was waiting, hoping for a possible five-franc piece. 'Bon soir, madame,' said she.

'Oh, indeed,' said Miss Dampier, staring at her, and she passed out with a sort of sniff, and then she walked home quietly through the dark back-streets, only, as she went along, she said to herself every now and then, she hardly knew why, 'Poor Elly—poor child!'

Meanwhile, M. Tourneur was taking Elizabeth gently to task. Elizabeth was pouting her red lips and sulking, and looking at him defiantly from under her drooped eyelids; and all the time Anthony Tourneur sat admiring her, with his eyes wide open, and his great mouth open too. He was a big young man, with immense hands and feet, without any manners to speak of, and with thick hair growing violently upon end. There was a certain distinction about his father which he had not inherited. Young Frenchmen of this class are often singularly rough and unpolished in their early youth; they tone down with time however, as they see more of men and of women. Anthony had never known much of either till now; for his young companions at the Protestant college were rough cubs like himself; and as for women, his mother was dead (she had been an Englishwoman, and died when he was ten years old), and old Françoise, the *cuisinière*, at home, was almost the only woman he knew. His father was more used to the world and its ways: he fancied he scorned them all, and yet the pomps and vanities and the pride of life had a horrible attraction for this quiet pasteur. He was humble and ambitious: he was tender-hearted, and hard-headed, and narrow-minded. Though stern to himself, he was weak to others, and yet feebly resolute when he met with opposition. He was not a great man; his qualities neutralized one another, but he had a great reputation. The Oratoire was crowded on the days when he was expected to preach, his classes were thronged, his pamphlets went through three or four editions. Popularity delighted him. His manner had a great charm, his voice was sweet, his words well chosen; his head was a fine melancholy head, his dark eyes flashed when he was excited. Women especially admired and respected Stephén Tourneur.

Mrs. Gilmour was like another person when she was in his presence. Look at her to-night, with her smooth black hair, and her grey silk gown, and her white hands busied pouring out his tea. See how she is appealing to him, deferentially listening to his talk. I cannot write his talk down here. Certain allusions can have no place in a little story like this one, and yet they were allusions so frequently in his thoughts and in his mouth that it was almost unconsciously that he used them. He and his brethren like him have learned to look at this life from a loftier point of view than Elly Gilmour and worldlings like her, who feel that to-day they are in the world and of it, not of their own will, indeed—though they are glad that they are here—but waiting a further dispensation. Tourneur, and those like him, look at this life only in comparison with the next, as though they had already passed beyond, and had but little concern with the things of to-day. They speak chiefly of sacred subjects; they have put aside our common talk, and thought, and career. They have put them away, and yet they are men and women after all. And Stephen Tourneur, among the rest, was a soft-hearted man. To-night, as indeed often before, he was full of sympathy for the poor mother who had so often spoken of her grief and care for her daughter, of her loneliness. He understood her need; her want of an adviser, of a friend whom she could reverence and defer to. How meekly she listened to his words, with what kindling interest she heard him speak of what was in his heart always, with what gentleness she attended to his wants. How womanly she was, how much more pleasant than any of the English, Scotch, Irish old maids who were in the habit of coming to consult him in their various needs and troubles. He had never known her so tender, so gentle, as to-night. Even Elly, sulking, and beating the tattoo with her satin shoes, thought that her mother's manner was very strange. How could any one of the people sitting round that little tea-table guess at the passion of hopelessness, of rage, of despair, of envy, that was gnawing at the elder woman's heart? at the mad, desperate determination she was making? And yet every now and then she said odd, imploring things—she seemed to be crying wildly for sympathy—she spoke of other people's troubles with a startling earnestness.

De Vaux, who arrived about nine o'clock, and asked for a *soupçon de thé*, and put in six lumps of sugar, and so managed to swallow the mixture, went away at ten, without one idea of the tragedy with which he had been spending his evening—a tragical farce, a comedy—I know not what to call it.

Elly was full of her own fancies; Monsieur Tourneur was making up his mind; Anthony's whole head was rustling with pink silk, or dizzy with those downcast, bright, bewildering blue eyes of Elly's, and he sat stupidly counting the little bows on her skirt, or watching the glitter of the rings on her finger, and wishing that she would not look so cross when he spoke to her. She had brightened up considerably while De Vaux was there; but now, in truth, her mind was travelling away, and she was picturing to herself the Dampiers at their tea-table—Tishy, pale and listless, over her feeble cups; Lady Dampier, with her fair hair and her hook nose, lying on the sofa; and John in the arm-chair by the fire, cutting dry jokes at his aunt. Elly's spirits had travelled away like a ghost, and it was only her body that was left sitting in the little gaudy drawing-room; and, though she did not know it, there was another ghost flitting alongside with hers. Strangely enough, the people of whom she was thinking were assembled together very much as she imagined them to be. Did they guess at the two pale phantoms that were hovering about them? Somehow or other, Miss Dampier, over her knitting, was still muttering, 'Poor child!' to the click of her needles; and John Dampier was haunted by the woman in red, and by a certain look in Elly's eyes, which he had seen yesterday when he found her under the tree.

Meanwhile, at the other side of Paris, the other little company was assembled round the fire; and Mrs. Gilmour, with her two hands folded tightly together, was looking at M. Tourneur with her great soft eyes, and saying, 'The woman was never yet born who could stand alone, who did not look for some earthly counsellor and friend to point out the road to better things—to help her along the narrow thorny way. Wounded, and bruised, and weary, it is hard, hard for us to follow our lonely path.' She spoke with a pathetic passion, so that Elizabeth could not think what had come to her. Mrs. Gilmour was generally quite capable of standing, and going, and coming, without any assistance whatever. In her father's time, Elly could remember that there was not the slightest need for his interference in any of their arrangements. But the mother was evidently in earnest to-night, and the daughter quite bewildered. Later in the evening, after Monsieur de Vaux was gone, Mrs. Gilmour got up from her chair and flung open the window of the balcony. All the stars of heaven shone splendidly over the city. A great, silent, wonderful night had gathered round about them unawares; a great calm had come after the noise and business of the careful day. Caroline Gilmour stepped out with a gasping sigh, and stood looking upwards; they could see her grey figure dimly against the darkness. Monsieur Tourneur remained sitting by the fire, with his eyes cast down and his hands folded. Presently he too rose and walked slowly across the room, and stepped out upon the balcony; and Elizabeth and Anthony remained behind, staring vacantly at one another. Elizabeth was yawning and wondering when they would go.

'You are sleepy, miss,' said young Tourneur, in his French-English.

Elly yawned in a very unmistakable language, and showed all her even white teeth:—'I always get sleepy when I have been cross, Mr. Anthony. I have been cross ever since three o'clock to-day, and now it is long past ten, and time for us all to go to bed: don't you think so?'

'I am waiting for my father,' said the young man. He watches late at night, but we are all sent off at ten.'

'"We!"—you and old Françoise?'

'I and the young Christians who live in our house, and study with my father and read under his direction. There are five, all from the south, who are, like me, preparing to be ministers of the gospel.'

Another great wide yawn from Elly.

'Do you think your father will stop much longer—if so, I shall go to bed. Oh, dear me!' and with a sigh she let her head fall back upon the soft cushioned chair, and then, somehow, her eyes shut very softly, and her hands fell loosely, and a little quiet dream came, something of a garden and peace, and green trees, and Miss Dampier knitting in the sunshine. Click, click, click, she heard the needles, but it was only the clock ticking on the mantel-piece. Anthony was almost afraid to breathe, for fear he should wake her. It seemed to him very strange to be sitting by this smouldering fire, with the stars burning outside, while through the open window the voices of the two people talking on the balcony came to him in a low murmuring sound. And there opposite him Elly, asleep, breathing so softly and looking so wonderfully pretty in her slumbers. Do you not know the peculiar peaceful feeling which comes to anyone sitting alone by a sleeping person? I cannot tell which of the two was for a few minutes the most tranquil and happy.

Elly was still dreaming her quiet, peaceful dreams, still sitting with Miss Dampier in her garden, under a chestnut-tree, with Dampier coming towards them, when suddenly some voice whispered 'Elizabeth' in her ear, and she awoke with a start of chill surprise. It was not Anthony who had called her, it was only fancy; but as she woke he said,—

'Ah! I was just going to wake you.'

What had come to him. He seemed to have awakened too—to have come to himself suddenly. One word which had reached him—he had very big sharp ears—one word distinctly uttered amid the confused murmur on the balcony, brought another word of old Françoise's to his mind. And then in a minute—he could not tell how it was—it was all clear to him. Already he was beginning to learn the ways of the world. Elly saw him blush up, saw his eyes light with intelligence, and his ears grow very red; and then he sat up straight in his chair, and looked at her in a quick, uncertain sort of way.

'You would not allow it,' said he, suddenly, staring at her fixedly with his great flashing eyes. 'I never thought of such a thing till this minute. Who ever would?'

'Thought of what? What are you talking about?' said Elly, startled.

'Ah! that is it.' And then he turned his head impatiently: 'How stupid you must have been. What can have put such a thing into his head and hers. Ah, it is so strange I don't know what to think or to say;' and he sank back in his chair. But, somehow or other, the idea which had occurred to him was not nearly so disagreeable as he would have expected it to be. The notion of some other companionship besides that of the five young men from the south, instead of shocking him, filled him with a vague, delightful excitement. 'Ah! then she would come and live with us in that pink dress,' he thought. And meanwhile Elizabeth turned very pale, and she too began dimly to see what he was thinking of, only she could not be quite sure. 'Is it that I am to marry him?' she thought; 'they cannot be plotting that.'

'What is it, M. Anthony?' said she, very fierce. 'Is it——they do not think that I would ever—ever dream or think of marrying you?' She was quite pale now, and *her* eyes were glowing.

Anthony shook his head again. 'I know that,' said he; 'it is not you or me.'

'What do you dare to imply?' she cried, more and more fiercely. 'You can't mean—you would never endure, never suffer that—that——' The words failed on her lips.

'I should like to have you for a sister, Miss Elizabeth,' said he, looking down; 'it is so *triste* at home.'

Elly half started from her chair, put up her white hands, scarce knowing what she did, and then suddenly cried out, 'Mother! mother!' in a loud, shrill, thrilling voice, which brought Mrs. Gilmour back into the room. And Monsieur Tourneur came too. Not one of them spoke for a minute. Elizabeth's horror-stricken face frightened the pasteur, who felt as if he was in a dream, who had let himself drift along with the feeling of the moment, who did not know even now if he had done right or wrong, if he had been carried away by mere earthly impulse and regard for his own happiness, or if he had been led and directed to a worthy helpmeet, to a Christian companion, to one who had the means and the power to help him in his labours. Ah, surely, surely he had done well, he thought, for himself, and for those who depended on him. It was not without a certain dignity at last, and nobleness of manner, that he took Mrs. Gilmour's hand, and said—

'You called your mother just now, Elizabeth; here she is. Dear woman, she has consented to be my best earthly friend and companion, to share my hard labours; to share a life poor and arduous, and full of care, and despised perhaps by the world; but rich in eternal hope, blessed by prayer, and consecrated by a Christian's faith.' He was a little man, but he seemed to grow tall as he spoke. His eyes kindled, his face lightened with enthusiasm. Elizabeth could not help seeing this, even while she stood shivering with indignation and sick at heart. As for Anthony he got up, and came to his father and took both his hands, and then suddenly flung his arms round his neck. Elizabeth found words at last:

'You can suffer this?' she said to Anthony. 'You have no feelings, then, of decency, of fitness of memory for the dead. You, mamma, can degrade yourself by a second marriage? Oh! for shame, for shame!' and she burst into passionate tears, and flung herself down on a chair. Monsieur Tourneur was not used to be thwarted, to be reproved; he got very pale, he pushed Anthony gently aside, and went up to her. 'Elizabeth,' said he, 'is this the conduct of a devoted daughter; are these the words of good will and of peace, with which your mother should be greeted by her children? I had hoped that you would look upon me as a friend. If you could see my heart, you would know how ready I am; how gladly I would love you as my own child,' and he held out his hand. Elly Gilmour dashed it away.

'Go,' she said; 'you have made me wretched; *I* hate your life and your ways, and your sermons, and we shall all be miserable, every one of us; I know well enough it is for her money you marry her. Oh, go away out of my sight.' Tourneur had felt doubts. Elizabeth's taunts and opposition reassured him and strengthened him in his purpose. This is only human nature, as well as pasteur nature in particular. If everything had gone smoothly, very likely he would have found out a snare of the devil in it, and broken it off, not caring what grief and suffering he caused to himself in so doing. Now that the girl's words brought a flush into his pale face and made him to wince with pain, he felt justified, nay, impelled to go on— to be firm. And now he stood up like a gentleman, and spoke:

'And if I want your mother's money, is it hers, is it mine, was it given to me or to her to spend for our own use? Was it not lent, will not an account be demanded hereafter? Unhappy child! where have you found already such sordid thoughts, such unworthy suspicions? Where is your Christian charity?'

'I never made any pretence of having any,' cried Elizabeth, stamping her foot and tossing her fair mane. 'You talk and talk about it and about the will of heaven, and suit yourselves, and break my heart, and look up quite scandalized, and forgive me for my wickedness. But I had rather be as wicked as I am than as good as you.'

'Allons, taisez-vous, Mademoiselle Elizabeth!' said Anthony, who had taken his part; 'or my father will not marry your mother, and then *you* will be in the wrong, and have made everybody unhappy. It is very, very sad and melancholy in our house; be kind and come and make us happy. If I am not angry, why should you mind? but see here, I will not give my consent unless you do, and I know my father will do nothing against my wishes and yours.'

Poor Elizabeth looked up, and then she saw that her mother was crying too; Caroline had had a hard day's work. No wonder she was fairly harassed and worn out. Elizabeth herself began to be as bewildered, as puzzled, as the rest. She put her hand wearily to her head. She did not feel angry any more, but very tired and sad. 'How can I say I think it right when I think it wrong? It is not me you want to marry, M. Tourneur; mamma is old enough to decide. What need you care for what a silly girl like me says and thinks? Good-night, mamma, I am tired and must go to bed. Good-night, Monsieur Tourneur. Good-night, M. Anthony. Oh, dear!' sighed Elizabeth, as she went out of the room with her head hanging, and with pale cheeks and dim eyes. You could hardly have believed it was the triumphant young beauty of an hour ago. But it had always been so with this impetuous, sensitive Elizabeth; she suffered as she enjoyed, more keenly than anybody else I ever knew; she put her whole heart into her life without any reserve, and then, when failure and disappointment came, she had no more heart left to endure with.

I am sure it was with a humble spirit that Tourneur that night, before he left, implored a benediction on himself and on those who were about to belong to him. He went away at eleven o'clock with Anthony, walking home through the dark, long streets to his house, which was near one of the gates of the city. And Caroline sat till the candles went out, till the fire had smouldered away, till the chill night breezes swept round the room, and then went stupefied to bed, saying to herself, 'Now he will learn that others do not despise me, and I—I will lead a good life.'

CHAPTER III.

> Le temps emporte sur son aile
> Et le printemps et l'hirondelle,
> Et la vie et les jours perdus ;
> Tout s'en va comme la fumée,
> L'espérance et la renommée,
> Et moi qui vous ai tant aimée,
> Et toi qui ne t'en souviens plus!

A LOW, one-storied house standing opposite a hospital, built on a hilly street, with a great white *porte-cochère* closed and barred, and then a garden wall; nine or ten windows only a foot from the ground, all blinded and shuttered in a row; a brass plate on the door, with *Stephen Tourneur* engraved thereon, and grass and chickweed growing between the stones and against the white walls of the house. Passing under the archway, you come into a grass-grown courtyard; through an iron grating you see a little desolate garden with wall-flowers and stocks, and tall yellow weeds all flowering together, and fruit-trees running wild against the wall. On one side there are some empty stables, with chickens pecketting in the sun. The house is built in two long low wings; it has a dreary moated-grange sort of look: and see, standing at one of the upper windows, is not that

Elizabeth looking out? An old woman in a blue gown and a white coif is pumping water at the pump, some miserable canaries are piping shrilly out of green cages, the old woman clacks away with her sabots echoing over the stones, the canaries cease their piping, and then nobody else comes. There are two or three tall poplar-trees growing along the wall, which shiver plaintively; a few clouds drift by, and a very distant faint sound of military music comes borne on the wind.

'Ah, how dull it is to be here! Ah, how I hate it, how I hate them all!' Elizabeth is saying to herself; 'There is some music, all the Champs Elysées are crowded with people, the soldiers are marching along with glistening bayonets and flags flying. Not one of them thinks that in a dismal house not very far away there is anybody so unhappy as I am. This day year—it breaks my heart to think of it—I was nineteen; to-day I am twenty, and I feel a hundred. Oh, what a sin and shame it is to condemn me to this hateful life. Oh, what wicked people these good people are. Oh, how dull, oh, how stupid, oh, how prosy, oh, how I wish I was dead, and they were dead, and it was all over!'

How many weary yawns, I wonder, had poor Elizabeth yawned since that first night when M. Tourneur came to tea? With what distaste she set herself to live her new life I cannot attempt to tell you. It bored her, and wearied and displeased her, and she made no secret of her displeasure, you may be certain. But what annoyed her most of all, what seemed to her so inconceivable that she could never understand or credit it, was the extraordinary change which had come over her mother. Mme. Tourneur was like Mrs. Gilmour in many things, but so different in others that Elly could hardly believe her to be the same woman. The secret of it all was a love of power and admiration, purchased no matter at what sacrifice, which had always been the hidden motive of Caroline's life. Now she found that by dressing in black, by looking stiff, by attending endless charitable meetings, prayer-meetings, religious meetings, by influencing M. Tourneur, who was himself a man in authority, she could eat of the food her soul longed for. 'There was a man once who did not care for me, he despised me,' she used to think sometimes; 'he liked that silly child of mine better ; he shall hear of me one day.'

Lady Dampier was a very strong partisan of the French Protestant Church. Mme. Tourneur used to hope that she would come to Paris again and carry home with her the fame of her virtues, and her influence, and her conversion; and in the meanwhile the weary round of poor Elly's daily existence went on. To-day, for two lonesome hours, she stood leaning at that window with the refrain of the distant music echoing in her ears long after it had died away. It was like the remembrance of the past pleasures of her short life. Such a longing for sympathy, for congenial spirits, for the pleasures she loved so dearly, came over her, that the great hot tears welled into her eyes, and the bitterest tears are those which do not fall. The gate bell rang at last, and Clementine walked across the yard to unbolt, to unbar, and to let in Monsieur Tourneur, with books under his arm, and a big stick. Then the bell rang again, and Madame Tourneur followed, dressed in prim scant clothes, accompanied by another person even primmer and scantier than herself; this was a widowed step-sister of M. Tourneur's who, unluckily, had no home of her own, so the good man received her and her children into his. Lastly, Elizabeth, from her window, saw Anthony arrive with four of the young Protestants, all swinging their legs and arms. (The fifth was detained at home with a bad swelled face.) All the others were now coming back to dinner, after attending a class at the Pasteur Boulot's. They clattered past the door of Elly's room—a bare little chamber, with one white curtain she had nailed up herself, and a straight bed and a chair. A clock struck five. A melancholy bell presently sounded through the house, and a strong smell of cabbage came in at the open window. Elly looked in the glass; her rough hair was all standing on end curling, her hands were streaked with chalk and brick from the window, her washed-out blue cotton gown was creased and tumbled. What did it matter? she shook her head, as she had a way of doing, and went downstairs as she was. On the way she met two untidy-looking little girls, and then clatter, clatter, along the uncarpeted passage, came the great big nailed boots of the pupils; and then at the dining-room door there was Clementine in a yellow gown—much smarter and trimmer than Elizabeth's blue cotton—carrying a great long loaf of sour bread.

Madame Tourneur was already at her post, standing at the head of the table, ladleing out the cabbage soup with the pieces of bread floating in every plate. M. Tourneur was eating his dinner quickly; he had to examine a class for confirmation at six, and there was a prayer-meeting at seven. The other prim lady sat opposite to him with her portion before her. There was a small table-cloth, streaked with blue, and not over clean; hunches of bread by every plate, and iron knives and forks. Each person said grace to himself as he came and took his place. Only Elizabeth flung herself down in a chair, looked at the soup, made a face, and sent it away untasted.

'Elizabeth, ma fille, vous ne mangez pas,' said M. Tourneur, kindly.

'I can't swallow it!' said Elizabeth.

'When there are so many poor people starving in the streets, you do not, I suppose, expect us to sympathise with such pampered fancies?' said the prim lady.

Although the sisters-in-law were apparently very good

friends, there was a sort of race of virtue always being run between them, and just now Elly's shortcomings were a thorn in her mother's side, so skilfully were they wielded by Mrs. Jacob. Lou-Lou and Tou-Tou, otherwise Louise and Thérèse, *her* daughters, were such good, stupid, obedient, uninteresting little girls, that there was really not a word to say against them in retort; and all that Elly's mother could do, was to be even more severe, more uncompromising than Madame Jacob herself. And now she said,—

'Nonsense, Elizabeth; you must really eat your dinner. Clementine, bring back Miss Elizabeth's plate.'

M. Tourneur looked up—he thought the soup very good himself, but he could not bear to see anybody distressed. 'Go and fetch the bouillie quickly, Clementine. Why should Elizabeth take what she does not like? Rose,' said he to his sister, 'do you remember how our poor mother used to make us breakfast off—*porridge* I think she called it—and what a bad taste it had, and how we used to cry?'

'We never ungratefully objected to good soup,' said Rose. 'I make a point of never giving in to Lou-Lou and Tou-Tou when they have their fancies. I care more for the welfare of their souls than for pampering their bodies.'

'And I only care for my body,' Elly cried. 'Mamma, I like porridge, will you have some for me?'

'Ah! hush! hush! Elizabeth. You do not think what you say, my poor child,' said Tourneur. 'What is mere eating and drinking, what is food, what is raiment, but dust and rottenness? You only care for your body!—for that mass of corruption. Ah, do not say such things, even in jest. Remember, that for every idle word——'

'And is there to be no account for spiteful words?' interrupted Elizabeth, looking at Mrs. Jacob.

Monsieur Tourneur put down the glass of wine he was raising to his lips, and with sad, reproachful glances, looked at the unruly step-daughter. Madame Jacob, shaking with indignation, cast her eyes up and opened her mouth, and Elizabeth began to pout her red lips. One minute and the storm would have burst, when Anthony upset a jug of water at his elbow, and the stream trickled down and down the table-cloth. These troubled waters restored peace for the moment. Poor Tourneur was able to finish his meal, in a puddle truly, but also in silence. Mrs. Jacob, who had received a large portion of the water in her lap, retired to change her dress, the young Christians sniggered over their plates, and Anthony went on eating his dinner.

I don't offer any excuse for Elizabeth. She was worried, and vexed, and tried beyond her powers of endurance, and she grew more wayward, more provoking every day. It is very easy to be good-natured, good-tempered, thankful and happy, when you are in the country you love, among your own people, living your own life. But if you are suddenly transplanted, made to live someone else's life, expected to see with another man's eyes, to forget your own identity almost, all that happens is, that you do not do as you were expected. Sometimes it is a sheer impossibility. What is that rare proverb about the shoe? Cinderella slipped it on in an instant; but you know her poor sisters cut off their toes and heels, and could not screw their feet in, though they tried ever so. Well, they did their best; but Elly did not try at all, and that is why she was to blame. She was a spoiled child, both by good and ill fortune. Sometimes, when she sat sulking, her mother used to look wondering at her with her black eyes, without saying a word. Did it ever occur to her that this was *her* work, that Elizabeth might have been happy now, honoured, prosperous, well loved, but for a little lie which had been told—but for a little barrier which had been thrown, one summer's day, between her and John Dampier? Caroline had long ceased to feel remorse—she used to say to herself that it would be much better for Elizabeth to marry Anthony, she would make anybody else miserable with her wayward temper. Anthony was so obtuse, that Elizabeth's fancies would not try him in the least. Mrs. Gilmour chose to term obtuseness a certain chivalrous devotion which the young man felt for her daughter. She thought him dull and slow, and so he was; but at the same time there were gleams of shrewdness which came quite unexpectedly, you knew not whence; there was a certain reticence and good sense of which people had no idea. Anthony knew much more about her and about his father than they knew about him. Every day he was learning to read the world. Elly had taught him a great deal, and he in return was her friend always.

Elly went out into the courtyard after dinner, and Anthony followed her—one little cousin had hold of each of his hands. If the little girls had not been little French Protestant girls, Elizabeth would have been very fond of them, for she loved children; but when they ran up to her, she motioned them away impatiently, and Anthony told them to go and run round the garden. Elizabeth was sitting on a tub which had been overturned, and resting her pretty dishevelled head wearily against the wall. Anthony looked at her for a minute.

'Why do you never wear nice dresses now,' said he at last, 'but this ugly old one always?'

'Is it not all vanity and corruption?' said Elizabeth, with a sneer; 'how can you ask such a question? Everything that is pretty is vanity. Your aunt and my mother only like ugly things. They would like to put out my eyes because they don't squint; to cut off my hair because it is pretty.'

'Your hair! It is not at all pretty like that,' said Anthony; 'it is all rough, like mine.'

Elizabeth laughed and blushed very sweetly. 'What is the use, who cares?'

'There are a good many people coming to-night,' said Anthony. 'It is our turn to receive the prayer-meeting. Why should you not smooth your curls and change your dress?'

'And do you remember what happened once, when I did dress, and make myself look nice?' said Elizabeth, flashing up, and then beginning to laugh.

Anthony looked grave and puzzled; for Elizabeth had caused quite a scandal in the community on that occasion. No wonder the old ladies in their old dowdy bonnets, the young ones in their ill-made woollen dresses, the preacher preaching against the vanities of the world, had all been shocked and outraged, when after the sermon had begun, the door opened, and Elizabeth appeared in the celebrated pink silk dress, with flowers in her hair, white lace falling from her shoulders, a bouquet, a gold fan, and glittering bracelets. Mme. Jacob's head nearly shook off with horror. The word was with the Pasteur Boulot, who did not conceal his opinion, and whose strictures introduced into the sermon were enough to make a less hardened sinner quake in her shoes. Many of the great leaders of the Protestant world in Paris had been present on that occasion. Some would not speak to her, some did speak very plainly. Elizabeth took it all as a sort of triumph, bent her head, smiled, fanned herself, and when ordered out of the room at last by her mother, left it with a splendid curtsey to the Rev. M. Boulot, and thanked him for his beautiful and improving discourse. And then, when she was upstairs in her own room again, where she had been decking herself for the last hour—the tallow candle was still spluttering on the table—her clothes all lying about the room—she locked the door, tore off her ornaments, her shining dress, and flung herself down on the floor, crying and sobbing as if her heart would break. 'Oh, I want to go! I want to go! Oh, take me away!' she prayed and sobbed. 'Oh, what harm is there in a pink gown more than a black one! Oh, why does not John Dampier come and fetch me? Oh, what dolts, what idiots, those people are! What a heart-broken girl I am! Poor Elly, poor Elly, poor, poor girl!' said she, pitying herself, and stroking her tear-stained cheeks. And so she went on, until she had nearly worn herself out, poor child. She really was almost heart-broken. This uncongenial atmosphere seemed to freeze and chill her best impulses. I cannot help being sorry for her, and sympathising with her against that rigid community down below, and yet, after all, there was scarcely one of the people whom she so scorned who was not a better Christian than poor Elizabeth, more self-denying, more scrupulous, more patient in effort, more diligent,—not one of them that did not lead a more useful life than hers. It was in vain that her mother had offered her classes in the schools, humble neighbours to visit, sick people to tend.

'Leave me alone,' the girl would say. 'You know how I hate all that cant!' Mme. Tourneur herself spent her whole days doing good, patronising the poor, lecturing the wicked, dosing the sick, superintending countless charitable communities. Her name was on all the committees, her decisions were deferred to, her wishes consulted. She did not once regret the step she had taken; she was a clever, ambitious, active-minded woman; she found herself busy, virtuous, and respected; what more could she desire? Her daughter's unhappiness did not give her any very great concern. 'It would go off in time,' she said. But days went by, and Elly was only more hopeless, more heart-broken; black lines came under the blue eyes; from being a stout hearty girl, she grew thin and languid. Seeing her day by day, they none of them noticed that she was looking ill, except Anthony, who often imagined a change would do her good; only how was this to be managed? He could only think of one way. He was thinking of it, as he followed her out into the courtyard to-day. The sun was low in the west, the long shadows of the trees flickered across the stones. Say what he would, the blue gown, the wall, the yellow hair, made up a pretty little piece of colouring. With all her faults, Anthony loved Elly better than any other human being, and would have given his life to make her happy.

'I cannot bear to see you so unhappy,' said he, in French, speaking very simply, in his usual voice. 'Elizabeth, why don't you do as your mother has done, and marry a French pasteur, who has loved you ever since the day he first saw you? You should do as you liked, and leave this house, where you are so miserable, and get away from aunt Rose, who is so ill-natured. I would not propose such a scheme if I saw a chance for something better; but anything would be an improvement on the life you are leading here. It is wicked and profitless, and you are killing yourself and wasting your best days. You are not taking up your cross with joy and with courage, dear Elizabeth. Perhaps by starting afresh——' His voice failed him, but his eyes spoke and finished the sentence.

This was Anthony's scheme. Elly opened her round eyes, and looked at him all amazed and wondering. A year ago it would have been very different, and so she thought as she scanned him. A year ago she would have scorned the poor fellow, laughed at him, tossed her head, and turned away. But was this the Elly of a year ago? This unhappy, broken-spirited girl, with dimmed beauty, dulled spirits, in all her ways so softened, saddened, silenced. It was almost another person than the Elizabeth Gilmour of former times, who spoke, and said, still looking at him steadfastly, 'Thank you, Anthony; I will think about it, and tell you to-morrow what—what I think.'

Anthony blushed, and faltered a few unintelligible words, and turned away abruptly, as he saw Madame

Jacob coming towards them. As for Elly, she stood quite still, and perfectly cool, and rather bewildered, only somewhat surprised at herself. 'Can this be me?' she was thinking. 'Can that kind fellow be the boy I used to laugh at so often? Shall I take him at his word? Why not—— ?'

But Madame Jacob's long nose came and put an end to her wonderings. This lady did not at all approve of gossiping; she stepped up with an enquiring sniff, turned round to look after Anthony, and then said, rather viciously, 'Our Christian brothers and sisters will assemble shortly for their pious Wednesday meetings. It is not by exchanging idle words with my nephew that you will best prepare your mind for the exercises of this evening. Retire into your own room, and see if it is possible to compose yourself to a fitter frame of mind. Tou-Tou, Lou-Lou, my children, what are you about?'

'I am gathering pretty flowers, mamma,' shouted Lou-Lou.

'I am picking up stones for my little basket,' said Tou-Tou, coming to the railing.

'I will allow four minutes,' said their mother, looking at her watch. 'Then you will come to me, both of you, in my room, and apply yourselves to something more profitable than filling your little baskets. Elizabeth, do you mean to obey me?'

Very much to Madame Jacob's surprise, Elizabeth

walked quietly before her into the house without saying
one word. The truth was, she was preoccupied with other
things, and forgot to be rebellious. She was not even rebellious in her heart when she was upstairs sitting by the
bedside, and puzzling her brains over Anthony's scheme.
It seemed a relief certainly to turn from the horrible
monotony of her daily life, and to think of his kindness.
He was very rough, very uncouth, very young; but he was
shrewd, and kind, and faithful, more tolerant than his
father,—perhaps because he felt less keenly;—not sensitive, like him, but more patient, dull over things which
are learnt by books, but quick at learning other not less
useful things which belong to the experience of daily life.
When Elly came down into the réfectoire where they were
all assembled, her mother was surprised to see that she had
dressed herself, not in the objectionable pink silk, but in
a soft grey stuff gown, all her yellow hair was smooth and
shining, and a little locket hung round her neck tied with
a blue ribbon. The little bit of colour seemed reflected
somehow in her eyes. They looked blue to-night, as they
used to look once when she was happy. Madame Tourneur
was quite delighted, and came up and kissed her, and said,
'Elly, this is how I like to see you.'

Madame Jacob tossed her head, and gave a rough pull
at the ends of the ribbon. '*This* was quite unnecessary,'
said she.

'Ah!' cried Elly, 'you have hurt me.'

'Is not that the locket Miss Dampier gave you?' said Madame Tourneur. 'You had best put such things away in your drawer another time. But it is time for you to take your place.'

CHAPTER IV.

Unhappier are they to whom a higher instinct has been given, who struggle to be persons, not machines ; to whom the universe is not a warehouse, or at best a fancy bazaar, but a mystic temple and hall of doom.

A NUMBER of straw chairs were ranged along the room, with a row of seats behind, for the pasteurs who were to address the meeting.

The people began to arrive very punctually: One or two grand-looking French ladies in cashmeres, a good many limp ones, a stray man or two, two English clergymen in white neckcloths, and five or six Englishwomen in old bonnets. A little whispering and chattering went on among the young French girls, who arrived guarded by their mothers. The way in which French mothers look after their daughters, tie their bonnet-strings, pin their collars, carry their books and shawls, &c., and sit beside them, and always answer for them if they are spoken to, is very curious. Now and then, however, they relax a little, and allow a little whispering with young companions. There was a low murmur and a slight bustle as four pasteurs of unequal heights walked in and placed themselves in the reserved seats. M. Stephen Tourneur followed and took his place. With what kind steadfast glances he greeted his audience! Even Elizabeth could not resist the charm of his manner, and she admired and respected him, much as she disliked the exercise of the evening.

His face lit up with Christian fervour, his eyes shone and gleamed with kindness, his voice, when he began to speak, thrilled with earnestness and sincerity. There was at times a wonderful power about the frail little man, the power which is won in many a desperate secret struggle, the power which comes from a whole life of deep feeling and honest endeavour. No wonder that Stephen Tourneur, who had so often wrestled with the angel and overcome his own passionate spirit, should have influence over others less strong, less impetuous than his own. Elly could not but admire him and love him, many of his followers worshipped him with the most affecting devotion; Anthony, his son, loved him too, and would have died for him in a quiet way, but he did not blindly believe in his father.

But listen! What a host of eloquent words, of tender thoughts come alive from his lips to-night. What reverent faith, what charity, what fervour! The people's eyes were fixed upon his kind, eloquent face, and their hearts all beat in sympathy with his own.

One or two of the Englishwomen began to cry. One French lady was swaying herself backwards and forwards in rapt attention; the two clergymen sat wondering in their white neckcloths. What would they give to preach such sermons? And the voice went on uttering, entreating, encouraging, rising and sinking, ringing with passionate cadence. It ceased at last, and the only sounds in the room were a few sighs, and the suppressed sobs of one or two women. Elizabeth sighed among others, and sat very still with her hands clasped in her lap. For the first time in her life she was wondering whether she had not perhaps been in the wrong hitherto, and Tourneur, and Madame Jacob, and all the rest in the right—and whether happiness was not the last thing to search for, and those things of which he had spoken, the first and best and only necessities. Alas! what strange chance was it that at that moment she raised her head and looked up with her great blue eyes, and saw a strange familiar face under one of the dowdy English bonnets—a face, thin, pinched, with a hooked nose, and sandy hair—that sent a little thrill to her heart, and made her cry out to herself eagerly, as a rush of old memories and hopes came over her, that happiness was sent into the world for a gracious purpose, and that love meant goodness and happiness too sometimes. And, yes—no—yes—that was Lady Dampier! and was John in Paris, perhaps? and Miss Dampier? and were the dear, dear old days come back? . . .

After a few minutes the congregation began to sing a hymn, the English ladies joining in audibly with their queer accents. The melody swayed on, horribly out of tune and out of time, in a wild sort of minor key. Tou-Tou and Lou-Lou sang, one on each side of their mother, exceedingly loud and shrill, and one of the clergymen attempted a second, after which the discordance reached its climax. Elly had laughed on one or two occasions, and indeed I do not wonder. To-day she scarcely heard the sound of the voices. Her heart was beating with hope, delight, wonder; her head was in a whirl, her whole frame trembling with excitement, that increased every instant. Would M. Boulot's sermon never come to an end? Monsieur Bontemps' exposition, Monsieur de Marveille's reports, go on for ever and ever?

But at last it was over: a little rustling, a little pause, and all the voices beginning to murmur, and the chairs scraping; people rising, a little group forming round each favourite pasteur, hands outstretched, thanks uttered, people coming and going. With one bound Elly found herself standing by Lady Dampier, holding both her hands, almost crying with delight. The apathetic English lady was quite puzzled by the girl's exaggerated expressions. She cared very little for Elly Gilmour herself: she liked her very well, but she could not understand her extraordinary warmth of greeting. However, she was carried away by her feelings to the extent of saying, 'You must come and see us to-morrow. We are only passing through Paris on our way to Schlangenbad for Lætitia; she has been sadly out of health and spirits lately, poor dear. We are at the Hôtel du Louvre. You must come and lunch with us. Ah! here is your mother. How d'ye do, dear Madam Tourneur? What a privilege it has been! What a treat Mossu Tourneur has given us to-night. I have been quite delighted, I assure you,' said her ladyship, bent on being gracious.

Mme. Tourneur made the most courteous of salutations. 'I am glad you came, since it was so,' said she.

'I want you to let Elly come and see me,' continued Lady Dampier; 'she must come to lunch; I should be so glad if you would accompany her. I would offer to take her to the play, but I suppose you do not approve of such things any more.'

'My life is so taken up with other more serious duties,' said Mme. Tourneur, with a faint superior smile, 'that I have little time for mere worldly amusements. I cannot say that I desire them for my daughter.'

'Oh, of course,' said Lady Dampier. 'I myself——but it is only *en passant*, as we are all going on to Schlangenbad in two days. It is really quite delightful to find you settled here so nicely. What a privilege it must be to be so constantly in Mossu Tourneur's society!'

Madame Tourneur gave a bland assenting smile, and turned to speak to several people who were standing near. 'Monsieur de Marveille, are you going? Thanks, I will be at the committee on Thursday without fail. Monsieur

Boulot, you must remain a few minutes; I want to consult you about that case in which la Comtesse de Glaris takes so deep an interest. Lady Macduff has also written to me to ask my husband's interest for her. Ah, Lady Sophia! how glad I am you have returned; is Lady Matilda better?'

'Well, I'll wish you good-by, Madame Tourneur,' said Lady Dampier, rather impressed, and not much caring to stand by quite unnoticed while all these greetings were going on. 'You will let Elly come to morrow?'

'Certainly,' said Mme. Tourneur. 'You will understand how it is that I do not call. My days are much occupied. I have little time for mere visits of pleasure and ceremony. Monsieur Bontemps, one word——'

'Elly, which is the way out?' said Lady Dampier, abruptly, less and less pleased, but more and more impressed.

'I will show you,' said Elly, who had been standing by all this time, and she led the way bare-headed into the court, over which the stars where shining tranquilly. The trees looked dark and rustled mysteriously along the wall, but all heaven was alight. Elly looked up for an instant, and then turned to her companion and asked her, with a voice that faltered a little, if they were all together in Paris?

'No; Miss Dampier is in Scotland still,' said my lady. It was not Miss Dampier's name of which Elizabeth

Gilmour was longing to hear, she did not dare ask any more; but it seemed as if a great weight had suddenly fallen upon her heart, as she thought that perhaps, after all, he was not come; she should not hear of him; see him, who knows, perhaps never again?

Elly tried to unbar the great front door to let out her friend; but she could not do it, and called to old Françoise, who was passing across to the kitchen, to come and help her. And suddenly the bolt, which had stuck in some manner, gave way, the gate opened wide, and as it opened Elly saw that there was somebody standing just outside under the lamp-post. The foolish child did not guess who it was, but said 'Good-night,' with a sigh, and held out her soft hand to Lady Dampier. And then, all of a sudden, the great load went away, and in its place came a sort of undreamt-of peace, happiness, and gratitude. All the stars seemed suddenly to blaze more brightly; all the summer's night to shine more wonderfully; all trouble, all anxiousness, to melt away; and John Dampier turned round and said,—

'Is that you, Elizabeth?'

'And you?' cried Elly, springing forward, with both her hands outstretched. 'Ah! I did not think who was outside the door.'

'How did you come here, John?' said my lady, very much flustered.

'I came to fetch you,' said her son. 'I wanted a walk,

and Letty told me where you were gone.' Lady Dampier did not pay much attention to his explanations; she was watching Elly with a dissatisfied face; and glancing round too, the young man saw that Elly was standing quite still under the archway, with her hands folded, and with a look of dazzled delight in her blue eyes that there was no mistaking.

'You don't forget your old friends, Elly?' said he.

'I! never, never,' cried Elizabeth.

'And I, too, do not forget,' said he, very kindly, and held out his hand once more, and took hers, and did not let it go. 'I will come and see you, and bring Lætitia,' he added, as his mother looked up rather severely. 'Goodnight, dear Elly? I am glad you are unchanged.'

People, however slow they may be naturally, are generally quick in discovering admiration, or affection, or respectful devotion to themselves. Lady Dampier only suspected, her son was quite sure of poor Elly's feelings, as he said good-night under the archway. Indeed he knew a great deal more about them than did Elizabeth herself. All she knew was that the great load was gone; and she danced across the stones of the yard, clapping her hands in her old happy way. The windows of the salle were lighted up. She could see the people within coming and going, but she did not notice Anthony, who was standing in one of them. He, for his part, was watching the little dim figure dancing and flitting about in the starlight.

Had he, then, anything to do with her happiness? Was he indeed so blessed? His heart was overflowing with humble gratitude, with kindness, with wonder. He was happy at the moment, and was right to be grateful. She was happy, too—as thoroughly happy now, and carried away by her pleasure, as she had been crushed and broken by her troubles. 'Ah! to think that the day has come at last, after watching all this long, long, cruel time! I always knew it would come. Everybody gets what they wish for sooner or later. I don't think anybody was ever so miserable as I have been all this year, but at last—at last——' No one saw the bright, happy look that came into her face, for she was standing in the dark outside the door of the house. She wanted to dream, she did not want to talk to anybody; she wanted to tell herself over and over again how happy she was; how she had seen him again; how he had looked; how kindly he had spoken to her. Ah! yes, he had cared for her all the time; and now he had come to fetch her away. She did not think much of poor Anthony; if she did, it was to say to herself that somehow it would all come right, and everybody would be as well contented as she was. The door of the house opened while she still stood looking up at the stars. This time it was not John Dampier, but the Pasteur Tourneur, who came from behind it. He put out his hand and took hold of hers.

'You there, Elizabeth! Come in, my child; you will

be cold.' And he drew her into the hall, where the Pasteurs Boulot and De Marveille were pulling on their cloaks and hats, and bidding everybody good-night.

The whole night Elizabeth lay starting and waking —so happy that she could not bear to go to sleep, to cease to exist for one instant. Often it had been the other way, and she had been thankful to lay her weary head on her pillow, and close her aching eyes, and forget her troubles. But all this night she lay wondering what the coming day was to bring forth. She had better have gone to sleep. The coming day brought forth nothing at all, except, indeed, a little note from Lætitia, written on a half-sheet of paper, which was put into her hand about eleven o'clock, just as she was sitting down to the *déjeûner à la fourchette*.

'Hôtel du Rhin, Place Vendôme.
'Wednesday Evening.

'My dear Elizabeth,— I am so disappointed to think that I shall not perhaps see you after all. Some friends of ours have just arrived, who are going on to Schlangenbad to-morrow, and aunt Catherine thinks it will be better to set off a little sooner than we had intended, so as to travel with them. I wish you might be able to come and breakfast with us about nine to-morrow; but I am afraid this is asking almost too much, though I should greatly enjoy seeing you again. Good-by. If we do not meet now, I trust that on our return in a couple of months we may be more fortunate, and see much of each other. We start at ten, and shall reach Strasbourg about eight.

'Ever, dear Elizabeth,

'Affectionately yours,

'LÆTITIA MALCOLM.'

'What has happened?' said Madame Tourneur, quite frightened, for she saw the girl's face change and her eyes suddenly filling with tears.

'Nothing has happened,' said Elizabeth. 'I was only disappointed to think I should not see them again.' And she put out her hand and gave her mother the note.

'But why care so much for people who do not care for you?' said her mother. 'Lady Dampier is one of the coldest women I ever knew; and as for Lætitia, if she loved you in the least, would she write you such a note as this?'

'Mamma! it is a very kind note,' said Elizabeth. 'I know she loves me.'

'Do you think she cried over it, as you did?' said her mother. '"So disappointed"—"more fortunate on our return through Paris"?'

'Do not let us judge our neighbours so hastily, my wife,' said M. Tourneur. 'Let Elizabeth love her friend. What can she do better?'

Caroline looked up with an odd expression, shrugged her shoulders, and did not answer.

Until breakfast was over, Elly kept up pretty well; but when M. Tourneur rose and went away into his writing-room, when Anthony and the young men filed off by an opposite door, and Mme. Tourneur disappeared to look to her household duties—then, when the room was quiet again, and only Madame Jacob remained sewing in a window, and Lou-Lou and Tou-Tou whispering over their lessons, suddenly the canary burst out into a shrill piping jubilant song, and the sunshine poured in, and Elly's heart began to sink. And then suddenly the horrible reality seemed realised to her. . . .

They were gone—those who had come, as she thought, to rescue her. Could it be true—could it be really true? She had stood lonely on the arid shore waving her signals of distress, and they who should have seen them, never heeded, but went sailing away to happier lands, disappearing in the horizon, and leaving her to her fate. That fate which—it was more than she could bear. It seemed more terrible than ever to her to-day. . . . Ah! silly girl, was her life as hard as the lives of thousands struggling along with her in the world, tossed and broken against the rocks, while she, at least, was safely landed on the beach? She had no heart to think of others. She sat sickening with disappointment, and once more her eyes filled up with stinging tears.

'Lou-Lou, Tou-Tou, come up to your lessons,' said Mrs. Jacob. 'I do not wish you to see such a wicked example of discontent.' The little girls went off on tiptoe; and when these people were gone, Elizabeth was left quite alone.

'I daresay I am very wicked,' she was saying to herself. 'I was made wicked. But this is more than I can bear— to live all day with the people I hate, and then when I do love with my whole heart, to be treated with such cruel indifference—such coldness. He *ought* to know, he must know that he has broken my heart. Why does he look so kindly, and then forget so heartlessly? . . .'

She hid her face in her hands, and bent her head over the wooden table. She did not care who knew her to be unhappy—what pain her unhappiness might give. The person who was likely to be most wounded by her poignant grief came into the room at the end of half-an-hour, and found her sitting still in the same attitude, with her head hanging, and her tears dribbling on the deal table. This was enough answer for poor Anthony.

'Elizabeth,' he faltered, 'I see you cannot make up your mind.'

'Ah! no, no, Anthony, not yet,' said Elizabeth; 'but you are the only person in the world who cares for me; and indeed, indeed, I am grateful.'

And then the poor little head sank down again overwhelmed with its load of grief.

'Tell me, Elizabeth, is there anything in the world I can do to make you more happy?' said Anthony. 'My prayers, my best wishes are yours. Is there nothing else?'

'Only not to notice me,' said Elly; 'only to leave me alone.'

And so Anthony, seeing that he could do nothing, went away very sad at heart. He had been so happy and confident the night before, and now he began to fear that what he longed for was never to be his. Poor boy, he buried his trouble in his own heart, and did not say one word of it to father, or mother, or young companions.

Five or six weeks went by, and Elly heard no more of the Dampiers. Every day she looked more ill, more haggard; her temper did not mend, her spirits did not improve. In June the five young men went home to their families. M. and Madame Tourneur went down to Fontainebleau for a week. Anthony set off for the South of France to visit an uncle. He was to be ordained in the autumn, and was anxious to pay this visit before his time should be quite taken up by his duties. Clementine asked for a holiday, and went off to her friends at Passy; and Elly remained at home. It was her own fault: Monsieur Tourneur had begged her to come with them; her mother had scolded and remonstrated, all in vain. The wayward girl declared that she wanted no change, no company, that she was best where she was. Only for a week? she would stay, and there was an end of it. I think the secret was, that she could not bear to quit Paris, and waited and waited, hoping against hope.

'I am afraid you will quarrel with Madame Jacob,' said her mother, as she was setting off.

'I shall not speak to her,' said Elly; and for two days she was as good as her word. But on the third day, this salutary silence was broken. Madame Jacob, coming in with her bonnet on, informed Elizabeth that she was going out for the afternoon.

'I confess it is not without great apprehensions, lest you should get into mischief,' says the lady.

'And pray,' says Elly, 'am I more likely to get into mischief than you are? *I* am going out.'

'You will do nothing of the sort,' says Madame Jacob.

'I will do exactly as I choose,' says Elizabeth.

In a few minutes, a battle royal was raging; Tou-Tou and Lou-Lou look on, all eyes and ears; old Françoise comes up from the kitchen, and puts her head in at the door.

Madame Jacob was desiring her, on no account, to let Elizabeth out that afternoon, when Lou-Lou said, 'There, that was the street-door shutting;' and Tou-Tou said, 'She is gone.' And so it was.

The wilful Elizabeth had brushed past old Françoise, rushed up to her own room, pulled out a shawl, tied on her bonnet, defiantly, run down stairs and across the yard, and, in a minute, was walking rapidly away without once looking behind her. Down the hill, past the hospital—they were carrying a wounded man in at the door as she passed, and she just caught a glimpse of his pale face, and turned shrinking away. Then she got into the Faubourg St. Honoré, with its shops and its cab-stands, and busy people coming and going; and then she turned up the Rue d'Angoulême. In the Champs Elysées the afternoon sun was streaming; there was a crowd, and, as it happened, soldiers were marching along to the sound of martial music. She saw an empty bench, and sat down for a minute to regain breath and equanimity. The music put her in mind of the day when she had listened at her window—of the day when her heart was so heavy and then so light—of the day when Anthony had told her his scheme, when John Dampier had waited at the door: the day, the only one —she was not likely to forget it—when she had been so happy, just for a little. And now——? The bitter remembrance came rushing over her; and she jumped up, and walked faster and faster, trying to escape from it.

She got into the Tuileries, and on into the Rue de Rivoli, but she thought that people looked at her strangely, and she turned homewards at last. It was lonely, wandering about this busy city by herself. As she passed by the columns of St. Philip's Church, somebody came out, and the curtain swung back, and Elly, looking up, saw a dim quiet interior, full of silent rays of light falling from the yellow windows and chequering the marble. She stopped, and went in with a sudden impulse. One old woman was kneeling on the threshold, and Elly felt as if she, too, wanted to fall upon her knees. What tranquil gloom, and silence, and repose! Her own church was only open at certain hours. Did it always happen that precisely at eleven o'clock on Sunday mornings she was in the exact frame of mind in which she most longed for spiritual communion and consolation? To be tightly wedged in between two other devotees, plied with *chaufferettes* by the pew-opener, forced to follow the extempore supplications of the preacher—did all this suffice to her wants? Here was silence, coolness, a faint, half-forgotten smell of incense, there were long, empty rows of chairs, one or two people kneeling at the little altars, five or six little pious candles burning in compliment to the various saints and deities to whom they were dedicated. The rays of the little candles glimmered in the darkness, and the foot-falls fell quietly along the aisle. I, for my part, do not blame this poor foolish heart, if it offered up a humble supplication here in the shrine of the stranger. Poor Elly was not very eloquent; she only prayed to be made a good girl and to be happy. But, after all, eloquence and long words do not mean any more.

She walked home, looking up at the sunset lines which were streaking the sky freshly and delicately; she thought she saw Madame Jacob's red nose up in a little pink cloud, and began to speculate how she would be received. And she had nearly reached her own door, and was toiling wearily up the last hilly piece of road, when she heard some quick steps behind; somebody passed, turned round, said, 'Why, Elly! I was going to see you.'

In an instant, Elly's blue eyes were all alight, and her ready hand outstretched to John Dampier—for it was he.

CHAPTER V.

In looking backward, they may find that several things which were not the charm have more reality to this groping memory than the charm itself which embalmed them.

HE had time to think, as he greeted her, how worn she looked, how shabbily she was dressed. And yet what a charming, talking, brightening face it was. When Elly smiled, her bonnet and dress became quite new and becoming, somehow. In two minutes he thought her handsomer than ever. They walked on, side by side, up the hilly street. She, trying to hide her agitation, asked him about Lætitia, about his mother, and dear Miss Dampier.

'I think she does care for me still,' said Elly; 'but you have all left off.'

'My dear child,' said he, 'how can you think anything so foolish.'

'I have nothing else to do,' said Elly, plaintively; 'all day long I think about those happy times which are gone. I thought you had forgotten me when you did not come.'

Dampier laughed a little uneasily. 'I have had to take them to their watering-place,' said he; 'I could not help it. But tell me about yourself. Are you not comfortable?' he asked.

'I am rather unhappy,' said Elizabeth. 'I am not good, like they are, and oh! I get so tired;' and then she went on and told him what miserable days she spent, and how she hated them, and she longed for a little pleasure, and ease, and happiness.

He was very much touched, and very, very sorry. 'You don't look well,' he said. 'You should have some amusement—some change. I would take you anywhere you liked. Why not come now, for a drive? See, here is a little open carriage passing. Surely, with an old friend like me, there can be no harm.' And he signed to the driver to stop.

Elizabeth was quite frightened at the idea, and said, 'Oh, no, no! indeed.' Whereas Dampier only said, 'Oh, yes! indeed, you must. Why, I knew you when you were a baby—and your father and your grandmother—and I am a respectable middle-aged man, and it will do you good, and it will soon be a great deal too dark for any of your pasteurs to recognise you and report. We have been out riding together before now—why not come for a little drive in the Bois? Why not?'

So said Elly to herself, doubtfully; and she got in, still hesitating, and in a minute they were rolling away swiftly out at the gates of Paris, out towards the sunset— so it seemed to Elizabeth—and she forgot all her fears.

The heavens glowed overhead; her heart beat with intensest enjoyment. Presently, the twilight came falling with a green glow, with stars, with evening perfumes, with lights twinkling from the carriages reflected on the lakes as they rolled past.

And so at last she was happy, sometimes silent from delight, sometimes talking in her simple, foolish way, and telling him all about herself, her regrets, her troubles—about Anthony. She could not help it—indeed, she could not. Dampier, for his part, cried out at the notion of her marrying Anthony, made fun of him, laughed at him, pitied him. The poor fellow, now that she compared him to John Dampier, did indeed seem dull and strangely uncouth, and commonplace.

'Marry that cub,' said Sir John; 'you mustn't do it, my dear. You would be like the princess in the fairy tale, who went off with the bear. It's downright wicked to think of such a thing. Elizabeth, *promise* me you won't. Does he ever climb up and down a pole? is he fond of buns? is he tame? If your father were alive, would he suffer such a thing? Promise me, Elly, that you will never become Mrs. Bruin.'

'Yes; I promise,' said Elly, with a sigh. 'But he is so kind. Nobody is as——' And then she stopped, and thought, 'Yes; here was some one who was a great deal kinder.' Talking to Dampier was so easy, so pleasant, that she scarcely recognised her own words and sentences:

it was like music in tune after music out of tune : it was like running on smooth rails after rolling along a stony road: it was like breathing fresh air after a heated stifling atmosphere. Somehow, he met her half-way; she need not explain, recapitulate, stumble for words, as she was forced to do with those practical, impracticable people at home. He understood what she wanted to say before she had half finished her sentence; he laughed at her fine little jokes; he encouraged, he cheered, he delighted her. If she had cared for him before, it was now a mad adoration which she felt for this man. He suited her; she felt now that he was part of her life—the better, nobler, wiser part; and if he was the other half of her life, surely, somehow, she must be as necessary to him as he was to her. Why had he come to see her else? Why had he cared for her, and brought her here? Why was his voice so gentle, his manner so kind and sympathetic? He had cared for her once, she knew he had; and he cared for her still, she knew he did. If the whole world were to deceive her and fail her, she would still trust him. And her instinct was not wrong : he was sincerely and heartily her friend. The carriage put them down a few doors from M. Tourneur's house, and then Elly went boldly up to the door and rang at the bell.

'I shall come at four o'clock to-morrow, and take you for a drive,' said John; 'you look like another woman already.'

'It is no use asking Madame Jacob,' said Elly; 'she would lock me up into my room. I will come somehow. How shall I thank you?'

'By looking well and happy again. I shall be so glad to have cured you.'

'And it is so pleasant to meet with such a kind doctor,' said Elly, looking up and smiling.

'Good-by, Elly,' repeated Sir John, quite affected by her gentle looks.

Old Françoise opened the door. Elly turned a little pale.

'Ah, ha! vous voilà,' says the old woman; 'méchante fille, you are going to get a pretty scolding. Where have you been?'

'Ah, Françoise!' said Elly, 'I have been so happy. I met Sir John Dampier: he is an old, old friend. He took me for a drive in the Bois. Is Madame Jacob very, very angry?'

'Well, you are in luck,' says the old woman, who could never resist Elizabeth's pretty pleading ways; 'she came home an hour ago and fetched the children, and went out to dine in town, and I told her you were in your room.'

'Ah, you dear kind old woman!' said Elly, flinging her arms round her neck, and giving her a kiss.

'There, there!' said the unblushing Françoise; 'I will put your couvert in the salle.'

'Ah! I am very glad. I am so hungry, Françoise,' said Elly, pulling off her bonnet, and shaking her loose hair as she followed the old woman across the courtyard.

So Elizabeth sat down to dine off dry bread and cold mutton. But though she said she was hungry, she was too happy to eat much. The tallow candle flickered on the table. She thought of the candles in St. Philip's Church; then she went over every word, every minute which she had spent since she was kneeling there. Old Françoise came in with a little cake she had made her, and found Elizabeth sitting, smiling, with her elbows on the table. 'Allons, allons!' thought the old cook. 'Here, eat, mamzelle,' said she; 'faut plus sortir sans permission—hein?'

'Thank you, Françoise. How nice! how kind of you!' said Elizabeth, in her bad French—she never would learn to talk properly; and then she ate her cake by the light of the candle, and this little dim tallow wick seemed to cast light and brilliance over the whole world, over her whole life, which seemed to her as if it would go on for ever and ever. Now and then a torturing doubt, a misgiving, came over her, but these she put quickly aside.

Madame Jacob was pouring out the coffee when Elly came down to breakfast next morning, conscious and ashamed, and almost disposed to confess. 'I am surprised,' said Madame Jacob, 'that you have the impudence to sit down at table with me;' and she said it in such an acid tone that all Elly's sweetness, and ashamedness, and penitence turned to bitterness.

'I find it very disagreeable,' says Elly; 'but I try and resign myself.'

'I shall write to my brother about you,' continued Madame Jacob.

'Indeed!' says Elizabeth. 'Here is a letter which he has written to me. What fun if it should be about you!' It was like Tourneur's handwriting, but it did not come from him. Elly opened it carelessly enough, but Tou-Tou and Lou-Lou exchanged looks of intelligence. Their mother had examined the little missive, and made her comments upon it:—

'Avignon, Rue de la Clochette,
'Chez le Pasteur Ch. Tourneur.

'My dear Elly,—I think of you so much and so constantly that I cannot help wishing to make you think of me, if only for one minute, while you read these few words. I have been telling my uncle about you; it is he who asks me why I do not write. But there are some things which are not to be spoken or to be written—it is only by one's life that one can try to tell them; and you, alas! do not care to hear the story of my life. I wonder will the day ever come when you will listen to it?

'I have been most kindly received by all my old friends down in these parts. Yesterday I attended the service in the Temple, and heard a most soul-stirring and eloquent oration from the mouth of M. le Pasteur David. I receive cheering accounts on every side. A new temple has been opened at Beziers, thanks to the munificence of one of our *coréligionnaires*. The temple was solemnly opened on the Monday of the Pentecost. The discourse of dedication was pronounced by M. le Pasteur Borrel, of Nismes. Seven pasteurs *en robe* attended the ceremony. They tell me that the interdiction which had weighed for some years upon the temple at Fouqueure (Charente) has been taken off, and that the faithful were able to reopen their temple on the first Sunday in June. Need I say what vivid actions of grace were uttered on this happy occasion? A Protestant school has also been established at Montauban, which seems to be well attended. I am now going to visit two of my uncle's *confrères*, MM. Bertoul and Joseph Aubré. Of M. Bertoul I have heard much good.

'Why do I tell you all this? Do you care for what I care? Could you ever bring yourself to lead the life which I propose to lead? Time only will show, dear Elizabeth. It will also show to you the faithfulness and depth of my affection.

'A. T.'

Elly put the letter down with a sigh, and went on drinking her coffee and eating her bread. Madame Jacob hemmed and tried to ask her a question or two on the subject, but Elly would not answer. Elly sometimes wondered at Anthony's fancy for her, knowing how little suited she was to the way of life she was leading; she was surprised that his rigid notions should allow him to entertain such an idea for an instant. But the truth was that Anthony was head over ears in love with her, and thought her perfection at the bottom of his heart.

Poor Anthony! This is what he got in return for his letter:—

'My dear Anthony,—It cannot be—never—never. But I do care for you, and I mean to always. For you are my brother in a sort of way.

'I am your affectionate, grateful

'ELLY.

'P.S.—Your father and my mother are away at Fontainebleau. Madame Jacob is here, and more disagreeable than anything you can imagine.'

And so it was settled; and Elly never once asked herself if she had been foolish or wise; but, after thinking compassionately about Anthony for a minute or two, she began to think about Dampier, and said to herself that she had followed his advice, and he must know best; and Dampier himself, comfortably breakfasting in the coffee-room of the hotel, was thinking of her, and, as he thought, put away all unpleasant doubts or suggestions. 'Poor

little thing! dear little thing!' he was saying to himself.
'I will not leave her to the tender mercies of those fanatics. She will die—I see it in her eyes—if she stays there. My mother or aunt Jean must come to her help; we must not desert her. Poor, poor, little Elly, with her wistful face! Why did not she make me marry her a year ago? I was very near it.'

He was faithful next day to his appointment, and Elly arrived breathless. 'Madame Jacob had locked her up in her room,' she said, only she got out of window and clambered down by the vine, and here she was. 'But it is the last time,' she added. 'Ah! let us make haste; is not that Françoise?' He helped her in, and in a minute they were driving away along the Faubourg. Elly let down the veil. John saw that her hand was trembling, and asked if she was afraid?

'I am afraid, because I know I am doing wrong,' said Elly; 'only I think I should have died for want of fresh air in that hateful prison, if I had not come.'

'You used to like your little apartment near the Madeleine better,' said Dampier; 'that was not a prison.'

'I grow sick with regret when I think of those days,' Elly said. 'Do you know that day you spoke to us in the Tuileries was the last happy day in my life, except——'

'Except?' said Dampier.

'Except yesterday,' said Elly. 'It is so delightful to do something wrong again.'

'Why should you think that this is doing wrong?' said Dampier. 'You know me, and can trust me—can't you, Elly?'

'Have I shown much mistrust?' said Elly, laughing; and then she added more seriously, 'I have been writing to Anthony this morning—I have done as you told me. So you see whether I trust you or not.'

'You have refused him?' said Dampier.

'Yes; are you satisfied?' said Elly, looking with her bright blue-eyed glance.

'He was unworthy of you,' cried Dampier, secretly rather dismayed to find his advice so quickly acted upon. What had he done? would not that marriage, after all, have been the very best thing for Elly perhaps? He was glad and sorry, but I think he would rather have been more sorry and less glad, and have heard that Elly had found a solution to all her troubles. He thought it necessary to be sentimental; it was the least he could do, after what she had done for him.

'Why wouldn't you let me in when I came to see you one day long ago, just before I left Paris?' he asked suddenly. 'Do you know what I wanted to say to you?'

Elly blushed up under her veil. 'Mamma had desired Clementine to let no one in. Did you not know I would have seen you if I could?'

'I knew nothing of the sort,' said Dampier, rather sadly. 'I wish—I wish—I had known it.' He forgot that, after all, that was not the real reason of his going away without speaking. He chose to imagine that this was the reason—that he would have married Elly but for this. He forgot his own careful scruples and hesitations; his doubts and indecision; and now to-day he forgot everything, except that he was very sorry for Elly, and glad to give her a little pleasure. He did not trouble himself as to what people would say of her—of a girl who was going about with a man who was neither her brother nor her husband. Nobody would know her. The only people to fear were the people at home, who should never hear anything about it. He would give her and give himself a little happiness, if he could; and he said to himself that he was doing a good action in so doing; he would write to his aunt about her, he would be her friend and her doctor, and if he could bring a little colour in those wasted cheeks and happiness into those sad eyes, it would be wicked and cruel not to do so.

And so, like a quack doctor, as he was, he administered his drug, which soothed and dulled her pain for the moment, only to increase and hasten the progress of the cruel malady which was destroying her. They drove along past the Madeleine, along the broad glittering Boulevards, with their crowds, their wares, people thronging the pavements, horses and carriages travelling alongside with them; the world, the flesh, and the devil jostling and pressing past.

'There is a theatre,' cried Elly, as they came to a sudden stop. 'I wonder, shall I ever go again? What fun it used to be.'

'Will you come to-night?' asked Dampier, smiling, 'I will take care of you.'

Elly, who had found her good spirits again, laughed and clasped her hands. 'How I should like it. Oh! how I wish it was possible, but it would be quite, quite impossible.'

'Have you come to think such vanities wrong?' said Dampier.

'Not wrong. Where is the harm? Only unattainable. Imagine Madame Jacob; think of the dragons, who would tear me to pieces if they found me out—of Anthony—of my step-father.'

'You need not show them the play-bill,' said Dampier, laughing. 'You will be quite sure of not meeting any of the pasteurs there. Could you not open one of those barred windows and jump out? I would come with a ladder of ropes, if you will let me.'

'I should not want a ladder of ropes,' said Elly; 'the windows are quite close to the ground. What fun it would be! but it is quite, quite impossible, of course.'

Dampier said no more. He told the driver to turn back, and to stop at the Louvre; and he made her get out, and took her upstairs into the great golden hall with the tall windows, through which you can see the Seine as it rushes under the bridges, and the light as it falls on the ancient stately quays and houses, on the cathedral, on the towers of Paris. It was like enchantment to Elly; all about the atmosphere was golden, was bewitched. She was eagerly drinking her cup of happiness to the dregs, she was in a sort of glamour. She hardly could believe that this was herself.

They went and sat down on the great round sofa in the first room, opposite the 'Marriage of Cana,' with 'St. Michael killing the Dragon' on one side, and the green pale wicked woman staring at them from behind: the pale woman with the unfathomable face. Elly kept turning round every now and then, fascinated by her cold eyes. Dampier was a connoisseur, and fond of pictures, and he told Elizabeth all about those which he liked best; told her about the painters—about their histories. She was very ignorant, and scarcely knew the commonest stories. How she listened; how she treasured up his words, how she remembered, in after days, every tone as he spoke, every look in his kind eyes! He talked when he should have been silent, looked kind when he should have turned his eyes away. What cruel kindness! what fatal friendship! He imagined she liked him; he knew it, indeed: but he fancied that she liked him and loved him in the same quiet way in which he loved her—hopelessly, regretfully, resignedly. As he walked by her side along these wonderful galleries, now and then it occurred to him that, perhaps, after all, it was scarcely wise; but he put the thought quickly away, as I have said already, and blinded himself, and said, surely it was right. They were standing before a kneeling abbess in white flannel, painted by good old Philip of Champagne, and laughing at her droll looks and her long nose, when Sir John, happening to turn round, saw his old acquaintance De Vaux coming directly towards them with his eye-glasses stuck over his nose, and his nose in the air. He came up quite close, stared at the abbess, and walked on without apparently seeing or recognising them. Elly had not turned her head, but Dampier drew a long breath when he was gone. Elly wondered to see him looking so grave when she turned round with a smile and made some little joke. 'I think we ought to go, Elly,' said he. 'Come; this place will soon be shut.'

They drove home through the busy street, once more, through the golden sunset. They stopped at the corner by the hospital, and Elly said 'Good-by,' and jumped out. As Elly was reluctantly turning to go away, Dampier felt that he *must* see her once more; that he *couldn't* part from her now. 'Elly,' he said, 'I shall be here at six o'clock on Friday. This is Tuesday, isn't it? and we must go to the play just once together. Won't you come? Do, please, come.'

'Shall I come? I will think about it all to-morrow,' said Elly, 'and make up my mind.' And then Dampier watched the slim little figure disappear under the doorway.

Fortune was befriending Elly to-day. Old Françoise had left the great door open, and now she slipped in and ran up to her own room, where she found the key in the lock. She came down quite demurely to dinner when Lou-Lou came to summon her to the frugal repast.

All dinner-time she thought about her scheme, and hesitated, and determined, and hesitated, and wished wistfully, and then suddenly said to herself that she would be happy her own way, come what might. 'We will eat, drink, and be merry,' said Elly to herself, with a little wry face at the cabbage, 'for to-morrow we die.'

And so the silly girl almost enjoyed the notion of running wild in this reckless way. Her whole life, which had been so dull and wearisome before, glittered with strange happiness and bewildering hope. She moved about the house like a person in a dream. She was very silent, but that of late had been her habit. Madame Jacob looked surprised sometimes at her gentleness, but thought it was all right, and did not trouble herself about much else besides Tou-Tou's and Lou-Lou's hymns and lessons. She had no suspicion. She thought that Elizabeth's first escapade had been a mere girlish freak; of the second she knew nothing; of the third not one dim imagination entered her head. She noticed that Elly did not eat, but she looked well and came dancing into

the room, and she (Mme. Jacob) supposed it was all right.
Was it all right? The whole summer nights Elly used to
lie awake with wide-open eyes, or spring from her bed,
and stand for long hours leaning from her window, staring
at the stars and telling them all her story. The life she
was leading was one of morbid excitement and feverish
dreams.

CHAPTER VI.

> What are we sent on earth for? Say to toil,
> Nor seek to leave the tending of the vines,
> For all the heat of day till it declines,
> And death's mild curfew shall from work assoil.

MADAME JACOB had a friend at Asnières, an old maiden lady, Tou-Tou's godmother, who was well to do in the world, with her 200*l.* a year, it was said, and who lived in a little Chinese pagoda by the railway. Now and then this old lady used to write and invite Tou-Tou and Lou-Lou and their mother to come and see her, and you may be sure her invitations were never disregarded.

Mme. Jacob did look at Elizabeth rather doubtfully when she found on Wednesday morning the usual ill-spelt, ill-written little letter. But, after all, Tou-Tou's prospects were not to be endangered for the sake of looking after a young woman like Elizabeth, were she ten times more wayward and ill-behaved, and so the little girls were desired to make up their paquets. It was a great event in Mme. Jacob's eyes; the house echoed with her directions; Françoise went out to request assistance, and came back with a friend, who helped her down with the box. The little girls stood at the door to stop the omnibus, which was to take them to the station. They were off at last. The house door closed upon them with a satisfactory bang, and Elly breathed freely and ran through the deserted rooms clapping and waving her hands, and dancing her steps, and feeling at last that she was free. And so the morning hours went by. Old Françoise was not sorry either to see everybody go. She was sitting in the kitchen in the afternoon peeling onions and potatoes, when Elly came wandering in in her restless way, with her blue eyes shining and her curly hair pushed back. What a tranquil little kitchen it was, with a glimpse of the courtyard outside, and the cocks and the hens, and the poplar-trees waving in the sunshine, and the old woman sitting in her white cap busy at her homely work. Elly did not think how tranquil it was, but said to herself as she looked at Françoise, how old she was, and what a strange fate hers, that she should be there quietly peeling onions at the end of her life. What a horrible fate, thought Elizabeth, to be sitting by one's grave, as it were, paring vegetables and cooking broth to the last day of one's existence. Poor Françoise! And then she said out loud, 'Françoise, tell me, are cooks like ladies; do they get to hate their lives sometimes? Are you not tired to death of cooking *pot-au-feu?*'

'I am thankful to have *pot-au-feu* to cook,' said Françoise. 'Mademoiselle, I should like to see you *éplu-*

cher vegetables sometimes, as I do, instead of running about all day. It would be much better for you.'

'Ecoutez, Françoise,' said Elly, imploringly; 'when I am old like you, I will sit still by the fire; now that I am young I want to run about. I am the only young person in this house. They are all old here, and like dead people, for they only think of heaven.'

'That is because they are on the road,' said Françoise. 'Ah! they are good folks—they are.'

'I see no merit in being good,' Elizabeth said, crossly, sitting down on the table and dabbling her fingers in a bowl of water, which stood there; 'they are good because they like it. It amuses them, it is their way of thinking — they like to be better than their neighbours.'

'*Fi donc*, Elizabeth!' said Françoise. 'You do not amuse them; but they are good to you. Is it Anthony's way of thinking when he bears with all your caprices? When my master comes home quite worn out and exhausted, and trudges off again without so much as waiting for his soup, if he hears he is wanted by some poor person or other, does he go because it pleases him, or because he is serving the Lord in this world, as he hopes to serve Him in the next?'

Elly was a little ashamed, and said, looking down, 'Have you always lived here with him, Françoise?'

'Not I,' said Françoise; 'ten years, that is all. But that is long enough to tell a good man from a bad one.

Good people live for others, and don't care about themselves. I hope when I have known you ten years, that you too will be a good woman, mademoiselle.'

'Like Madame Jacob?' said Elly.

Françoise shrugged her shoulders rather doubtfully, and Elly sat quite still watching her. Was it not strange to be sitting there in this quiet everyday kitchen, with a great unknown world throbbing in her heart. 'How little Françoise guesses,' thought Elly; 'Françoise, who is only thinking of her marmite and her potatoes.' Elly did not know it, but Françoise had a very shrewd suspicion of what was going on in the poor little passionate heart. 'The girl is not suited here,' thought the old woman. 'If she has found someone, so much the better; Clementine has told me something about it. If madame were to drive him off again, that would be a pity. But I saw them quite plainly that day I went to Martin, the chemist's, driving away in that little carriole, and I saw him that night when he was waiting for his mother.'

So old Françoise peels potatoes, and Elly sits wondering and saying over to herself, 'Good people live for others.' Who had she ever lived for but for herself? Ah! there was one person whom she would live and die for now. Ah! at last she would be good. 'And about the play?' thought Elly; 'shall I go—shall I send him word that I will not? There is no harm in a play; why should I not please him and accept his kindness? it is not the first time that we have been there together. I know that plays are not wrong, whatever these stupid people say. Ah! surely if happiness is sent to me, it would be wicked to turn away, instead of being always—always grateful all my life.' And so, though she told herself that it could not be wrong to go, she forgot to tell herself that it was wrong to go with him; her scruples died away one by one; once or twice she thought of being brave and staying away, and sending a message by old Françoise, but she only thought of it.

All day long, on Friday, she wandered about the empty house, coming and going, like a girl bewitched. She went into the garden; she picked flowers and pulled them to pieces, trying to spell out her fate; she tried to make a wreath of vine-leaves, but got tired, and flung it away. Old Françoise, from her kitchen window, watched her standing at the grating and pulling at the vine; but the old woman's spectacles were somewhat dim, and she did not see Elly's two bright feverish eyes and her burning cheeks from the kitchen window. As the evening drew near, Elly's cheeks became pale, and her courage nearly failed her, but she had been three days at home. Monsieur and Madame Tourneur were expected the next morning; she had not seen Dampier for a long, long time —so it seemed to her. Yes, she would go; she did not care. Wrong? Right? It was neither wrong nor right, —it was simply impossible to keep away. She could not

think of one reason in the world why she should stop.
She felt a thousand in her heart urging, ordering, compelling her to go. She went up to her own room after dinner, and began to dress, to plait, and to smoothe her pretty curly hair. She put on a white dress, a black lace shawl, and then she found that she had no gloves. Some of her ancient belongings she kept in a drawer, but they were not replaced as they wore out. And Elly possessed diamond rings and bracelets in abundance; but neither gloves, nor money to buy them. What did it matter? She did not think about it twice; she put on her shabby bonnet and ran downstairs. She was just going out, when she remembered that Françoise would wonder what had become of her, and so she went to the kitchen-door, opened it a little way, and said, 'Good-night, Françoise! don't disturb me to-night, I want to get up early to-morrow.'

Françoise, who had invited a friend to spend the evening, said, 'Bon soir, mamzelle!' rather crossly,—she did not like her kitchen invaded at all times and hours,—and then Elly was free to go.

She did not get out by the window, there was no need for that, but she unfastened it, and unbarred the shutter on the inside, so that, though everything looked much as usual on the outside, she had only to push, and it would fly open.

As she got to the door, her heart began to beat, and she stopped for an instant to think. Inside, here, where she was standing, was dulness, weariness, security, death; outside, wonderful happiness, dangerous happiness, and life —so it seemed to her. Inside were cocks and hens, and sermons, weary exhortations, old Françoise peeling her onions. Outside, John Dampier waiting, the life she was created for, fresh air, congenial spirits, light and brightness,—and heaven there as well as here, thought Elly, clasping her hands ; heaven spreading across the housetops as well as over this narrow courtyard. 'What shall I do? Oh! shall I be forgiven? Oh! it will be forgiven me, surely, surely!' the girl sighed, and, with trembling hands, she undid the latch, and went out into the dusky street.

The little carriole, as Françoise called it, was waiting, a short way down, at the corner of the hospital; and Dampier came to meet her, looking very tall and straight through the twilight. She wondered at his grave, anxious face; but, in truth, he too was exceedingly nervous, though he would not let her know it: he was beginning to be afraid for her, and had resolved that he would not take her out again; it might, after all, be unpleasant for them both; he had seen De Vaux, and found out, to his annoyance, that he had recognised them in the Louvre the day before, and had passed them by on purpose. There was no knowing what trouble he might not get poor Elly into. And, besides, his aunt Jean was on her way to Paris. She had been keeping house for Will Dampier, she wrote, and she was coming. Will was on his way to Switzerland, and she should cross with him.

That very day John had received a letter from her, in answer to the one he had written about Elly. He had written it three days ago; but he was not the same man he had been three days ago. He was puzzled, and restless, and thoroughly wretched, that was the truth, and he was not used to be unhappy, and he did not like it. Elly's face haunted him day and night; he thought of her continually; he tried, in vain, to forget her, to put her out of his mind. Well, on the whole he was glad that his aunt was coming, and very glad that his mother and Lætitia were still away, and unconscious of what he was thinking about.

'So you did not lose courage?' he said, as they were driving off. 'How did you escape Madame Jacob?'

'I have been all alone,' said Elly, 'these two days. How I found courage to come I cannot tell you. I don't quite believe that it is I myself who am here. It seems impossible. I don't feel like myself. I have not for some days past. All I know is, that I am certain those horrible long days have come to an end.' John Dampier was frightened—he hardly knew why—when he heard her say this.

'I hope so, most sincerely,' said he. 'But, after all, Elly, we men and women are rarely contented; and there are plenty of days, more or less tiresome, in store for me and for you, I hope. We must pluck up our courage and go through with them. You are such a sensitive, weak-minded little girl that you will go on breaking your heart a dozen times a day to the end of your life.'

Dampier looked very grave as he spoke, though it was too dark for her to see him. He was angry and provoked with himself, and an insane impulse came over him to knock his head violently against the sides of the cab. Insane, do I say? It would have been the very best thing he could have done. But they drove on all the same: Elly in rapture. She was not a bit afraid now. Her spirits were so high and so daring that they would carry her through anything; and when she was with Dampier she was content to be happy, and not to trouble herself with vague apprehensions. And she was happy now: her eyes danced with delight, her heart beat with expectation, she seemed to have become a child again, she was not like a woman any more.

'Have you not a veil?' said Dampier, as they stopped before the theatre. There was a great light, a crowd of people passing and repassing; other carriages driving up.

'No,' said Elly. 'What does it matter? Who will know me?'

'Well, make haste. Here, take my arm,' said Sir John, hurriedly; and he hastily sprang down and helped her out.

'Look at the new moon,' said Elly, looking up smiling.

'Never mind the new moon. Come, Elly,' said Dampier. And so they passed on into the theatre.

Dampier was dreading recognition. He had a feeling that they would be sure to come against someone. Elly feared no one. When the play began she sat entranced, thrilling with interest, carried away. *Faust* was the piece which they were representing; and as each scene was played before her, as one change after another came over the piece, she was lost more and more in wonder. If she looked up for an instant it was to see John Dampier's familiar face opposite; and then outside the box, with its little curtain, great glittering theatre-lights, crystals reflecting the glitter, gilding, and silken drapery; everywhere hundreds of people, silent, and breathless too, with interest, with excitement. The music plays, the scene shifts and changes, melting into fresh combinations. Here is *Faust*. Listen to him as he laments his wasted life. Of what use is wisdom? What does he care for knowledge? A lonely man without one heart to love, one creature to cherish him. Has he not wilfully wasted the best years of his life? he cries, in a passion of rage and indignation—wasted them in the pursuit of arid science, of fruitless learning? Will these tend him in his old age, soothe his last hours, be to him wife, and children, and household, and holy home ties? Will these stand by his bedside, and close his weary, aching eyes, and follow him to his grave in the churchyard?

Faust's sad complaint went straight to the heart of his hearers. The church bell was ringing up the street. Fathers, mothers, and children were wending their way obedient to its call. And the poor desolate old man burst into passionate and hopeless lamentation.

It was all so real to Elly that she almost began to cry herself. She was so carried away by the play, by this history of Faust and of Margaret, that it was in vain Dampier begged her to be careful, to sit back in the shade of the curtain, and not to lean forward too eagerly. She would draw back for a minute or two, and then by degrees advance her pretty, breathless head, turning to him every now and then. It was like a dream to her. Like a face in a dream, too, did she presently recognise the face of De Vaux, her former admirer, opposite, in one of the boxes. But Margaret was coming into the chapel with her companions, and Elly was too much interested to think of what he would think of her. Just at that moment it was Margaret who seemed to her to be the important person in the world.

De Vaux was of a different opinion; he looked towards them once or twice, and at the end of the second act, Dampier saw him get up and leave his seat. Sir John was provoked and annoyed beyond measure. He did not want him, De Vaux, least of all people in the world. Every moment he felt as he had never felt before—how wrong it was to have brought Elly, whom he was so fond

H

of, into such a situation. For a moment he was undecided, and then he rose, biting his lips, and opened the door of the box, hoping to intercept him; but there was his Mephistopheles, as ill luck would have it, standing at the door ready to come in.

'I thought I could not be mistaken,' De Vaux began, with a smirk, bowing, and looking significantly from one to the other. 'Did you see me in the gallery of the Louvre the other day?'

Elly blushed up very red, and Dampier muttered an oath as he caught sight of the other man's face. He was smiling very disagreeably. John glanced a second time, hesitated, and then said, suddenly and abruptly, 'No, you are not mistaken. This is Miss Gilmour, my *fiancée*, M. de Vaux. I dare say you are surprised that I should have brought her to the play. It is the custom in our country.' He did not dare look at Elly as he spoke. Had he known what else to say he would have said it.

De Vaux was quite satisfied, and instantly assumed a serious and important manner. The English miss was to him the most extraordinary being in creation, and he would believe anything you liked to tell him of her. He was prepared to sit down in the vacant chair by Elizabeth, and make himself agreeable to her.

The English miss was scarcely aware of his existence. Faust, Margaret, had been the whole world to her a minute ago. Where was she now? . . . where were they? . . .

Was she the actress? and were they the spectators looking on? . . . Was that the Truth which he had spoken? Did he mean it? Was there such wonderful, wonderful happiness in store for a poor little wretch like herself? Ah! could it be—could it be true? Her whole soul shone in her trembling eyes, as she looked up for one instant, and upturned her flashing, speaking, beaming face. Dampier was very pale, and was looking vacantly at the stage. Margaret was weeping, for her troubles had begun. Mephistopheles was laughing, and De Vaux chatting on in an agreeable manner, with his hat between his knees. After some time, he discovered that they were not paying attention to one single word he was saying; upon which he rose in an *empressé* manner, wished them good-by politely, and went away, very well pleased with his own good breeding. And then, when he was gone, when the door was shut, when they were alone together, there was a silence, and Elly leant her head against the side of the box; she was trembling so that she could not sit up. And Dampier, looking white and grey in the face somehow, said, in an odd, harsh voice,—

'Elly, you must not mind what I was obliged to say just now. You see, my dear child, that it doesn't do. I ought never to have brought you, and I could think of no better way to get out of my scrape than to tell him that lie.'

'It was—it was a lie?' repeated Elly, slowly raising herself upright.

'What could I do?' Sir John continued, very nervously and exceedingly agitated. 'Elly, my dear little girl, I could not let him think you were out upon an unauthorised escapade We all know how it is, but he does not. You must, you do forgive me—only say you do.'

'And it is not true?' said Elly, once more, in a bewildered, piteous way.

'I—I belong to Lætitia. It was settled before we came abroad,' faltered Dampier; and he just looked at her once, and then he turned away. And the light was gone out of her face; all the sparkle, the glitter, the amazement of happiness. Just as this shining theatre, now full of life, of light, of excitement, would be in a few hours black, ghastly, and void. John Dampier did not dare to look at her again—he hesitated, he was picking and choosing the words which should be least cruel, least insulting; and while he was still choking and fumbling, he heard a noise outside, a whispering, as the door flew open. Elly looked up and gave a little low plaintive cry, and two darkling, frowning men in black coats came into the box.

They were the Pasteurs Boulot and Tourneur.

Who cares to witness, who cares to read, who cares to describe scenes such as these? Reproach, condemnation, righteous wrath, and indignation, and then one crushed, bewildered, almost desperate little heart.

She was hurried out into the night air. She had time to say good-bye, not one other word. He had not stretched out a hand to save her. The play was going on, all the people were sitting in their places, one or two looked up as she passed by the open doors. Then they came out into the street; the stars were all gone, the night was black with clouds, and a heavy rain was pouring down upon the earth. The drops fell wet upon her bare, uncovered head. 'Go under shelter,' said the Pasteur Boulot; but she paid no heed, and in a minute a cab came up, the two men clasped each other's hands in the peculiar silent way to which they were used. Boulot walked away. And Elly found herself alone, inside the damp vehicle, driving over the stones. Her stepfather had got upon the box; he was in a fury of indignation, so that he could not trust himself to be with her.

His indignation was not what she most feared. Another torturing doubt filled her whole heart. Her agony of hopelessness was almost unendurable: she was chilled through and through, but she did not heed it—and faint, and sick, and wearied, but too unhappy to care. Unhappy is hardly the word—bewilderment, a sort of crushed dull misery, would better describe her state. She felt little remorse: she had done wrong, but not very wrong, she thought. She sat motionless in the corner of the jolting cab, with the rain beating in at the open window, as they travelled through the black night and the splashing streets.

By what unlucky chance had M. Boulot been returning home along the Boulevards about half-past seven, at the very moment when Elly, jumping from the carriage, stopped to look up at the little new moon? He, poor man, could hardly believe his eyes. He did not believe them, and went home wondering, and puzzling, and asking himself if that audacious girl could be so utterly lost as to set her foot in that horrible den of iniquity. Ah! it was impossible; it was some one strangely like her. She could not be so lost—so perverted. But the chances were still against Elly; for when he reached the modest little apartment where he lived, his maid-servant told him that M. Tourneur had been there some time, and was waiting to see him. And there in the study, reading by the light of the green lamp, sat Tourneur, with his low-crowned hat lying on the table. He had come up on some business connected with an appointment he wanted to obtain for Anthony. His wife was to follow him next day, he said, and then he and Boulot fell to talking over their affairs and Anthony's prospects and chances.

'Poor Anthony, he has been sorely tried and proved of late,' said his father. 'Elizabeth will never make him happy.'

'Never—never—never!' cried Boulot. 'Elizabeth!—

she!—the last person in the world a pastor ought to think of as a wife!'

'If she were more like her mother,' sighed Tourneur.

'Ah! that would be different,' said Boulot; 'but the girl causes me deep anxiety, my friend. Hers is, I fear an unconverted spirit. Her heart is of this world; she requires much earnest teaching. Did you take her to Fontainebleau with you?'

'She would not come,' said Tourneur; 'she is at home with my sister, Madame Jacob; or rather by herself, for my sister went away a day or two ago.'

'Tourneur, you do not do wisely to leave that girl alone; she is not to be trusted,' said the other, suddenly remembering all his former doubts. And so, when Tourneur asked what he meant, he told him what he had seen. The mere suspicion was a blow for our simple-minded pasteur. He loved Elly; with all her waywardness, there was a look in her eyes which nobody could resist. In his heart of hearts he liked her better for a daughter-in-law than any one of the decorous young women who were in the habit of coming to be catechized by him. But to think that she had deceived him, to think that she had forgotten herself so far, forgotten his teaching, his wishes, his firm convictions, sinned so outrageously! Ah, it was too much; it was impossible, it was unpardonable. He fired up, and in an agitated voice said that it could not be; that he knew her to be incapable of such horrible conduct, and then seizing his hat, he rushed downstairs and called a carriage which happened to be passing by.

'Where are you going?' asked Boulot, who had followed him, somewhat alarmed.

'I am going home, to see that she is there. Safe in her room, and sheltered under her parents' roof, I humbly pray. Far away from the snares, and dangers, and temptations of the world.'

Alas! poor Elly was not at home, peacefully resting or reading by the lamp light. Françoise, to be sure, told them she was in bed, and Tourneur went hopefully to her door and knocked—

'Elly,' he cried, 'mon enfant! êtes-vous là, ma fille? Répondez, Elizabeth!' and he shook the door in his agitation.

Old Françoise was standing by, holding the candle; Boulot was leaning against the wall. But there came no answer. The silence struck chill. Tourneur's face was very pale, his lips were drawn, and his eyes gleamed as he raised his head. He went away for a minute and came back with a little tool; it did not take long to force back the lock—the door flew open, and there was the empty room all in disorder! In silence truly, but emptiness is not peace always, silence is not tranquillity; a horrible dread and terror came over poor Tourneur; Françoise's hand, holding the light, began to tremble guiltily. Boulot was dreadfully shocked—

'My poor friend! my poor friend!' he began.

Tourneur put his hand to his head—

'How has this come to pass—am I to blame?' said he. 'Oh! unhappy girl, what has she done?—how has she brought this disgrace upon us?' and he fell on his knees by the bedside, and buried his head in the clothes—kneeling there praying for Elly where she had so often knelt and poured out all her sad heart. . . .

Elly, at that minute—sitting in the little box, wondering, delighted, thrilling with interest, with pleasure—did not guess what a strange scene was taking place in her own room at home; she did not once think of what trouble, what grief, she was causing to others, and to herself, poor child, most of all. Only a few minutes more—all the music would cease abruptly for her; all the lights go out; all the sweetness turn to gall and to bitterness. Nearer and nearer comes the sad hour, the cruel awakening; dream on still for a few happy minutes, poor Elly!—nearer and nearer come these two angry silent men, in their black, sombre clothes—nearer and nearer the cruel spoken word which will chill, crush, and destroy. Elizabeth's dreams lasted a little longer, and then she awoke at last

CHAPTER VII.

> Not a flower, not a flower sweet,
>   On my black coffin let there be strown
> Not a friend, not a friend greet
>   My poor corpse where my bones shall be thrown.
> A thousand, thousand sighs to save,
>   Lay me, oh! where
> Sad true lover never find my grave,
>   To weep there.

IT was on the evening of the Monday after that Miss Dampier arrived in Paris, with her bonnet-box, her knitting, her carpet-bag. She drove to Meurice's, and hired a room, and then she asked the servants there who knew him whether Sir John Dampier was still staying in the house. They said he had left the place some time before, but that he had called twice that day to ask if she had arrived. And then Miss Dampier, who always liked to make herself comfortable and at home, went up to her room, had the window opened, light brought, and ordered some tea. She was sitting at the table in her cap, in her comfortable black gown, with her knitting, her writing-desk, her books, all set out about the room. She was pouring out tea for herself, and looking as much at home as if she had lived there for months, when the door opened, and her nephew walked in. She was delighted to see him.

'My dear Jack, how good of you to come,' said the old lady, looking up at him, and holding out her hand. 'But you don't look well. You have been sitting up late and racketing. Will you have some tea to refresh you? I will treat you to anything you like.'

'Ah! don't make jokes,' said Dampier. 'I am very unhappy. Look here, I have got into the most horrible scrape; and not myself only.' And the room shook, and the tea-table rattled, as he went pacing up and down the room with heavy footsteps. 'I want to behave like a gentleman, and I wake up one morning and find myself a scoundrel. Do you see?'

'Tell me about it, my dear,' said Miss Dampier, quietly.

And then poor John burst out and told all his story, confounding himself, and stamping, flinging himself about into one chair after another. 'I meant no harm,' he said. 'I wanted to give her a little pleasure, and this is the end. I think I have broken her heart, and those *pasteurs* have murdered her by this time. They won't let me see her; Tourneur almost ordered me out of the house. Aunt Jean, do say something; do have an opinion.'

'I wish your cousin was here,' said Miss Dampier; 'he is the parson of the family, and bound to give us all good advice; let me write to him, Jack. I have a certain reliance on Will's good sense.'

'I won't have Will interfering with my affairs,' cried the other, testily. 'And you—you will not help me, I see?'

'I will go and see Elizabeth,' said Miss Dampier, 'to-night, if you like. I am very, very sorry for her, and for you too, John. What more can I say? Come again in an hour, and I will tell you what I think.'

So Miss Dampier was as good as her word, and set off on her pilgrimage, and drove along the lighted streets, and then past the cab-stand and the hospital to the house with the shuttered windows. Her own heart was very sad as she got out of the carriage and rang at the bell. But looking up by chance, she just saw a gleam of light which came from one of the upper windows and played upon the wall. She took this as a good omen, and said to herself that all would be well. Do you believe in omens? The light came from a room where Elly was lying asleep, and dreaming gently,—calm, satisfied, happy for once, heedless of the troubles, and turmoils, and anxieties of the waking people all round about her. She looked very pale, her hands were loosely clasped, the light was in the window, flickering; and meanwhile, beneath the window, in the street, Miss Dampier stood waiting under the stars. She did not know that Elly saw her in her dim dreams, and somehow fancied that she was near.

The door opened at last. How black the courtyard looked behind it! 'What do you want?' said Clementine, in a hiss. 'Who is it?'

'I want to know how Miss Gilmour is,' said Miss Dampier, quite humbly, 'and to see Monsieur or Madame Tourneur.'

'Vous êtes Madame Dampierre,' said Clementine. 'Madame est occupée. Elle ne reçoit pas.'

'When will she be disengaged?' said the old lady.

'*Ma foi!*' said Clementine, shrugging her shoulders, 'that I cannot tell you. She has desired me to say that she does not wish to see anybody.' And the door was shut with a bang. Elly woke up, startled from her sleep; and old Françoise, happening to come into the room, carried the candle away.

Miss Dampier went home very sad and alarmed, she scarcely knew why. She wrote a tender little letter to Elly next day. It was :—

'Dear Child,—You must let me come and see you. We are very unhappy, John and I, to think that his imprudence has caused you such trouble. He does not know how to beg you to forgive him—you and M. Tourneur and your mother. He should have known better; he has been unpardonably thoughtless, but he is nearly broken-hearted about it. He has been engaged to Lætitia for three or four months, and you know how long she has loved him.

Dearest Elly, you must let me come and see you, and perhaps one day you may be trusted to the care of an old woman, and you will come home with me for a time, and brighten my lonely little house. Your affectionate old friend,   'JEAN DAMPIER.'

But to this there came no answer. Miss Dampier went again and could not get in. She wrote to Madame Tourneur, who sent back the letter unopened. John Dampier walked about pale and haggard, and remorseful.

One evening he and his aunt were dining in the public room of the hotel, and talking over this affair, when the waiter came and told them that a gentleman wanted to speak to Miss Dampier, and the old lady got up and went out of the room. She came back in an instant, looking very agitated. 'John!' she said—'oh, John!' and then began to cry. She could not speak for a minute, while he, quite frightened for his part, hastily went to the door. A tall young man was standing there, wrapped in a loose coat, who looked into his face and said—

'Are you Sir John Dampier? My sister Elizabeth would like to see you again. I have come for you.'

'Your sister Elizabeth!' said Dampier, looking surprised.

The other man's face changed as he spoke again. 'I am Anthony Tourneur; I have come to fetch you, because it is her wish, and she is dying, we fear.'

The two men stood looking at one another for one horrible moment, then Dampier slowly turned his face round to the wall. In that one instant, all that cruel weight which had almost crushed poor Elly to death came and fell upon his broad shoulders, better able, in truth, to bear it, than she had ever been.

He looked up at last. 'Have I done this?' said he to Tourneur, in a sort of hoarse whisper. 'I meant for the best.'

'I don't know what you have done,' said the other, very sadly. 'Life and death are not in your hands or mine. Let us pray that our mistakes may be forgiven us. Are you ready now?'

Elly's visions had come to an end. The hour seemed to be very near when she should awake from the dream of life. Dim figures of her mother, her step-father, of old Françoise, came and stood by her bed-side. But how far-off they appeared; how distant their voices sounded. Old Françoise came into her room the morning after Elly had been brought home, with some message from Tourneur, desiring her to come downstairs and speak to him: he had been lying awake all night, thinking what he should say to her, praying for her, imploring grace, so that he should be allowed to touch the rebellious spirit, to point out all its errors, to bring it to the light. And, meanwhile, Elly, the rebellious spirit, sat by her bedside in a sort of bewildered misery. She scarcely told herself why she was so unhappy. She wondered a little that there was agony so great to be endured; she had never conceived its existence before. Was he gone for ever—was it Lætitia whom he cared for? 'You know that I belong to Lætitia,' he had said. How could it be? all heaven and earth would cry out against it. Lætitia's—Lætitia, who cared so little, who was so pale, and so cold, and so indifferent? How could he speak such cruel words? Oh, shame, shame! that she should be so made to suffer. 'A poor little thing like me,' said Elly, 'lonely and friendless, and heart-broken.' The pang was so sharp that it seemed to her like physical pain, and she moaned, and winced, and shivered under it—was it she herself or another person that was here in the darkness? She was cold too, and yet burning with thirst; she groped her way to the jug, and poured out a little water, and drank with eager gulps. Then she began to take off her damp clothes; but it tired her, and she forgot to go on; she dropped her cloak upon the floor, and flung herself upon the bed, with a passionate outcry. Her mouth was dry and parched, her throat was burning, her hands were burning too. In the darkness she seemed to see his face and Lætitia's glaring at her, and she turned sick and giddy at the sight; presently, not theirs only, but a hundred others—Tourneur's, Boulot's, Faust's, and Mephistopheles'—crowding upon her and glaring furiously. She fell into a short, uneasy sleep once, and woke up with a moan as the hospital clock struck three. The moon was shining into her room, ineffably grey, chill, and silent, and as she woke, a horror, a terror, came over her—her heart scarcely beat; she seemed to be sinking and dying away. She thought with a thrill that her last hour was come; the terror seemed to bear down upon her, nearer and closer and irresistible—and then she must have fallen back senseless upon her bed. And so when Françoise came with a message in the morning, which was intended to frighten the rebellious spirit into submission, she found it gone, safe, far away from reproach, from angry chiding and the poor little body lying lifeless, burnt with fierce fever, and racked with dull pain. All that day Elly was scarcely sensible, lying in a sort of stupor. Françoise, with tender hands, undressed her and laid her within the sheets; Tourneur came and stood by the poor child's bedside. He had brought a doctor, who was bending over her.

'It is a sort of nervous fever,' said the doctor, 'and I fear that there is some inward inflammation as well; she is very ill. This must have been impending for some time past.'

Tourneur stood, with clasped hands and a heavy heart, watching the changes as they passed over the poor little face. Who was to blame in this? He had not spoken one word to her the night before. Was it grief? was it repentance? Ah me! Elly was dumb now, and could not answer. All his wrath was turned against Dampier; for Elly he only felt the tenderest concern. But he was too unhappy just now to think of his anger. He went for Madame Tourneur, who came back and set to work to nurse her daughter; but she was frightened and agitated, and seemed scarcely to know what she was about. On the morning of the second day, contrary to the doctor's expectations, Elly recovered her consciousness; on the third day she was better. And when Tourneur came into the room, she said to him, with one of her old pretty, sad smiles, 'You are very angry with me, are you not? You think I ought not to have gone to the play with John Dampier?'

'Ah, my child,' said Tourneur, with a long-drawn, shivering sigh, 'I am too anxious to be angry.'

'Did he promise to marry you, Elly?' said Madame Tourneur, who was sitting by her bedside. She was looking so eagerly for an answer that she did not see her husband's look of reproach.

'How could he?' said Elly, simply. 'He is going to marry Lætitia.'

'Tell me, my child,' said Tourneur, gently taking her hand, 'how often did you go with him?'

'Three times,' Elly answered, faintly. 'Once to the Bois, and once to the Louvre, and then that last time;' and she gasped for breath. Tourneur did not answer, but bent down gently, and kissed her forehead.

It was on that very day that Dampier called. Elly seemed somehow to know that he was in the house. She got excited, and began to wander, and to call him by his name. Tourneur heard her, and turned pale, and set his teeth as he went down to speak to Sir John. In the evening the girl was better, and Anthony arrived from the south. And I think it was on the fifth day that Elly told Anthony that she wanted to see Dampier once again.

'You can guess how it has been,' she said, 'and I love him still, but not as I did. Anthony, is it not strange? Perhaps one is selfish when one is dying. But I want to see him—just once again. Everything is so changed. I cannot understand why I have been so unhappy all this time. Anthony, I have wasted all my life; I have made nobody happy—not even you.'

'You have made me love you, and that has been my happiness,' said Anthony. 'I have been very unhappy too; but I thank heaven for having known you, Elly.'

Elly thought that she had but a little time left. What was there in the solemn nearness of death that had changed her so greatly? She had no terror: she was ready to lie down and go to sleep like a tired child in its mother's arms. Worldly! we call some folks worldly, and truly they have lived for to-day and cared for to-day; but for them, as for us, the great to-morrow comes, and then they cease to be worldly—is it not so? Who shall say that such and such a life is wasted, is purposeless? that such and such minds are narrow, are mean, are earthly? The day comes, dawning freshly and stilly, like any other day in all the year, when the secret of their life is ended, and the great sanctification of Death is theirs.

Boulot came to see Tourneur, over whom he had great influence, and insisted upon being shown to Elizabeth's bedside. She put out her hand and said, 'How-d'ye-do, Monsieur Boulot?' very sweetly, but when he had talked to her for some little time, she stopped him and said,— 'You cannot know how near these things seem, and how much more great, and awful, and real they are, when you are lying here like me, than when you are standing by another person's sick bed. Nobody can speak of them to me as they themselves speak to me.' She said it so simply, with so little intention of offence, that Boulot stopped in the midst of his little sermon, and said farewell quite kindly and gently. And then, not long after he was gone, Anthony came back with the Dampiers.

They walked up the wooden stairs with hearts that ached sorely enough. Miss Dampier was calm and composed again; she had stood by many a death-bed—she was expecting to go herself before very long—but John was quite unnerved. Little Elly, whom he had pitied, and looked down upon, and patronised, was she to be to him from this minute a terror, a life-long regret and remorse? —he could hardly summon courage to walk into the room when the door was opened and Anthony silently motioned him to pass through it.

And yet there was nothing very dreadful. A pale, sweet face lying on the little white bed; the gentle eyes, whose look he knew so well, turned expectantly towards him; a cup with some flowers; a little water in a glass by the bedside; an open window; the sun setting behind the poplar-trees.

Old Françoise was sitting in the window, sewing; the birds were twittering outside. John Dampier thought it strange that death should come in this familiar guise— tranquilly, with the sunset, the rustling leaves of the trees, the scent of the geraniums in the court below, the cackle of the hens, the stitching of a needle—he almost envied Elly, lying resting at the end of her journey: Elly, no longer the silly little girl he had laughed at, chided, and played with—she was wise now, in his eyes.

She could not talk much, but what she said was in her own voice and in her old manner,—' You kind people, to come and see me,' she said, and beckoned to them to approach nearer.

Miss Dampier gave her nephew a warning touch; she saw how agitated he was, and was afraid that he would disturb Elizabeth. But what would he not have done for her? He controlled himself, and spoke quietly, in a low voice—

' I am very grateful to you, dear Elly, for sending for

me. I was longing to hear about you. I want to ask you to forgive me for the ill I have done you. I want to tell you just once that I meant no harm, only it was such a pleasure to myself that I persuaded myself it was right. I know you will forgive me. All my life I will bless you.' And his head fell as he spoke.

'What have I to forgive?' faltered Elly. 'It seems so long ago!—Faust and Margaret, and those pleasant drives. Am I to forgive you because I loved you? That was a sort of madness; but it is gone. I love you still, dear John, but differently. I am not mad now, but in my senses. If I get well, how changed it will be—if I die——'

If she died? Dampier, hating himself all the while, thought, with a chill pang, that here would be a horrible solution to all his perplexities. Perhaps Elly guessed something of what was passing in his mind, for she gave him her hand once more, and faltered,—

'My love to Lætitia,' and, as she spoke, she raised her eyes, with the old familiar look in them.

It was more than he could bear; he stooped and kissed her frail, burning fingers, and then, with scorched, quivering lips, turned aside and went softly out of the room. Anthony and Madame Tourneur were standing outside, and as Dampier passed she looked at him piteously, and her lips trembled too, but she did not speak. It seemed to him somehow—only he was thinking of other things—as if Elly's good and bad angels were waiting there. He himself passed on with a hanging head; what could he say to justify himself?—his sorrow was too real to be measured out into words, his penitence greater almost than the offence had been. Even Tourneur, whom he met in the courtyard, almost forgave him as he glanced at the stricken face that was passing out of his house into the street.

After he was gone, Elly began to wander. Françoise, who had never taken such a bad view of Elly's condition as the others, and who strongly disapproved of all this leave-taking, told Miss Dampier that if they wanted to kill her outright, they need only let in all Paris to stare at her, as they had been doing for the last two days; and Miss Dampier, meekly taking the hint, rose in her turn to go. But Elly, from her bed, knew that she was about to leave her, and cried out piteously, and stretched out her hands, and clutched at her gown.

'Faut rester,' whispered Françoise.

'I mean to stay,' said Miss Dampier, after a moment's deliberation, sitting down at the bedside and untying her bonnet.

Under her bonnet she wore a little prim cap, with loops of grey ribbon; out of her pocket she pulled her knitting and a pair of mittens. She folded up her mantlet and put it away; she signed to Françoise to leave her in charge. When Tourneur came in he found her installed.

and as much at home as if she were there by rights. Elly wished it, she told him, and she would stay were ten pasteurs opposed to it.

Tourneur reluctantly consented at last, much against his will. It seemed to him that her mother ought to be Elly's best nurse, but Madame Tourneur eagerly implored him to let Miss Dampier remain; she seemed strangely scared and helpless, and changed and odd. 'Oh, if you will only make her well!' said she to the old Scotchwoman.

'How can I make her well?' Miss Dampier answered. 'I will try and keep her quiet, that is the chief thing; and if M. Tourneur will let me, I should like to send for my old friend, Dr. Bertin.'

And her persistency overcame Tourneur's bewildered objections; her quiet good sense and determination carried the day. Doctor Bertin came, and the first doctor went off in a huff, and Elly lay tossing on her bed. What a weary rack it was to her, that little white bed! There she lay, scorched and burning—consumed by a fierce fire. There she lay through the long days and the nights, as they followed one by one, waiting to know the end. Not one of them dared think what that end might be. Doctor Bertin himself could not tell how this queer illness might turn; such fevers were sometimes caused by mental disquietude, he said. Of infection there was no fear; he came day after day, and stood pitifully by the bedside.

He had seen her once before in her brilliance and health; he had never cared for her as he did now that she was lying prostrate and helpless in their hands.

Madame Jacob had carried off her children at the first alarm of fever; the house was kept darkened and cool and quiet; and patient Miss Dampier sat waiting in the big chair for good or for ill fortune. Sometimes of an evening she would creep downstairs and meet her nephew in the street outside and bring him news.

And besides John, there was poor Anthony wandering about the house, wretched, anxious, and yet resigned. Often, as a boy, he had feared death; the stern tenets to which he belonged made him subject to its terrors, but now it seemed to him so simple a thing to die, that he wondered at his own past fears. Elly thought it a simple thing to die, but of this fever she was weary—of this cruel pain and thirst and misery; she would moan a little, utter a few complaining words, and wander off into delirium again. She had been worse than usual one evening, the fever higher. It was a bad account that Miss Dampier had to give to the doctor when he came, to the anxious people waiting for news. All night long Elly's kind nurse sat patiently in the big arm-chair, knitting, as was her way, or sometimes letting the needles fall into her lap, and sitting still with clasped hands and a wistful heart. The clocks of the city struck the dark hours as they passed—where these Elly's last upon earth? Jean Dampier sadly wondered. The stars set behind the poplar-trees, a night breeze came shivering now and then through the open window. The night did not appear so very long; it seemed hastening by, dark and silent, relentless to the wearied nurse; for presently, before she knew it almost, it seemed as if the dawn had begun; and somehow, as she was watching still, she fell asleep for a little. While she slept the shadows began to tremble and fade, and fly hither and thither in the death-like silence of the early morning, and when she awoke it was with a start and a chill terror, coming, she knew not whence. She saw that the room was grey, and black no longer. Her heart began to beat, and with a terrified glance she looked round at the bed where Elly was lying.

She looked once, and then again, and then suddenly her trembling hands were clasped in humblest thanksgiving, and the grey head bent lower and lower.

There was nothing to fear any more. Elly was sleeping quietly on her pillow, the fiery spots had faded out of her cheeks, her skin looked fresh and moist, the fever had left her. Death had not yet laid his cold hand on the poor little prey, he had not come while the nurse was sleeping—he had not called her as yet. I speak in this way from long habit and foolishness. For in truth, had he come, would it have been so sad, would it have been so hard a fate—would it have been death with his skeleton's head, and his theatrical grave-clothes and his scythe, and his hour-glass? Would it have been this, or simply the great law of Nature working peacefully in its course — only the seed falling into the ground, only the decree of that same merciful Power which sent us into the world?—us men and women, who are glad to exist, and grateful for our own creation, into a world where we love to tarry for a while?

Jean Dampier, sitting there in the dawning, thought something of all this, and yet how could she help acknowledging the mercy which spared her and hers the pang of having fatally injured this poor little Elly, whom she had learnt to love with all her tender old heart? It seemed a deliverance, a blessing a hundred times beyond their deserts.

She had been prepared for the worst, and yet she had shrunk with terror from the chastisement. Now, in this first moment of relief—now that, after all, Elly was, perhaps, given back to them, to youth, to life—she felt as if she could have borne the blow better than she had ever dared to hope. The sun rose, the birds chirped freshly among the branches, the chill morning spread over the city. Sleepers began to stir, and to awake to their daily cares, to their busy life. Elizabeth's life, too, began anew from this hour.

Someone said to me just now that we can best make others happy by the mere fact of our own existence; as she got well day by day, Elly found that it was so. How had she deserved so much of those about her? she often wondered to herself. A hindrance, a trouble, a vexation to them, was all she had ever been; and yet as one by one they came to greet her, she felt that they were glad. Anthony's eyes were full of tears; Tourneur closed his for an instant, as he uttered a silent thanksgiving—she herself did not know how to thank them all.

And here, perhaps, my story ought to end, but in truth it is not finished, though I should cease to write it down, and it goes on and on as the years go by.

CHAPTER VIII.

> Move eastward, happy earth, and leave
>   Yon orange sunset, waning slow
> From fringes of the faded eve.
>   O happy planet, eastward go,
>   Till over thy dark shoulder glow
> Thy silver sister-world, and rise
> To glass herself in dewy eyes,
>   That watch me from the glen below.

AND so she had left all behind, Elizabeth thought. Paris, the old house, mother, stepfather, and pasteur, the courtyard, the familiar wearisome life, the dull days breaking one by one, John Dampier, her hopeless hopes, and her foolish fancies—she had left them all on the other side of the sea for a time, and come away with kind Miss Dampier.

Here, in England, whither her good friend had brought her to get well, the air is damp with sea breezes; the atmosphere is not keen and exciting as it is abroad; the sky is more often grey than blue; it rarely dazzles and bewilders you with its brilliance; there is humidity and vegetation, a certain placidity and denseness, and moisture of which some people complain. To Elizabeth—nervous, eager, excitable—this quiet green country, these autumn mists, were new life. Day by day she gained strength, and flesh, and tone, and health, and good spirits.

But it was only by slow degrees that this good change was effected; weaknesses, faintnesses, relapses,—who does not know the wearisome course of a long convalescence?

To-night, though she is by way of being a strong woman again, she feels as if she was a very very old one, somehow, as she sits at the window of a great hotel looking out at the sunset. It seems to her as if it was never to rise again. There it goes sinking, glorying over the sea, blazing yellow in the west. The place grows dark; in the next room through the open door her white bed gleams chilly; she shudders as she looks at it, and thinks of the death-bed from which she has scarce risen. There are hours, especially when people are still weak and exhausted by sickness, when life seems unbearable, when death appears terrible, and when the spirit is so weary that it seems as if no sleep could be deep enough to give it rest. 'When I am dead,' thought Elizabeth; 'ah me! my body will be at rest, but I myself, shall I have forgotten—do I want to forget . . . ?'

Meanwhile Miss Dampier, wrapped in her grey cloak, is taking a brisk solitary little walk upon the wooden pier which Elly sees reflected black against the sea. Aunt Jean is serenely happy about her charge; delighted to have carried her off against all opposition; determined that somehow or other she shall never go back; that she shall be made happy one day.

It is late in the autumn. Tourists are flocking home; a little procession of battered ladies and gentlemen carrying all sorts of bundles, and bags, and parcels, disembarks every day; and then another procession of ladies and gentlemen goes to see them land. Any moment you may chance to encounter some wan sea-sick friend staggering along with the rest of the sufferers, who are more or less other people's friends. The waves wash up and down, painted yellow by the sunset. There is no wind, but it has been blowing hard for a day or two, and the sea is not yet calm. How pleasant it is, Miss Dampier thinks; chill, fresh, wholesome. This good air is the very thing for Elly. Along the cliffs the old lady can see the people walking against the sky like little specks. There are plenty of fishing-boats out and about. There is the west still blazing yellow, and then a long grey bank of clouds; and with a hiss and a shrill clamour here comes the tossing dark-shadowed steamer across the black and golden water. All the passengers are crowding on deck and feebly gathering their belongings together; here the *Frederick William* comes close alongside, and as everybody else rushes along the pier to inspect the new comers, good old Jean trots off, too to see what is what. In a few minutes the passengers appear, slowly rising through a trap like the ghost in the *Corsican Brothers*.

First, a lilac gentleman, then a mouldy green gentleman (evidently a foreigner), then an orange lady.

Then a ghostly blue gentleman, then a deadly white lady, then a pale lemon-coloured gentleman, with a red nose.

Then a stout lady, black in the face, then a faltering lady's-maid, with a band-box.

Then a gentleman with an umbrella.

Jean Dampier is in luck to-night, as, indeed, she deserves to be: a more kindly, tender-hearted, unselfish old woman does not exist—if that is a reason for being lucky—however, she has been my good friend for many a long year, and it is not to-day that I am going to begin to pay her compliments.

I was saying she is in luck, and she finds a nephew among the passengers—it is the gentleman with the umbrella; and there they are, greeting one another in the most affectionate manner.

The Nephew.—'Let me get my portmanteau, and then I will come and talk to you as much as you like.'

The Aunt.—'Never mind your portmanteau, the porter will look after it. Where have you been, Will? Where do you come from? I am at the "Flag Hotel," close by.'

The Nephew.—'So I hear.'

The Aunt.—'Who told you that?'

The Nephew.—'A sour-faced woman at Paris. I asked for you at Meurice's, and they sent me to this Madame

Tourneur. She told me all about you. What business is it of yours to go about nursing mad girls?'

Aunt Jean.—'Elly is not mad. You have heard me talk of her a hundred times. I do believe I saved her life, Will; it was my business, if anybody's, to care for her. Her heart was nearly broken.'

The Nephew.—'John nearly broke her heart, did he? I don't believe a word of it' (*smiling very sweetly*). 'You are always running away with one idea after another, you silly old woman. Young ladies' hearts are made of india-rubber, and Lady Dampier says this one is an artful— designing—horrible—abominable——'

Aunt Jean (*sadly*).—'Elly nearly died, that is all. You are like all men, Will——'

The Nephew (*interrupting*).—'Don't! Consider, I'm just out of the hands of the steward. Let me have something to eat before we enter into any sentimental discussion. Here (*to a porter*), bring my portmanteau to the hotel.— Nonsense (*to a flyman*), what should I do with your carriage?'

Will Dampier was a member of the Alpine Club, and went year by year to scramble his holiday away up and down mountain sides. He was a clergyman, comfortably installed in a family living. He was something like his cousin in appearance, but, to my mind, better looking, browner, broader, with bright blue eyes and a charming smile. He looked like a gentleman. He wore a clerical waistcoat. He had been very much complimented upon his good sense; and he liked giving advice, and took pains about it, as he was anxious not to lose his reputation. Now and then, however, he did foolish things, but he did them sensibly, which is a very different thing from doing sensible things foolishly. It seems to me that is just the difference between men and women.

Will was Miss Dampier's ideal of what a nephew should be. They walked back to the hotel together, chattering away very comfortably. He went into the coffee-room and ordered his dinner, and then he came back to his aunt, who was walking on the lawn outside. Meanwhile the sun went on setting; the windows lighted up one by one. It was that comfortable hour when people sit down in little friendly groups and break bread, and take their ease, the business of the day being over. Will Dampier and his aunt took one or two turns along the gravel path facing the sea; he had twenty minutes to wait, and he thought they might be well employed in giving good counsel.

'It seems to me a very wild scheme of yours, carrying off this unruly young woman,' he began; 'she will have to go home sooner or later. What good will you have done?'

'I don't know, I'm sure,' says Miss Dampier, meekly; 'a holiday is good for us at all times. Haven't you enjoyed yours, Will?'

'I should rather think I had. You never saw anything so pretty as Berne the other morning as I was coming away. I came home by the Rhine, you know. I saw aunt Dampier and Tishy for an hour or two.'

'And did you see John at Paris?'

'No; he was down at V——, staying with the M——s. And now tell me about the young lady with the heart. Is she upstairs tearing her hair? Aunt Dampier was furious.'

'So she had heard of it?' said Miss Dampier, thoughtfully. And then she added rather sharply, 'You can tell her that the young lady is quite getting over her fancy. In fact, John doesn't deserve that she should remember him. Now, listen, Will, I am going to tell you a story.' And then, in her quiet, pleasant, old-fashioned way, she told him her version of all that had been happening.

Will listened and laughed, and said, 'You will think me a brute, but I agree with aunt Dampier. Your young woman has behaved as badly as possible; she has made a dead set at poor John, who is so vain that any woman can get him into her clutches.'

'What do you mean?' cries the aunt, quite angry.

'If she had really cared for him, would she have forgotten all about him already? I warn you, aunt Jenny; I don't approve of your heroine.'

'I must go and look after my heroine,' says Miss Dampier, dryly. 'I dare say your dinner is ready.'

But Will Dampier, whose curiosity at all events was excited, followed his aunt upstairs and along the passage, and went in after her as she opened a door; went into a dim chill room, with two wide-set windows, through which the last yellow streaks of the sunset were fading, and the fresh evening blast blew in with a gust as they entered. It was dark, and nothing could be seen distinctly, only something white seemed crouching in a chair, and as the door opened they heard a low sobbing sigh, which seemed to come out of the gloom; and then it was all very silent.

'Elly, my dear child,' said Miss Dampier, 'what is the matter?'

There was no answer.

'Why don't you speak?' said the kind old lady, groping about, and running up against chairs and tables.

'Because I can't speak without crying.' gasps Elly, beginning to cry. 'And it's so ungrateful——'

'You are tired, dear,' says aunt Jean, 'and cold'—taking her hand; and then turning round and seeing that her nephew had come in with her, she said, 'Ring the bell, Will, and go to your dinner. If you will tell them downstairs to send up some tea directly I shall be obliged to you.' William Dampier did as he was bid, and walked away considerably mollified towards poor Elly. 'One is so apt to find fault with people,' he was thinking. 'And there she was crying upstairs all the time, poor wretch.'

He could never bear to see a woman cry. His parishioners—the women, I mean—had found this out, and used to shed a great many tears when he came to see them. He had found them out—he knew that they had found him out, and yet as sure as the apron-corner went up, the half-crown came out of the pocket.

9.30.—*Reading Room, Flag Hotel, Boatstown.*—Mr. William Dampier writing at a side-table to a married sister in India. Three old gentlemen come creaking in : select limp neswpapers, and take their places. A young man who is going to town by the 10.30 train lies down on the sofa and falls asleep, and snores gently. A soothing silence. Mr. Dampier's blunt pen travels along the thin paper. . . . 'What a dear old woman aunt Jenny is. How well she tells a story. Lady Dampier was telling me the same story the other day. I was very much bored I thought each one person more selfish and disagreeable than the other. Now aunt Jenny takes up the tale. The personages all brighten under her friendly old spectacles, and become good, gentle-hearted, romantic, and heroic all at once—as she is herself. I was a good deal struck by her report of poor John's sentimental imbroglio. I drank tea with the imbroglio this evening, and I can't help rather liking her. She has a sweet pretty face, and her voice, when she talks, pipes and thrills like a musical snuff-box. Aunt Jenny wants her for a niece, that is certain, and says that a man ought to marry the wife he likes best. You are sure to agree to that; I wonder what Miles says? But she's torn with sympathy, poor old dear, and first cries over one girl, and then over the other. She says John came to her one day at Paris in a great state of mind, declared he was quite determined to finish with all his uncertainty, and that he had made up his mind to break with Lætitia, and to marry Elizabeth, if she was still in her old way of thinking. Aunt Jean got frightened, refused to interfere, carried off the young lady, and has not spoken to her on the subject. John, who is really behaving very foolishly, is still at Paris, and has not followed them, as I know my aunt hoped he would have done. I can't help being very sorry for him. Lady Dampier has heard of his goings on. A Frenchman told some people, who told some people, who—you know how things get about. Some day when I don't wish it, you will hear all about me, and write me a thundering letter all the way from Lucknow. There is no doubt about the matter. It would be a thousand pities if John were to break off with Lætitia, to speak nothing of the cruelty and the insult to the poor child.

'And so Rosey and Posey are coming home. I am right sorry for their poor papa and mamma. I hope you have sometimes talked to my nieces about their respectable uncle Will. They are sure to be looked after and happy with aunt Jenny, but how you will be breaking your hearts after them! A priest ought perhaps to talk to you of one consolation very certain and efficacious. But I have always found my dear Prue a better Christian than myself, and I have no need to preach to her.'

Will Dampier wrote a close straight little handwriting, only one side of his paper was full, but he did not care to write any more that night: he put up his letter in his case, and walked out into the garden.

It was a great starlight night. The sea gloomed vast and black on the horizon. A few other people were walking in the garden, and they talked in hushed yet distinct voices. Many of the windows were open and alight. Will looked up at the window of the room where he had been to see his aunt. That was alight and open, too, and some one was sitting with clasped hands, looking at the sky. Dampier lit a cigar, and he, too, walked along gazing at the stars, and thinking of Prue's kind face as he went along. Other constellations clustered above her head, he thought; between them lay miles of land and sea, great countries, oceans rushing, plains arid and unknown; vast jungles, deserted cities, crumbling in a broiling sun: it gave him a little vertigo to try and realise what hundreds of miles of distance stretched between their two beating hearts. Distance so great, and yet so little; for he could love his sister, and think of her, and see her, and talk to her, as if she was in the next room. What was that distance which could be measured by miles, compared to the immeasurable gulf that separates each one of us from the nearest and dearest whose hands we may hold in our own?

Will walked on, his mind full of dim thoughts, such as come to most people on starlight nights; when constellations are blazing, and the living soul gazes with awe-stricken wonder at the great living universe, in the midst of which it waits, and trembles, and adores. 'The world all about has faded away,' he thought, 'and lies dark and dim, and indistinct. People are lying like dead people stretched out, unconscious on their beds, heedless, unknowing. Here and there in the houses, a few dead people are lying like the sleepers. Are they as unconscious as the living?' He goes to the end of the garden, and stands looking upward, until he cannot think longer of things so far above him. It seems to him that his brain is like the string of an instrument, which will break under the passionate vibration of harmonies so far beyond his powers to render. He goes back into the house. Everything suddenly grows strangely real and familiar, and yet it seemed, but a moment ago, as if to-day and its cares had passed away for ever.

CHAPTER IX.

> To humbler functions, awful Power,
>   I call Thee: I myself commend
> Unto thy guidance from this hour.
>   Oh, let my weakness have an end.
> Give unto me, made lowly wise,
> The spirit of self-sacrifice—
> The confidence of reason give,
> And in the light of truth *thy bondman* let me live.
> *Ode to Duty.*

ELLY had a little Indian box that her father had once given to her. It served her for a work-box and a treasure casket. She kept her scissors in it and her ruby ring; some lavender, a gold thimble, and her father's picture. And then in a lower tray were some cottons and tapes, one or two letters, a pencil, and a broken silver chain. She had a childish habit of playing with it still, sometimes, and setting it to rights. It was lying on the breakfast-table next morning when Will Dampier came in to see his aunt. Miss Dampier, who liked order, begged Elly to take it off, and Dampier politely, to save her the trouble, set it down somewhere else, and then came to the table and asked for some tea. The fishes had had no luck that morning, he told them; he had been out in a boat since seven o'clock, and brought back a basketful. The sea air made them hungry, no doubt, for they came by dozens —little feeble whiting—and nibbled at the bait. 'I wish you would come,' he said to his aunt; 'the boat bobs up and down in the sunshine, and the breeze is delightfully fresh, and the people come down on the beach and stare at you through telescopes.' As he talked to his aunt he glanced at Elly, who was pouring out his tea; he said to himself that she was certainly an uncommonly pretty girl; and then he began to speculate about an odd soft look in her eyes. 'When I see people with that expression,' he wrote to his sister, 'I always ask myself what it means? I have seen it in the glass, sometimes, when I have been shaving. Miss Gilmour was not looking at me, but at the muffins and tea-cups. She was nicely dressed in blue calico; she was smiling; her hair trim and shiny. I could hardly believe it was my wailing banshee of the previous night.' (What follows is to the purpose, so I may as well transcribe a little more of Will's letter.) 'When she had poured out my tea, she took up her hat and said she should go down to the station, and get *The Times* for my aunt. I should have offered my services, but aunt Jean made me a sign to stay. What for, do you think? To show me a letter she had received in the morning from that absurd John, who cannot make up his mind. "I do not," he says, "want you to talk poor Elly into a *grande passion*. But if her feelings are unchanged,

I will marry her to-morrow, if she chooses; and I daresay Tishy will not break her heart. Perhaps you will think me a fool for my pains; but I shall not be alone in the world. What was poor little Elly herself when she cried for the moon?" This is all rodomontade; John is not acting fairly by Lætitia, to whom he is bound by every possible promise.

'My aunt said just now that it would be hard for Tishy if he married her, liking Elizabeth best: and there is truth in that. But he mustn't like her best; Miss Gilmour will get over her fancy for him, and he must get over his for her. If he had only behaved like a man and married her right off two years ago, and never hankered after the flesh-pots of Egypt, or if he had only left her alone to settle down with her French pasteur——

' "If—if," cried my aunt, impatiently, when I said as much—(you know her way)—"he has done wrong and been sorry for it, Will, which of us can do more? I doubt whether you would have behaved a bit better in his place."

This portion of Mr. Will's letter was written at his aunt's writing-book immediately after their little talk. Elly came in rosy from her walk, and Will went on diligently, looking up every now and then with the sense of *bien-être* which a bachelor experiences when he suddenly finds himself domesticated and at home with kind women.

Miss Dampier was sitting in the window. She had got *The Times* in her hand, and was trying to read. Every now and then she looked up at her nephew, with his curly head bent over his writing, at Elly leaning lazily back in her chair, sewing idly at a little shred of work. Her hair was clipped, the colour had faded out of her cheeks, her eyes gleamed. Pretty as she was, still she was changed—how changed from the Elizabeth of eighteen months ago whom Miss Dampier could remember! The old lady went on with her paper, trying to read. She turned to the French correspondent, and saw something about the Chamber, the Emperor, about Italy; about M. X——, the rich banker, having resolved to terminate his existence, when fortunately his servant enters the room at the precise moment when he was preparing to precipitate himself . . . 'The servant to precipitate . . . the window . . . the . . . poor Tishy! At my age I did think I should have done with sentimental troubles. Heigho! heigho!' sighs Miss Dampier.

Elly wanted some thread, and rose with a soft rustle, and got her box and came back to her easy chair. Out of the window they could see all the pleasant idle business of the little seaport going on, the people strolling in the garden, or sitting in all sorts of queer corners, the boats, the mariners (I do believe they are hired to stand about in blue shirts, and shake their battered old noses as they prose for hours together). The waiter came and took away the breakfast, William went on with his letter, and Miss Dampier, with John's little note in her pocket, was, as I say, reading the most extraordinary things in *The Times* all about her own private concerns. Nobody spoke for some ten minutes, when suddenly came a little gasp, a little sigh from Elly's low chair, and the girl said, ' Aunt Jean! look here,' almost crying, and held out something in her thin hand.

' What is it, my dear?' said Miss Dampier, looking up hastily, and pulling off her spectacles: they were dim somehow and wanted wiping.

' Poor dear, dearest Tishy,' cried Elly, in her odd impetuous way. 'Why does he not go to her? Aunt Jean, look here, I found it in my box—only look here;' and she put a little note into Miss Dampier's hand.

Will looked up curiously from his writing. Elly had forgotten all about him. Miss Dampier took the letter, and when she had read what was written, and then turned over the page, she took off her glasses again with a click, and said, ' What nonsense !'

And so it was nonsense, and yet the nonsense touched Elizabeth, and brought tears into her eyes. They came faster and faster, and then suddenly remembering that she was not alone, and ashamed that Dampier should see her cry again, she jumped up with a shining, blushing, tear-dimmed tender face, and ran away out of the room. Aunt Jean looked at Will doubtfully, then hesitated, and gave him the little shabby letter that had brought these bright tears into the girl's eyes. Dear old soul! she made a sort of confessor of her nephew.

The confessor saw a few foolish words which Lætitia must have written days ago, never thinking that her poor little words were to be scanned by stranger eyes—written perhaps unconsciously on a stray sheet of paper. There was 'John. Dear John! Dear, dearest! I am so hap. . . John and Lætitia. John, my jo. Goose and gander.' And then, by some odd chance, she must have folded the blotted sheet together and forgotten what she had written, and sent it off to Elly Gilmour, with a little careless note about Schlangenbad, and ' more fortunate next time,' on the other side.

'Poor little Letty!' thought Dampier, and he doubled the paper up, and put it back into the lavender box as the door opened, and Miss Gilmour came back into the room. She had dried her eyes, she had fastened on her grey shawl. She picked up her hat, which was lying on the floor, and began pulling on two very formidable looking gauntlets over her slim white hands. 'I am going for a little walk,' she said to Miss Dampier. 'Will you'—hesitating and blushing—'direct that little note of Lætitia's to Sir John? I am going along the cliff towards the pretty little bay.'

Will was quite melted and touched. Was this the scheming young woman, against whom he had been warned? the woman who had entangled his cousin with her wiles?

'Aunt Jenny,' he says, with a sudden glance, 'are you going to tell her why John Dampier does not go to Lætitia?'

'Why does he not go?' Elly repeats, losing her colour a little.

'He says that if you would like him to stay, he thinks he ought not to go,' says Jean Dampier, hesitating, and tearing corners off *The Times* newspaper.

Will Dampier turned his broad back and looked out of window. There was a moment's silence. They could hear the tinkling of bells, the whistling of the sea, the voices of the men calling to each other in the port: the sunshine streamed in: Elly was standing in it, and seemed gilt with a golden background. She ought to have held a palm in her hand, poor little martyr!

It seemed a long time, it was only a minute, and then she spoke; a sweet honest blush came deepening into Elizabeth's pale cheeks: 'I don't want to marry him because I care for him,' she said, in a thrilling pathetic voice. 'Why should Lætitia, who is so fond of him, suffer because I behaved so badly?' The tears once more came welling up into her eyes. 'I shall think I ought to have died instead of getting well,' she said. 'Aunt Jean, send him the little note; make him go, dear aunt Jean.'

Miss Dampier gave Elly a kiss; she did not know

what to say; she could not influence her one way or another.

She wrote to John that morning, taking good care to look at the back of her paper first.

'Flag Hotel, Boatstown, Nov. 15th.

'My dear Jack,—I had great doubts about communicating your letter to Elizabeth. It seemed to me that the path you had determined upon was one full of thorns and difficulties, for her, for you, and for my niece Lætitia. But although Elly is of far too affectionate a nature ever to give up caring for any of her friends, let me assure you that her feelings are now only those of friendly regard and deep interest in your welfare. When I mentioned to her the contents of your letter (I think it best to speak plainly), she said, with her eyes full of tears, that she did not want to marry you—that she felt you were bound to return to Lætitia. She had been much affected by discovering the enclosed little note from your cousin. I must say that the part which concerns you interested me much, more so than her letter to her old friend. But she was evidently pre-occupied at the time, and Elly, far from feeling neglected, actually began to cry, she was so touched by this somewhat singular discovery. Girl's tears are easily dried. If it lies in my power she shall yet be made happy.

'There is nothing now, as you see, that need prevent your fulfilling your engagements. You are all very good children, on the whole, and I trust that your troubles are but fleeting clouds that will soon pass away. That you and Lætitia may enjoy all prosperity is the sincere hope and desire of your

'Affectionate old aunt,

'J. M. DAMPIER.'

Miss Dampier, having determined that she had written a perfectly impartial letter, put it up in an envelope, rang the bell, and desired a waiter to post it.

Number twenty-three's bell rang at the same moment; so did number fifteen; immediately after a quantity of people poured in by the eleven o'clock train; the waiter flung the letter down on his pantry table, and rushed off to attend to half-a-dozen things at once, of which posting the note was not one.

About three o'clock that afternoon Miss Dampier in her close bonnet was standing in the passage talking to a tall young man with a black waistcoat and wide-awake.

'What are you going to do?' he said. 'Couldn't we go for a drive somewhere?'

'I have ordered a carriage at three,' said Miss Dampier, smiling. 'We are going up on the hills. You might come, too, if you liked it.' And when the carriage drove up to the door there he was, waiting to hand her in.

He had always, until he saw her, imagined Elly a little flirting person, quite different from the tall young lady in the broad hat, with the long cloak falling from her shoulders, who was prepared to accompany them. She had gone away a little, and his aunt sent him to fetch her. She was standing against the railing, looking out at the sea with her sad eyes. There was the lawn, there was the sea, there was Elly. A pretty young lady always makes a pretty picture; but out of doors in the sunshine she looks a prettier young lady than anywhere else, thought Mr. Will, as Elizabeth walked across the grass. He was not alone in his opinion; more than one person looked up as she passed. He began to think that far from doing a foolish thing his aunt had shown her usual good sense in taking such good care of this sad, charming, beautiful young woman. It was no use trying to think ill of her. With such a face as hers, she has a right to fall in love with anybody she pleases, he thought; and so, as they were walking towards the carriage, Will Dampier, thinking that this was a good opportunity for a little confidential communication, said, somewhat in his professional manner, 'You seem out of spirits, Miss Gilmour. I hope that you do not regret your decision of this morning.'

'Yes, I do regret it,' said poor Elly; and two great tears came dribbling down her cheeks. 'Do you think that when a girl gives up what she likes best in the world she is not sorry? I am horribly sorry.'

Will was very much puzzled how to answer this unexpected confidence. He said, looking rather foolish,

'One is so apt to ask unnecessary questions. But, take my word for it, you have done quite right, and some day you will be more glad than you are now.'

I must confess that my heroine here got exceedingly cross.

'Ah, that is what people say who do not know of what they are talking. What business of yours is my poor unlucky bruised and broken fancy?' she said. 'Ah! why were you ever told? What am I? What is it to you?'

All the way she sat silent and dull, staring out at the landscape as they went along; suffering, in truth, poor child, more than either of her companions could tell; saying goodbye to the dearest hope of her youth, tearing herself away from the familiar and the well-loved dreams. Dreams, do I say? They had been the Realities to her, poor child! for many a day. And the realities had seemed to be the dreams.

They drove along a straight road, and came at last to some delightful fresh downs, with the sea sparkling in the distance, and a sort of autumnal glow on the hills all about. The breeze came in fresh gusts, the carriage jogged on, still up hill, and Will Dampier walked alongside, well pleased with the entertainment, and making endless jokes at his aunt. She rather liked being laughed at; but Elly never looked up once, or heeded what they said. They were going towards a brown church, that was standing on the top of a hill. It must have been built by the Danes a thousand years ago. There it stood, looking out at the sea, brown, grim, solitary, with its graveyard on the hillside. Trees were clustering down in a valley below; but here, up above, it was all bleak, bare, and solitary, only tinted and painted by the brown and purple sunshine.

They stopped the carriage a little way off, and got out and passed through a gate, and walked up the hill-top. Elly went first, Will followed, and Miss Dampier came slowly after. As Elly reached the top of the hill she turned round, and stood against the landscape, like a picture with a background, and looked back and said—

'Do you hear?'

The organ inside the church was playing a chaunt, and presently some voices began chaunting to the playing of the organ. Elly went across the graveyard, and leant against the porch, listening. Five minutes went by; her anger was melting away. It was exquisitely clear, peaceful, and tranquil here, up on this hill where the dead people were lying among the grass and daisies. All the bitterness went away out of her heart, somehow, in the golden glow. She said to herself that she felt now, suddenly, for the first time, as if she could bury her fancy and leave it behind her in this quiet place. As the chaunt went on, her whole heart uttered in harmony with it, though her lips were silent. She did not say to herself, what a small thing it was that had troubled her: what vast combinations were here to make her happy; hills, vales, light, with its wondrous refractions, harmony, colour; the great ocean, the great world, rolling on amid the greater worlds beyond!

But she felt it somehow. The voices ceased, and all was very silent.

'O give thanks,' the Psalm began again; and Elly felt that she could indeed give thanks for mercies that were more than she had ever deserved. When she was at home with her mother she thought—just now the thought of returning there scarce gave her a pang—she should remember to-day all the good hopes, good prayers, and aspirations which had come to her in this peaceful graveyard up among the hills. She had been selfish, discontented, and ungrateful all her life, angry and chafed but an hour ago, and here was peace, hers for the moment; here was tranquil happiness. The mad, rash delight she had felt when she had been with John Dampier was nothing compared to this great natural peace and calm. A sort of veil seemed lifted from her eyes, and she felt, for the first time, that she could be happy though what she had wished for most was never to be hers—that there was other happiness than that which she had once fancied part of life itself. Did she ever regret the decision she had made? Did she ever see occasion to think differently from this? If, in after times, she may have felt a little sad, a little lonely now and then—if she may have thought with a moment's regret, of those days that were now already past and over for ever—still she knew she had done rightly when she determined to bury the past with all kindness, with reverend hands. Somehow, in some strange and mysterious manner, the bitterness of her silly troubles had left her—left her a better girl than she had been ever before. She was more good, more happy, more old, more wise, now, and, in truth, there was kindness in store for her, there were suns yet to shine, friendly words to be spoken, troubles yet to be endured, other than those sentimental griefs which had racked her youth so fiercely.

While they were all on the hill-top the steamer came into the port earlier than on the day when Will Dampier arrived. One of the passengers walked up to the hotel and desired a waiter to show him to Miss Dampier's room. It was empty, of course; chairs pushed about, windows open, work and books on the table. The paper was lying on the floor—the passenger noticed that a corner had been torn off; a little box was open on the table, a ruby ring glittering in the tray. 'How careless!' he thought; and then went and flung himself into a great arm-chair.

So! she had been here a minute ago. There was a glove lying on a chair; there were writing materials on a side-table, a blotting-book open, pens with the ink scarcely dry; and in this room, in this place, he was going to decide his fate—rightly or wrongly he could not tell. 'Lætitia is a cold-blooded little creature,' he kept saying to himself; 'this girl, with all her faults, with all her impulses, has a heart to break or to mend. My mother will learn too late that I cannot submit to such dictation. By Jove, what a letter it is!' He pulled it out of his pocket, read it once more, and crumpled it up and threw it into the fireplace. It was certainly not a very wise composition—long, vicious, wiry tails and flourishes. 'John, words cannot,' &c. &c. 'What Lady Tomsey,' &c. &c. 'How horror-struck Major Potterton,' &c. &c.; and finally concluded with a command that he should instantly return to Schlangenbad; or, failing this, an announcement that she should immediately join him, *wherever* he might be!

So Sir John, in a rage, packed up and came off to Boatstown—his mother can follow him or not, as she chooses: and here he is walking up and down the room, while Elly, driving over the hills, is saying farewell, farewell, goodbye to her old love for ever.

Could he have really cared for anybody? By some strange contradiction, now that the die is cast, now that, after all these long doubts and mistrusts, he has made up his mind, somehow new doubts arise. He wonders whether he and Elly will be happy together? He pictures stormy scenes; he intuitively shrinks from the idea of her unconventionalities, her eagerness, her enthusiasm. He is a man who likes a quiet life, who would appreciate a sober, happy home — a gentle, equable companion, to greet him quietly, to care for his tastes and his ways, to sympathise, to befriend him. Whereas now it is he who will have to study his companion all the rest of his life; if he thwart her she will fall ill of sorrow, if he satisfy her she will ask more and more; if he neglect her—being busy, or weary, or what not—she will die of grief; if he want sympathy and common sense, she will only adore him. Poor Elly! it is hard upon her that he should make such a bugbear of her poor little love. His courage is oozing out at his finger-ends. He is in a rage with her, and with himself, and with his mother, and with his aunt. He and everybody else are in a league to behave as badly as possible. He will try and do his duty, he thinks, for all that, for my hero is an honest-hearted man, though a weak one. It is not Lady Dampier's letter that shall influence him one way or another; if Elly is breaking her heart to have him, and if Letty doesn't care one way or the other, as is likely enough, well then he will marry Elizabeth, he cries with a stout desperation, and he dashes up and down the room in a fury.

And just at this minute the waiter comes in, and says Miss Dampier has gone out for a drive, and will not be back for some time. Mr. Dampier is staying in the house, but he has gone out with her, and who shall he say? And Sir John, looking up, gives his name and says he will wait.

Upon which the waiter suddenly remembers the letter he left in his pantry, and, feeling rather guilty, proposes to fetch it. And by this time Elly, and Will, and Miss

Dampier have got into the carriage again and are driving homewards.

There was a certain humility about Elly, with all her ill-humours and varieties, which seemed to sweeten her whole nature. Will Dampier, who was rather angry with her for her peevishness, could not help forgiving her, when, as he helped her out of the carriage in the courtyard, she said,—

'I don't quite know how to say it--but I was very rude just now. I was very unhappy, and I hope you will forgive me;' and she looked up. The light from the hills was still in her face.

'It was I who was rude,' says Will, goodnaturedly holding out his hand; and of course he forgave her.

The band was playing, the garden was full of people; but aunt Jenny was cold, and glad to get home. The ladies went upstairs: Will remained down below, strolling up and down in the garden with the rest of the people; but at five o'clock the indefatigable bell began to ring once more; the afternoon boat was getting up its steam, and making its preparations to cross over to the other side.

Will met a friend of his, who was going over in it, and he walked down with him to see him off. He went on board with him, shook hands, and turned to come away. At that minute some one happened to look round, and Will, to his immense surprise, recognised his cousin. That was John; those were his whiskers; there was no doubt about it.

He sprang forward and called him by name. 'John,' he said, 'you here?'

'Well!' said John, smiling a little, 'why not me, as well as you? are you coming across?'

'Are you going across?' said Will, doubtfully.

'Yes,' the other answered; 'I came over on business; don't say anything of my having been here. Pray remember this. I have a particular reason.'

'I shall say nothing,' said Will. 'I am glad you are going, John,' he added, stupidly. 'I think I know your reason—a very nice, pretty reason too.'

'So those women have been telling you all about my private affairs?' said Sir John, speaking quick, and looking very black.

'Your mother told me first,' Will said. 'I saw her the other day. For all sakes, I am glad you are giving up all thoughts of Elly Gilmour.'

'Are you?' said John, dryly. They waited for a minute in awkward silence, but as they were shaking hands and saying 'Goodbye,' suddenly John melted and said, 'Look here, Will, I should like to see her once more. Could you manage this for me? I don't want her to know, you know; but could you bring her to the end of the pier? I am going back to Letty, as you see, so I don't think she need object.'

Will nodded, and went up the ladder and turned towards the house without a word, walking quickly and hurrying along. The band in the garden burst out into a pretty melancholy dance tune. The sun went down peg by peg into the sea; the steamer still whistled and puffed as it got up its steam.

Elly was sitting alone. She had lighted a candle, and was writing home. Her hat was lying on a chair beside her. The music had set her dreaming; her thoughts were far away, in the dismal old home again, with Françoise, and Anthony, and the rest of them. She was beginning to live the new life she had been picturing to herself; trying to imagine herself good and contented in the hateful old home; it seemed almost endurable just at this minute, when suddenly the door burst open, and Will Dampier came in with his hat on.

'I want you to come out a little way with me,' he said. 'I want you to come and see the boat off. There's no time to lose.'

'Thank you,' said Elly, ' but I'm busy.'

'It won't take you five minutes,' he said.

She laughed. 'I am lazy, and rather tired.'

Will could not give up. He persisted: he knew he had a knack of persuading his old women at home; he tried it on Miss Gilmour.

'I see you have not forgiven me,' he said; 'you won't trust yourself with me.'

'Yes, indeed,' said Elly; 'I am only lazy.'

The time was going. He looked at his watch; there were but five minutes—but five minutes for John to take leave of his love of many a year; but five minutes and it would be too late. He grew impatient.

'Pray, come,' he said. 'I shall look upon it as a sign that you have forgiven me. Will you do me this favour? —will you come? I assure you I shall not be ungrateful.'

Elly thought it odd, and still hesitated; but it seemed unkind to refuse. She got up, fetched her hat and cloak, and in a minute he was hurrying her along across the lawn, along the side of the dock, out to the pier's end.

They were only just in time. 'You are very mysterious,' said Elly. 'Why do you care so much to see the boat go out? How chilly it is! Are you not glad to be here on this side of the water? Ah! how soon it will be time for me to go back!'

Will did not answer, he was so busy watching the people moving about on board. Puff! puff! Cannot you imagine the great boat passing close at their feet, going out in the night into the open sea; the streaks of light in the west; Elly, with flushed, rosy-red cheeks, like the sunset, standing under the lighthouse, and talking in her gentle voice, and looking out, saying it would be fine to-morrow?

Can't you fancy poor Sir John leaning against a pile

of baggage, smoking a cigar, and looking up wistfully? As he slid past he actually caught the tone of her voice. Like a drowning man who can see in one instant years of his past life flashing before him, Sir John saw Elly—a woman with lines of care in her face,—there, standing in the light of the lamp, with the red streams of sunset beyond, and the night closing in all round about; and then he saw her as he had seen her once—a happy, unconscious girl, brightening, smiling at his coming; and as the picture travelled on, a sad girl, meeting him in the street by chance—a desperate, almost broken-hearted woman, looking up greyly into his face in the theatre. Puff! puff!—it was all over, she was still smiling before his eyes. One last glimpse of the two, and they had disappeared. He slipped away right out of her existence, and she did not even guess that he had been near. She stood unwitting for an instant, watching the boat as it tossed out to sea, and then said, 'Now we will go home.' A sudden gloom and depression seemed to have come over her. She walked along quite silently, and did not seem to heed the presence of her companion.

CHAPTER X.

> . . . Poor forsaken Flos!
> Not all her brightness, sportfulness, and bloom,
> Her sweetness and her wildness, and her wit,
> Could save her from desertion. No; their loves
> Were off the poise. Love competent
> Makes better bargains than love affluent.

BEFORE he went to bed that night Dampier wrote the end of his letter to Prue. He described, rather amusingly, the snubbing which Elly had given him, the dry way in which Sir John had received his advances, the glances of disfavour with which aunt Jean listened to his advice. 'So this is all the gratitude one gets for interfering in the most sensible manner. If you are as ungrateful, Prue, for this immense long letter, I shall, indeed, have laboured in vain. It is one o'clock. Bong! there it went from the tower. Good-night, dear; your beloved brother is going to bed. Love to Miles. Kiss the children all round for their and your affectionate W. D.'

Will Dampier was not in the least like his letter. I know two or three men who are manly enough, who write gentle, gossiping letters like women. He was a big, commonplace young man, straight-minded and tender-hearted, with immense energy, and great good spirits. He believed in himself; indeed, he tried so heartily and conscientiously to do what was right, that he could not help knowing more or less that he was a good fellow. And then he had a happy knack of seeing one side of a question, and having once determined that so and so was the thing to be done, he could do so and so without one doubt or compunction. He belonged to the school of athletic Christianity. I heard someone once say that there are some of that sect who would almost make out cock-fighting to be a religious ceremony. William Dampier did not go so far as this; but he heartily believed that nothing was wrong that was done with a Christian and manly spirit. He rode across country, he smoked pipes, he went out shooting, he played billiards and cricket, he rowed up and down the river in his boat, and he was charming with all the grumbling old men and women in his parish, he preached capital sermons —short, brisk, well-considered. He enjoyed life and all its good things with a grateful temper, and made most people happy about him.

One day, Elly began to think what a different creed Will Dampier's was from her stepfather's, only she did not put her thoughts into words. It was not her way.

Tourneur, with a great heart, set on the greatest truth, feeling the constant presence of those mightier dispensations, cared but little for the affairs of to-day: they seemed to him subordinate, immaterial; they lost all importance from comparison to that awful reality that this man had so vividly realised to himself. To Dampier, it was through the simple language of his daily life that he could best express what good was in him. He saw wisdom and mercy, he saw order and progression, he saw infinite variety and wonder in all natural things, in all life, at all places and hours. By looking at this world, he could best understand and adore the next.

And yet Tourneur's was the loftier spirit: to him had come a certain knowledge and understanding, of which Dampier had scarce a conception. Dampier, who felt less keenly, could well be more liberal, more forbearing. One of these two told Elly that we were put into the world to live in it, and to be thankful for our creation; to do our duty, and to labour until the night should come when no man can work. The other safe, sadly, you are born only to overcome the flesh, to crush it under foot, to turn away from all that you like most, innocent or not. What do I care? Are you an immortal spirit, or are you a clod of earth? Will you suffer this all-wondrous, all-precious gift should be clogged, and stifled, and choked, and destroyed, maybe, by despicable daily concerns? Tourneur himself set an example of what he preached by his devoted, humble, holy, self-denying-life. And yet Elly turned with a sense of infinite relief to the other creed: she could understand it, sympathise with it, try to do good, though to be good was beyond her frail powers. Already she was learning to be thankful, to be cheerful, to be unselfish, to be keenly penitent for her many shortcomings.

As the time drew near when an answer to her note might be expected, Miss Dampier grew anxious and fidgety, dropped her stitches, looked out for the post, and wondered why no letter came. Elly was only a little silent, a little thoughtful. She used to go out by herself and take long walks. One day Will, returning from one of his peregrinations, came upon her sitting on the edge of a cliff staring at the distant coast of France. It lay blue, pale, like a dream-country, and glimmered in the horizon. Who would believe that there was reality, busy life in all earnest going on beyond those calm, heavenly-looking hills! Another time his aunt sent him out to look for her, and he found her at the end of the pier, leaning against the chain, and still gazing towards France.

In his rough, friendly manner he said, 'I wish you would look another way sometimes, Miss Gilmour, up or down, or in the glass even. You make me feel very guilty, for to tell the truth I—I advised John——'

'I thought so,' Elly cried, interrupting. 'And you were quite right. I advised him too,' she said, with a smile. 'Don't you think he has taken your advice?'

Will looked down uncomfortably. 'I think so,' he said, in a low tone.

And, meanwhile, Miss Dampier was sitting in the window and the sunshine, knitting castles in the air.

M

'Suppose he does not take this as an answer? Suppose Lætitia has found somebody else, suppose the door opens and he comes in, and the sun shines into the room, and then he seizes Elly's hand, and says, "Though you give me up, I will not give up the hope of calling you mine," and Elly glances up bright, blushing, happy... Suppose Lady Dampier is furious, and dear Tishy makes peace? I should like to see Elizabeth mistress of the dear old house. I think my mother was like her. I don't approve of cousins' marriages... How charming she would look coming along the old oak gallery!' Look at the old maid in the window building castles in the air through her spectacles. But it is a ridiculous sight; she is only a fat, foolish old woman. All her fancies are but follies flying away with caps and jingling bells—they vanish through the window as the door opens and the young people come in.

'Here is a letter for you the porter gave me in the hall,' said Will, as carelessly as he could; Jean saw Elly's eyes busy glancing at the writing.

'My dear Aunt Jean,—Many thanks for your note, and the enclosure. My mother and Lætitia are with me, and we shall all go back to Friar's Bush on Thursday. Elly's decision is the wisest under the circumstances, and we had better abide by it. Give her my love. Lætitia knows nothing, as my mother has had the grace to be silent.

'Yours affectionately, J. C. D.

'P.S.—You will be good to her, won't you?'

Miss Dampier read the note imperturbably, but while she read there seemed to run through her a cold thrill of disappointment, which was so unendurable that after a minute she got up and left the room.

When she came back, Elly said with a sigh, 'Where is he?'

'At Paris,' said Miss Dampier. 'They have saved him all trouble and come to him. He sends you his love, Elly, which is very handsome of him, considering how much it is worth.'

'It has been worth a great deal to me,' said Elly, in her sweet voice. 'It is all over; but I am grateful still and always shall be. I was very rash; he was very kind. Let me be grateful, dear aunt Jean, to those who are good to me.' And she kissed the old woman's shrivelled hand.

Miss Gilmour cheered up wonderfully from that time. I am sure that if she had been angry with him, if she had thought herself hardly used, if she had had more of what people call self-respect, less of that sweet humility of nature, it would not have been so.

As the short, happy, delightful six weeks which she was to spend with Miss Dampier came to an end, she began to use all her philosophy and good resolves to reconcile herself to going home. Will Dampier was gone. He had only been able to stay a week. They missed him. But still they managed to be very comfortable together.

Tea-talk, long walks, long hours on the sands, novels and story-books, idleness and contentment—why couldn't it go on for ever? Elly said. Aunt Jean laughed and said they might as well be a couple of jelly-fish at once. And so the time went by, but one day just before she went away, Mr. Will appeared again unexpectedly.

Elly was sitting in the sun on the beach, throwing idle stones into the sea. She had put down her novel on the shingle beside her. It was 'Deerbrook,' I think—an old favourite of Jean Dampier's. Everybody knows what twelve o'clock is like on a fine day at the sea-side. It means little children, nurses in clean cotton gowns, groups of young ladies scattered here and there; it means a great cheerfulness and tranquillity, a delightful glitter, and life, and light: happy folks plashing in the water, bathing-dresses drying in the sun, all sorts of aches, pains, troubles, vanishing like mist in its friendly beams. Elly was thinking: 'Yes, how pleasant and nice it is, and how good, how dear aunt Jean is! Only six months, and she says I am to come to her in her cottage again.' (Splash a stone goes into the water.) 'Only six months! I will try and spend them better than I ever spent six months before. Eugh! If it was not for Mme. Jacob . . . . I really do love my stepfather, and could live happily enough with him.' (Splash.) Suddenly an idea came to Elly—the Pasteur Boulot was the idea. 'Why should not he marry Mme. Jacob? He admires her immensely. Ah! what fun that would be!' (Splash, splash—a couple of stones.) And then, tramp, tramp, on the shingle behind her, and a cheery man's voice says, 'Here you are!'

Elly stares up in some surprise, and looks pleased, and attempts to get up, but Will Dampier—he was the man—sits down beside her, opens his umbrella, and looks very odd. 'I only came down for the day,' he said, after a little preliminary talk. 'I have been with aunt Jean; she tells me you are going home to-morrow.'

'Yes,' says Elly, with a sigh; 'but I am to come back again and see her in a little time.'

'I am glad of that,' says the clergyman. 'What sort of place do you live in at Paris?'

'It is rather a dull place,' says Elly. 'I'm very fond of my stepfather; besides him, there is Anthony, and five young pupils, there is an old French cook, and a cross maid, and my mother, and a horri—— a sister of Monsieur Tourneur's, and Tou-Tou and Lou-Lou, and me.'

'Why, that is quite a little colony,' said Dampier. 'And what will you do there when you get back?'

'I must see,' said the girl, smiling. 'Till now I have done nothing at all; but that is stupid work. I shall teach Tou-Tou and Lou-Lou a little, and mind the house if my mother will let me, and learn to cook from Françoise. I have a notion that it may be useful some day or other.'

'Do, by all means,' said Will; 'it is a capital idea. But as years go on, what do you mean to do? Tou-Tou and Lou-Lou will grow up, and you will have mastered the art of French cookery——'

'How can you ask such things?' Elly said, looking out at the sea. 'I cannot tell, or make schemes for the future.'

'Pray forgive me,' said Will, 'for asking such a question, but have you any idea of marrying M. Anthony eventually?'

'He is a dear old fellow,' said Elly, flushing up. 'I am not going to answer any such questions. I am not half good enough for him—that is my answer.'

'But suppose—— ?'

'Pray don't suppose. I am not going to marry anybody, or to think much about such things ever again. Do you imagine that I am not the wiser for all my experience?'

'Are you wise now?' said Will, still in his odd manner.

'Look at that pretty little fishing-smack,' Elly interrupted.

'Show it,' he went on, never heeding, 'by curing yourself of your fancy for my cousin John; by curing yourself, and becoming some day a really useful personage and member of society.'

Elly stared at him, as well she might.

'Come back to England some day,' he continued, still looking away, 'to your home, to your best vocation in life, to be happy, and useful, and well-loved,' he said, with a sweet inflexion in his voice; 'that is no very hard fate.'

'What are you talking about?' said Elly. 'How can I cure myself? How can I ever forget what is past? I am not going to be discontented, or to be particularly happy at home. I am going *to try*—to try and do my best.'

'Well, then, do your best to get cured of this hopeless nonsense,' said Mr. William Dampier, 'and turn your thoughts to real good sense, to the real business of life, and to making yourself and others happy, instead of wasting and maudling away the next few best years of your life, regretting and hankering after what is past and unattainable. For some strong minds, who can defy the world, and stand alone without the need of sympathy and sustainment, it is a fine thing to be faithful to a chimera,' he said, with a pathetic ring in his voice. 'But I assure you infidelity is better still sometimes, more human, more natural, particularly for a confiding and uncertain person like yourself.' Was he thinking of to-day as he spoke? Was he only thinking of Elly, and preaching only to her?

'You mean I had better marry him?' said Elly, while her eyes filled up with tears, and she knocked one stone against another. 'And yet aunt Jean says, "No!"—that I need not think of it. It seems to me as if I—I had rather jump into the sea at once,' said the girl, dashing the stones away, 'though I love him dearly, dear old fellow!'

'I did not exactly mean M. Anthony,' said Will, looking round for the first time and smiling at her tears and his own talk.

Elizabeth was puzzled still. For, in truth, her sad experience had taught her to put but little faith in kindness and implications of kindness—to attach little meaning to the good-nature and admiration a beautiful young woman was certain to meet with on every side. It had not occurred to her that Will, who had done so little, seen her so few times, could be in love with her; when John, for whom she would have died, who said and looked so much, had only been playing with her, and pitying her as if she had been a child; and she said, still with tears, but not caring much—

'I shall never give a different answer. I believe you are right, but I have not the courage to try. I think I could try and be good if I stay as I am; but to be bound and chained to Anthony all the rest of my life—once I thought it possible; but now—— You who advise it do not know what it is.'

'But I never advised it,' Will said; 'you won't understand me. Dear Elizabeth, why won't you see that it is of myself that I am speaking?'

Elly felt for a moment as if the sea had rushed up suddenly, and caught her away on its billows, and then the next moment she found that she was only sitting crying in the sun, on the sands.

'Look here: every day I live, I get worse and worse,' she sobbed. 'I flirt with one person after another—I don't deserve that you should ever speak to me again—I can't try and talk about myself—I do like you, and—and yet I know that the only person I care for really is the one who does not care for me; and if I married you to-morrow, and I saw John coming along the street, I should rush away to meet him. I don't want to marry him, and I don't know what I want. But, indeed, I have tried to be good. You are stronger than me, don't be hard upon me.'

'My dear little girl,' said Will, loyally and kindly, 'don't be unhappy; you have not flirted with me. I couldn't be hard upon you if I tried: you are a faithful little soul. Shall I tell you about myself? Once, not so very long ago, I liked Tishy almost as well as you like John. There, now, you see that you have done no great harm, and only helped to cheer me up again, and I am sure that you and I will be just as good friends as ever. As for John,' he added, in quite a different tone, 'the sooner you forget all about him the better.'

Will took her hand which was lying limp on the shingle, said 'Goodbye,' took up his umbrella, and walked away.

And so, by some strange arrangement, Elly put away

from her a second time the love of a good and honourable man, and turned back impotently to the memory—it was no more—of a dead and buried passion. Was this madness or wisdom? Was this the decree of fate or of folly?

She sat all in a maze, staring at the sea and the wavelets, and in half an hour rushed into the sitting-room, flung her arms round Miss Dampier's neck, and told her all that happened.

CHAPTER XI.

Of all the gifts of Heaven to us below, that felicity is the sum and the chief. I tremble as I hold it, lest I should lose it, and be left alone in the blank world without it. Again, I feel humiliated to think that I possess it: as hastening home to a warm fireside, and a plentiful table, I feel ashamed sometimes before the poor outcast beggar shivering in the street.

ELLY expected, she did not know why, that there would be some great difference when she got back to the old house at Paris. Her heart sank as Clementine, looking just as usual, opened the great door, and stepped forward to help with the box. She went into the courtyard. Those cocks and hens were pecketting between the stones, the poplar-trees shivering, Françoise in her blue gown came out of the kitchen: it was like one of the dreams which used to haunt her pillow. This sameness and monotony was terrible. Already in one minute it seemed to her that she had never been away. Her mother and father were out. Mme. Jacob came downstairs with the children to greet her and see her. Ah! they had got new frocks, and were grown—that was some relief. Tou-Tou and Lou-Lou were not more delighted with their little check black-and-white alpacas than Elly was.

Anthony was away—she was glad. After the first shock the girl took heart and courage, and set herself to practise the good resolutions she had made when she was away. It was not so hard as she had fancied to be a little less ill-tempered and discontented, because you see she had really behaved so very badly before. But it was not so easy to lead the cheerful devoted life she had pictured to herself. Her mother was very kind, very indifferent, very unhappy, Elizabeth feared. She was ill too, and out of health, but she bore great suffering with wonderful patience and constancy. Tourneur looked haggard and worn. Had he begun to discover that he could not understand his wife, that he had not married the woman he fancied he knew so well, but some quite different person? Ill-temper, discontent, he could have endured and dealt with; but a terrible mistrust and doubt had come into his heart, he did not know how or when, and had nearly broken it.

A gloom seemed hanging over this sad house; a sort of hopeless dreariness. Do you remember how cheerful and contented Caroline had been at first? By degrees she began to get a little tired now and then—a little weary. All these things grew just a little insipid and distasteful. Do you know that torture to which some poor slaves have been subjected? I believe it is only a drop of water falling at regular intervals upon their heads. At first they scarcely heed it, and talk and laugh; then they become silent; and still the drop falls and drips. And then they moan and beg for mercy, and still it falls; and then scream out with horror, and cry out for death, for this is more than they can bear—but still it goes on falling. I have read this somewhere, and it seems to me that this applies to Caroline Tourneur, and to the terrible life which had begun for her.

Her health failed, and she daily lost strength and interest in the things by which she was surrounded; then they became wearisome. Her tired frame was not equal to the constant exertions she had imposed upon herself; from being wearisome, they grew hateful to her; and, one by one, she gave them up. Then the terrible sameness of a life in which her heart was no longer set, seemed to crush her down day by day: a life never lived from high and honourable motives, but for mean and despicable ends; a life lofty and noble to those who, with great hearts and good courage, knew how to look beyond it, and not to care for the things of the world, but dull and terrible beyond expression to a woman whose whole soul was set amidst the thorns and thistles; and who had only rushed by chance into this narrow path blindfold with passion and despair.

Now she has torn the bandage off her eyes; now she is struggling to get out of it, and beating against the thorns, and wearily trying to trace back her steps. Elly used to cry out in her childish way. Caroline, who is a woman, is silent, and utters not one word of complaint; only her cheeks fall away and her eyes glare out of great black rings.

Elly came home blooming and well, and was shocked and frightened at first to see the change which had come over her mother. She did not ask the reason of it, but, as we all do sometimes, accepted without much speculation the course of events. Things come about so simply and naturally that people are often in the midst of strangest histories without having once thought so, or wondered that it should be. Very soon all the gloomy house, though she did not know it, seemed brightened and cheered by her coming home. Even Mme. Jacob relented a little when she heard Tou-Tou and Lou-Lou's shouts of laughter one day coming through the open window. The three girls were at work in the garden. I do not know that they were doing much good except to themselves. It was a keen, clear, brilliant winter morning, and the sun out of doors put out the smouldering fires within.

The little girls were laughing and working with all their hearts. Elly was laughing too, and tearing up dried old plants, and heaping broken flower-pots together. Almost happy, almost contented, almost good. . . . And there is many a worse state of mind than this. She was sighing as she laughed, for she was thinking of herself, pacing round and round the neglected garden once not so long ago; then she thought of the church on the hill-top, then of Will Dampier, and then of John, and then she came upon a long wriggling worm, and she jumped away and forgot to be sentimental. Besides working in the garden, she set to teaching the children in her mother's school. What this girl turned her hand to, she always did well and thoroughly. She even went to visit some of the sick people, and though she never took kindly to these exercises, the children liked to say their lessons to her, and the sick people were glad when she came in. She was very popular with them all; perhaps the reason was, that she did not do these things from a sense of duty, and did not look upon the poor and the sick, as so many of us do, as a selfish means of self-advancement; she went to them because it was more convenient for her to go than for anybody else—she only thought of their needs, grumbled at the trouble she was taking, and it never occurred to her that this unconsciousness was as good as a good conscience.

My dear little Elizabeth! I am glad that at last she is behaving pretty well. Tourneur strokes her head sometimes, and holds out his kind hand to her when she comes into his room. His eyes follow her fondly as if he were her father. One day she told him about William Dampier. He sighed as he heard the story. It was all ordained for the best, he said to himself. But he would have been glad to know her happy, and he patted her cheek and went into his study.

Miss Dampier's letters were Elly's best treasures: how eagerly she took them from Clementine's hands, how she tore them open and read them once, twice, thrice! No novels interest people so much as their own—a story in which you have ever so little a part to enact thrills, and excites, and amuses to the very last. You don't skip the reflections; the descriptions do not weary. I can fancy Elly sitting in a heap on the floor, and spelling out Miss Dampier's; Tou-Tou and Lou-Lou looking on with respectful wonder.

But suddenly the letters seemed to her to change. They became short and reserved; they were not interesting any more. Looked for so anxiously, they only brought disappointment when they came, and no word of the people about whom she longed to hear, no mention of their doings. Even Lady Dampier's name would have been welcome. But there was nothing. It was in vain she read and re-read so eagerly, longing and thirsting for news.

Things were best as they were, she told herself a hundred times; and so, though poor Elly sighed and wearied, and though her heart sank, she did not speak to anyone of her trouble: it was a wholesome one, she told herself, one that must be surmounted and overcome by patience. Sometimes her work seemed almost greater than her strength, and then she would go upstairs and cry a little bit and pity herself, and sop up all her tears, and then run round and round the garden once or twice, and come back, with bright eyes and glowing cheeks, to chatter with Françoise, to look after her mother and Stephen Tourneur, to scold the pupils and make jokes at them, to romp with the little girls.

One day she found her letter waiting on the hall-table, and tore it open with a trembling hope. . . . Aunt Jean described the weather, the pigsty, made valuable remarks on the news contained in the daily papers, signed herself, ever her affectionate old friend. And that was all. Was not that enough? Elly asked herself, with such a sigh. She was reading it over in the doorway of the salle-à-manger, bonneted and cloaked, with all the remains of the mid-day meal congealing and disordered on the table.

'Es-tu prête, Elizabeth?' said Tou-Tou, coming in with a little basket—there were no stones in it this time. 'Tiens, voilà ce que ma tante envoie à cette pauvre Madame Jonnes.'

Madame Jonnes was only Mrs. Jones, only an old woman dying in a melancholy room hard-by—in a melancholy room in a deserted street, where there were few houses, but long walls, where the mould was feeding, and yellow placards were pasted and defaced and flapping in shreds, and where Elly, picking her little steps over the stone, saw blades of grass growing between them. There was a *chantier*—a great wood-yard—on one side; now and then a dark doorway leading into a black and filthy court, out of which a gutter would come with evil smells, flowing murkily into the street; in the distance, two figures passing; a child in a nightcap, thumping a doll upon a kerbstone; a dog snuffing at a heap; at the end of the street the placarded backs of tall houses built upon a rising ground; a man in a blouse wheeling a truck, and singing out dismally; and meanwhile, good old Mrs. Jones was dying close at hand, under this black and crumbling doorway, in a room opening with cracked glass-doors upon the yard.

She was lying alone upon her bed; the nurse they had sent to her was gossiping with the porter in his lodge. Kindly and dimly her eyes opened and smiled somehow at the girl, out of the faded bed, out of a mystery of pain, of grief, and solitude.

It was a mystery indeed, which Elizabeth, standing beside it, could not understand, though she herself had lain so lately and so resignedly upon a couch of sickness. Age, abandonment, seventy years of life—how many of grief and trouble? As she looked at the dying, indifferent face, she saw that they were almost ended. And in the midst of her pity and shrinking compassion Elly thought to herself that she would change all with the sick woman, at that minute, to have endured, to have surmounted so much.

She sat with her till the dim twilight came through the dirty and patched panes of the windows. Even as she waited there her thoughts went wandering, and she was trying to picture to herself faces and scenes that she could not see. She knew that the shadows were creeping round about those whom she loved, as quietly as they were rising here in this sordid room. It was their evening as it was hers; and then she said to herself that they who made up so large a part of her life must, perforce, think of her sometimes: she was part of their lives, even though they should utterly neglect and forget and abandon her; even though they should never meet again from this day; though she should never hear their names so much as mentioned; though their paths should separate for ever. For a time they had travelled the same road——ah! she was thankful even for so much; and she unconsciously pressed the wasted hand she was holding: and then her heart thrilled with tender, unselfish gladness as the feeble fingers tried to clasp hers, and the faltering whisper tried to bless.

She came home sad and tired from her sick woman's bedside, thinking of the last kind gleam of the eyes as she left the room. She went straight upstairs and took off her shabby dress, and found another, and poured out water and bathed her face. Her heart was beating, her hands trembling. She was remembering and regretting; she was despairing and longing, and yet resigned, as she had learnt to be of late. She leant against the wall for a minute before she went down; she was dressed in the blue dress, with her favourite little locket hanging round her neck. She put her hand tiredly to her head: and so she stood, as she used to stand when she was a child, in a sort of dream, and almost out of the world.

And as she was waiting a knock came at the door. It was Clementine who knocked, and who said, in the sing-song way in which Frenchwomen speak—'Mademoiselle, voilà pour vous.'

It was too dark to see anything, except that it was another familiar-looking letter. Elly made up her mind not to be disappointed any more, and went downstairs leisurely to the study, where she knew she should find Tourneur's lamp alight. And she crossed the hall and turned the handle of the door, and opened it and went in.

The lamp, with its green shade on the table, lit up one part of the room, but in the duskiness, standing by the stove and talking eagerly, were two people whom she could not distinguish very plainly. One of them was Tourneur, who looke round and came to meet her, and took her hand; and the other . . . .

Suddenly her heart began to beat so that her breath was taken away. What was this? Who was this——? What chance had she come upon? Such mad hopes as hers, were they ever fulfilled? Was this moment, so sudden, so unlooked for, the one for which she had despaired and longed; for which she had waited and lived through an eternity of grief? Was it John Dampier into whose hand Tourneur put hers? Was she still asleep and dreaming one of those delighting but terrible dreams, from which, ah me! she must awake? In this dream she heard the pasteur saying, 'Il a bien des choses à vous dire, Elizabeth,' and then he seemed to go away and to leave them.

In this dream, bewildered and trembling, with a desperate effort, she pulled her hand away, and said, 'What does it mean? Where is Tishy? Why do you come, John? Why don't you leave me in peace?'

And then it was a dream no longer, but a truth and a reality, when John began to speak in his familiar way, and she heard his voice, and saw him before her, and—yes, it was he; and he said, 'Tishy and I have had a quarrel, Elly. We are nothing to one another any more, and so I have come to you—to—to—tell you that I have behaved like a fool all this time.' And he turned very red as he spoke, and then he was silent, and then he took both her hands and spoke again: 'Tell me, dear,' he said, looking up into her sweet eyes,—'Elly, tell me, would you—won't you—be content with a fool for a husband?' And Elizabeth Gilmour only answered, 'Oh, John, John!' and burst into a great flood of happy tears: tears which fell raining peace and calm after this long drought and misery; tears which seemed to speak to him, and made him sad, and yet happier than he had ever dreamt of or imagined: tears which quieted her, soothed her, and healed all her troubles.

Before John went away that night, Elly read Miss Dampier's letter, which explained his explanations. The old lady wrote in a state of incoherent excitement.—It was some speech of Will's which had brought the whole thing about.

'What did he say?' Elly asked, looking up from the letter, with her shining eyes.

Sir John said, 'He asked me if I did not remember that church on the hill, at Boatstown? We were all out in the garden, by the old statue of the nymph. Tishy suddenly stopped, and turned upon me, and cried out, when was I last at Boatstown? And then I was obliged to confess, and we had a disagreeable scene enough, and she appealed to William—gave me my congé, and I was not sorry, Elly.'

'But had you never told her about——?'

'It was from sheer honesty that I was silent,' said Sir John; 'a man who sincerely wishes to keep his word doesn't say, "Madam, I like someone else, but I will marry you if you insist upon it;" only the worst of it is, that we were both uncomfortable, and I now find she suspected me the whole time. She sent me a note in the evening. Look here:'—

The note said—

'I have been thinking about what I said just now in the garden. I am more than ever decided that it is best we two should part. But I do not choose to say goodbye to you in an angry spirit, and so this is to tell you that I forgive you all the injustice of your conduct to me.

Everybody seems to have been in a league to deceive me, and I have not found out one true friend among you all. How could you for one moment imagine that I should wish to marry a man who preferred another woman? You may have been influenced and worked upon; but for all that I should never be able to place confidence in you again, and I feel it is best and happiest for us both that all should be at an end between us.

'You will not wonder that, though I try to forgive you, I cannot help feeling indignant at the way in which I have been used. I could never understand exactly what was going on in your mind. You were silent, you equivocated; and not you only, everybody seems to have been thinking of themselves, and never once for me. Even William, who professes to care for me still, only spoke by chance, and revealed the whole history. When he talked to you about Boatstown, some former suspicions of mine were confirmed, and by the most fortunate chance two people have been saved from a whole lifetime of regret.

'I will not trust myself to think of the way in which I should have been bartered had I only discovered the truth when it was too late. If I speak plainly, it is in justice to myself, and from no unkindness to you; for though I bid you farewell, I can still sincerely sign myself,

'Yours affectionately,

'LÆTITIA.

Elly read the letter, and gave it back to him, and sighed, then smiled, then sighed again, and then went on with Miss Dampier's epistle.

For some time past Jean Dampier wrote she had noticed a growing suspicion and estrangement between the engaged couple. John was brusque and morose at times, Tishy cross and defiant. He used to come over on his brown mare, and stop at the cottage gate, and ask about Elly, and then interrupt her before she could answer and change the talk. He used to give her messages to send, and then retract them. He was always philosophising and discoursing about first affections. Lætitia, too, used to come and ask about Elly.

Miss Dampier hoped that John himself would put an end to this false situation. She did not know how to write about either of them to Elly. Her perplexities had seemed unending.

'But I also never heard that you came to Boatstown,' Elly said.

'And yet I saw you there,' said John, 'standing at the end of the pier.' And then he went on to tell her a great deal more, and to confess all that he had thought while he was waiting for her.

Elly passed her hand across her eyes with the old familiar action.

'And you came to Boatstown, and you went away

when you read Tishy's writing, and you had the heart to be angry with me?' she said.

'I was worried, and out of temper,' said John. 'I felt I was doing wrong when I ran away from Tishy. I blamed you because I was in a rage with myself. I can't bear to think of it. But I was punished, Elly. Were you ever jealous?' She laughed and nodded her head. 'I daresay not,' he went on; 'when I sailed away and saw you standing so confidentially with Will Dampier, I won't try and tell you what I suffered. I could bear to give you up—but to see you another man's wife——Elly, I know you never were jealous, or you would understand what I felt at that moment.'

When their *tête-à-tête* was over they went into the next room. All the family congratulated them, Madame Tourneur among the rest; she was ill and tired that evening, and lying on the yellow Utrecht velvet sofa. But it was awkward for them and uncomfortable, and John went home early to his inn. As Elly went up to bed that night Françoise brought her one other piece of news—Madame Jonnes was dead. They had sent to acquaint the police. But Elly was so happy, that, though she tried, she could not be less happy because of this. All the night she lay awake, giving thanks and praise, and saying over to herself, a hundred times, 'At last—at last!'

At last! after all this long rigmarole. At last! after all these despairing adjectives and adverbs; at last! after all these thousands of hours of grief and despair. Did not that one minute almost repay her for them all? She went on telling herself, as I have said, that this was a dream—from which she need never awake. And I, who am writing her story, wonder if it is so—wonder if even to such dreams as these there may not be a waking one day, when all the visions that surround us shall vanish and disappear for ever into eternal silence and oblivion. Dear faces—voices whose tones speak to us even more familiarly than the tender words which they utter! It would, in truth, seem almost too hard to bear, if we did not guess—if we were not told—how the love which makes such things so dear to us endures in the eternity out of which they have passed.

Happiness like Elly's is so vague and so great that it is impossible to try to describe it. To a nature like hers, full of tenderness, faithful and eager, it came like a sea, ebbing and flowing with waves, and with the sun shining and sparkling on the water, and lighting the fathoms below. I do not mean to say that my poor little heroine was such a tremendous creature that she could compass the depths and wide extent of a sea in her heart. Love is not a thing which belongs to any one of us individually; it is everywhere, here and all round about, and sometimes people's hearts are opened, and they guess at it, and realise that it is theirs.

Dampier came early next morning, looking kind and

happy and bright, to fetch her for a walk; Elly was all blue ribbons and blue eyes; her feet seemed dancing against her will, she could hardly walk quietly along. Old Françoise looked after them as they walked off towards the Bois de Boulogne; Tou-Tou and Lou-Lou peeped from their bedroom window. The sun was shining, the sky had mounted Elly's favourite colours.

CHAPTER XII.

> O blessed rest, O royal night!
>   Wherefore seemeth the time so long
> Till I see yon stars in their fullest light,
>   And list to their loudest song?

WHEN I first saw Lady Dampier she had only been married a day or two. I had been staying at Guildford, and I drove over one day to see my old friend Jean Dampier. I came across the hills and by Coombe Bottom and along the lanes, and through the little village street, and when I reached the cottage I saw Elly, of whom I had heard so much, standing at the gate. She was a very beautiful young woman, tall and straight, with the most charming blue eyes, a sweet frank voice, and a taking manner, and an expression on her face that I cannot describe. She had a blue ribbon in her hair, which was curling in a crop. She held her hat full of flowers; behind her the lattices of the cottage were gleaming in the sun; the creepers were climbing and flowering about the porch.

All about rose a spring incense of light, of colour, of perfume. The country folks were at work in the fields and on the hills. The light shone beyond the church spire, beyond the cottages and glowing trees. Inside the cottage, through the lattice, I could see aunt Jean nodding over her knitting.

She threw down her needles to welcome me. Of course I was going to stay to tea—and I said that was my intention in coming. As the sun set, the clouds began to gather, coming quickly we knew not whence; but we were safe and dry, sitting by the lattice and gossiping, and meanwhile Miss Dampier went on with her work.

Elly had been spending the day with her, she told me. Sir John was to come for her, and presently he arrived, dripping wet, through the April shower which was now pouring over the fields.

The door of the porch opens into the little dining-room, where the tea was laid: a wood fire was crackling in the tall cottage chimney. Elizabeth was smiling by the hearth, toasting cakes with one hand and holding a book in the other, when the young man walked in.

He came into the room where we were sitting and shook hands with us both, and then he laughed and said he must go and dry himself by the fire, and he went back.

So Jean Dampier and I sat mumbling confidences in the inner room, and John and Elly were chattering to one another by the burning wood logs.

The door was open which led, with a step, into the dining-room, where the wood fire was burning. Darkness was setting in. The rain was over, the clouds swiftly breaking and coursing away, and such a bright, mild-eyed little star peeped in through the lattice at us two old maids in the window. It was a shame to hear, but how could we help it? Out of the fire-lit room the voices came to us, and when we ceased chattering for an instant, we heard them so plainly—

'I saw Will to-day,' said a voice. 'He was talking about Lætitia. I think there will be some news of them before long. Should you be glad?'

'Ah! so glad. I don't want to be the only happy woman in the world.'

'My dearest Elly!' said the kind voice. 'And you will never regret——And are you happy?'

'Can you ask?' said Elly. 'Come into the porch, and I will tell you.' And then there was a gust of fresh rain-scented air, and a soft rustle, and the closing click of a door. And then we saw them pass the window, and Jean clasped my hand very tightly, and flung her arms round my neck, and gave me a delighted kiss.

'You dear, silly woman,' said I, 'how glad I am they are so happy together.'

'I hope she won't catch cold,' said Jean, looking at the damp walks. 'Could not you take out a shawl?'

'Let her catch cold!' said I; 'and in the meantime give me some tea, if you please. Remember, I have got to drive home in the dark.'

So we went into the next room. Jean rang for the candles. The old silver candlesticks were brought in by Kitty on a tray.

'Don't shut the curtains,' said Miss Dampier; 'and come here, Mary, and sit by the fire.'

While Elizabeth and John Dampier were wandering up and down in the dark damp garden, Jenny and I were comfortably installed by the fire drinking hot, sweet tea, and eating toasted cakes, and preserves, and cream. I say *we*, but that is out of modesty, for she had no appetite, whereas I was very hungry.

'Heigho!' said Jean, looking at the fire. 'It's a good thing to be young, Mary. Tell me honestly: what would you give——'

'To be walking in the garden with young Dampier,' said I (and I burst out laughing), 'without a cloak, or an umbrella, or india-rubbers? My dear Jenny, where are your five wits?'

'Where indeed?' said Jean, with another sigh. 'Yet I can remember when you used to cry instead of laughing over such things, Mary.'

Her sadness had made me sad. Whilst the young folks were whispering outside, it seemed as if we two old women were sitting by the fire and croaking the elegy of all youth, and love, and happiness. 'The night is coming for you and me, Jenny,' I said. 'Dear me, how quickly.'

'The night is at hand,' echoed she softly, and she passed

her fingers across her eyes, and then sighed, and got up slowly and went to the door which opened into the porch. And then I heard her call me. 'Come here!' she said, 'Mary!' And then I, too, rose stiffly from my chair, and went to her. The clouds had cleared away. From the little porch, where the sweetbriar was climbing, we could see all the myriad worlds of heaven, alight and blazing, and circling in their infinite tracks. An awful, silent harmony, power and peace, and light and life eternal—a shining benediction seemed to be there hanging above our heads. 'This is the night,' she whispered, and took my hand in hers.

And so this is the end of the story of Elizabeth Gilmour, whose troubles, as I have said, were not very great; who is a better woman, I fancy, than if her life had been the happy life she prophesied to herself. Deeper tones and understandings must have come to her out of the profoundness of her griefs, such as they were. For when other troubles came, as they come to all as years go by, she had learnt to endure and to care for others, and to be valiant and to be brave. And I do not like her the less because I have spoken the truth about her, and written of her as the woman she is.

I went to Paris a little time ago. I saw the old grass-grown court; I saw Françoise and Anthony, and Tou-Tou and Lou-Lou, who had grown up two pretty and modest and smiling young girls. The old lady at Asnières had done what was expected, and died and left her fortune to Tou-Tou, her god-daughter. (The little Chinese pagoda is still to let.) Poor Madame Jacob did not, however, enjoy this good luck, for she died suddenly one day, some months before it came to them. But you may be sure that the little girls had still a father in Tourneur, and Caroline too was very kind to them in her uncertain way. She loved them because they were so unlike herself—so gentle, and dull, and guileless. Anthony asked me a great many questions about Elizabeth and her home, and told me that he meant to marry Lou-Lou eventually. He is thin and pale, with a fine head like his father, and a quiet manner. He works very hard, he earns very little—he is one of the best men I ever knew in my life. As I talked to him, I could not but compare him to Will Dampier and to John, who are also good men. But then they are prosperous and well-to-do, with well-stored granaries, with vineyards and fig-trees, with children growing up round them. I was wondering if Elizabeth, who chose her husband because she loved him, and for no better reason, might not have been as wise if she could have appreciated the gifts better than happiness, than well-stored granaries, than vineyards, than fig-trees, which Anthony held in his hand to offer? Who shall say? Self-denial and holy living are better than ease and prosperity? But for that reason some people wilfully turn away from the mercies of Heaven, and call the angels devils, and its gracious bounties temptation.

Anthony has answered this question to himself as we all must do. His father looks old and worn. I fear there is trouble still under his roof—trouble, whatever it may be, which is borne with Christian and courageous resignation by the master of the house: he seems, somehow, in these later years to have risen beyond it. A noble reliance and peace are his; holy thoughts keep him company. The affection between him and his son is very touching.

Madame Tourneur looks haggard and weary; and one day, when I happened to tell her I was going away, she gasped out suddenly—'Ah! what would I not give——' and then was silent and turned aside. But she remains with her husband, which is more than I should have given her credit for.

And so when the appointed hour came, I drove off, and all the personages of my story came out to bid me farewell. I looked back for the last time at the courtyard with the hens pecketting round about the kitchen door; at the garden with the weeds and flowers tangling together in the sun; at the shadows falling across the stones of the yard. I could fancy Elizabeth a prisoner within those walls, beating like a bird against the bars of the cage, and revolting and struggling to be free.

The old house is done away with and exists no longer. It was pulled down by order of the Government, and a grand new boulevard runs right across the place where it stood.

TWO HOURS.

> 'Girl, get you in!' She went, and in one month
> They wedded her to sixty thousand pounds,
> To lands in Kent, and messuages in York,
> And slight Sir Robert with his watery smile
> And educated whisker.

I.

WHAT restless genius is it that takes a malicious pleasure in shifting and mingling the various materials of which daily life is composed? No sooner are a set of people and circumstances comfortably sorted out together, than they are suddenly engulphed, dispersed, revolved away,—no sooner are they well dispersed than all the winds, and horses, and laws of gravitation are struggling to bring them together again. Take, for instance, a colony of people living next door to each other and happily established. How much time are they left in peace? Or let us even take a company of five or six persons comfortably talking round a fire. How long will their talk last on? An hour rarely—half-an-hour, perhaps—even ten minutes is something saved out of the rush of circumstance; and then a clock begins to strike any number from one to twelve; an organ to grind distractingly; a carriage to roll slowly, crushing the gravel outside. Visions flit in; of expectant wives and husbands, of impatient coachmen, of other semi-circles: enter Mrs. Grundy: five o'clock tea; the fire begins to smoke, or what not, and the comfortable little circles jar, break up, disperse in all directions. And, indeed, if a certain number of people are happily established together, the whole combination of accidental circumstances is against them, and nothing can happen that will not interfere more or less with their harmony.

Years ago a set of people had been sitting round the fire at Brand House, and had then dispersed east and west, and for a dozen years, and on the day about which I am writing, some of them had come together again by an odd accident. It is true they were sitting in stiffer attitudes than when they had last assembled, and some of them seemed to have wigs and masks on, compared to their old remembrance of each other. A little girl who had been playing in her pinafore then, was now dressed up as a real young lady, with a red petticoat, and looped grey dress, and round grey eyes, and a chignon; a young fox-hunting parson is disguised as an archdeacon; the hostess, who was a handsome and dignified person twelve years ago, has put on a black front and spectacles, which certainly do not improve her appearance; the least changed of the party is a young man, who had just come of age when they last met altogether. He has grown a thick beard, he has travelled, and learnt to smoke a narghilé since his last visit to Brand House; but, on the whole, he is not greatly altered.

They have been sitting for an hour, and reading and talking of one thing and another, while a log of wood has changed into blue and golden flames. Mrs. Brandiscombe, in the wig and spectacles, announces an arrival by the six-o'clock train. Her son-in-law, the Archdeacon, and his lady, who are returning home next day, talk about stations and cross-roads and convenient trains. The young traveller, it seems, is leaving too, and going to another country-house, called The Mount, about a mile off. The young lady is pressed to stay. 'Dear Caroline' (the expected guest) 'would be so disappointed to miss her.' The girl hesitates, blushes up, says she thinks she must go home with her uncle the Archdeacon ; she shall see her friend at dinner; she cannot stay here; she cannot accept the Merediths' invitation to The Mount ; she is wanted at home. They all try to persuade her to change her mind ; and just as she is giving way the carriage is announced. Mrs. Brandiscombe instantly rises to get ready, and they all disperse ; some go to their rooms, some out into the cold dim December world all round about ; their voices die away up the staircase and passages, and everything is silent.

Janet Ireton, the young lady in the chignon, is delayed

in the hall for a minute by Mr. Hollis of the beard, who asks her if she is going to walk with her uncle. Janet answers shyly and quickly, and springs upstairs lightfooted. She comes upon the two elder ladies leisurely proceeding down the passage.

'He is most to blame, if *those* are his real intentions,' says Mrs. Brandiscombe. 'He should not cause a young girl to be remarked upon; it is not the first time.'

'It is his way, mamma,' says Mrs. Debenham, the Archdeacon's second wife. 'The Archdeacon won't believe me. What does it matter? he is very nice. I assure you, he means nothing. Don't you remember how he flirted with me and with—— Oh, Janet, I didn't hear you.'

'Hm—ah!—girls cannot be too careful,' says Mrs. Brandiscombe, turning into her room, while Janet, with tingling ears and cheeks, flies down a side passage. The coachman, to his indignation, is actually kept waiting ten minutes.

Janet, who is in her great room at the end of the passage, fastening a black hat, with a smart red feather, becomingly on the top of her chignon, is surprised by a tap at the door, and an apparition of Mrs. Brandiscombe herself, ready veiled, and gloved, and caped, and prepared for her daily airing in the close carriage.

'Although it is against my custom to keep the horses waiting,' says the old lady, 'it has occurred to me that, as I am going to call upon Mrs. Meredith, you might like to send some message. Are you quite determined to return home to-morrow?'

'Almost quite,' Janet said, wistfully, looking into the old lady's wrinkled face. 'I have had a delightful holiday. Everybody has been so kind—I don't——'

'I merely wished to ascertain your intentions,' said the shrouded figure, preparing to go. 'We are only too glad to keep you, Janet; although I cannot but agree with my daughter in her opinion of our guest. He has, if I don't mistake, a very special reason for wishing to prolong his stay in this neighbourhood—a lady whom he knew... But I am not at liberty—I merely wish to express a hope that your name may not be coupled with his, and to approve of your self-respect and prudent consideration for other people's opinion.'

Mrs. Brandiscombe had been uttering dark oracles ever since Janet's arrival, but none so definite as this. The girl listened, half angry, half incredulous, half indignant. Then she ran downstairs in no very amiable frame of mind. Mr. Hollis was gone. Her uncle was waiting for her in the hall, rolling an umbrella, and prepared to start. Janet walked away still disturbed in her mind.

'What has become of Mr. Hollis?' said the Archdeacon, looking up and down the misty garden. 'He promised to wait for us here.'

'Who wants Mr. Hollis?' said Janet. 'Come along, uncle John; we shall lose the best part of the day.'

II.

Who does not know the look of furniture in a room lately vacated, as it stands about the chimney-piece in confidential proximity? A sort of faint image of the people who are gone is still in the deserted chamber. Stuffed arm-chairs with sprawling castored legs turned towards each other, a *duchesse* with a grand lace back in an affected attitude by the table, a sprinkling of light bachelor cane-chairs joining into the conversation, and then the hostess's state chair in its chintz dressing-gown by the chimney corner, with its work-basket, its paper-cutter, and its book by its side. The book at Brand House is 'Early Years of the Prince Consort.' There is a lozenge and a coat of arms upon the paper-cutter. One of the castored chairs has been reading the 'Guardian,' which is now lying in a dead faint upon the floor all doubled over. On the grand lace-covered cushion rests a little green book of poetry, with a sprig of holly to mark the place. Everything is quite silent, and a coal falls into the fender, which conscientiously reflects the fire. There is a distant roll (not so loud as that which announces the arrival of the carriage on the stage), then more silence; someone walking in the garden looks in through the tall window. You may see through the glass that it is the gentleman with the black beard and black eyes and country leggings who was lately established by the lace chair.

He walks away and disappears behind a laurel-bush, and then nothing more happens till the clock begins to strike. With the last stroke of four comes a sound of voices, a rustling of silks. The door opens wide, and a lady is standing in the middle of the room, looking curiously up and down with bright slow glances. Her glances are those of a well-esteemed and well-satisfied person. It is curious to note the different expressions with which people see the daily life-pictures that pass before them, the long portrait-galleries, the pictures of still life for housekeepers, the *tableaux de genre* in our homes. Some look critically, secure of their own standing, though it may be on a different level; others, wistfully, feeling that they have no share, and are always looking on; others— and to this class my lady belongs—with a half-sympathy and a half-indifference. People look what they *are,* gazing at other lives; they look what they *feel* when they are sitting being gazed at. She does not care to feel a whole sympathy, her life has been too complete and calm for that; and yet its very completeness and calmness, which have left no room for some things she may once have dreamt of, prevent her from feeling the whole indifference of very happy people; and now and then she gives a glance from her sheltered bower at the sun and the winds in which others are struggling in the plains without.

Slow as these glances are, they have noted everything: the chairs, the tall windows, across one of which gusty branches are brushing; she sees the distant corners of the room reflected in the dim looking-glasses; she looks back to ascertain if the butler has followed her, and then moves, with a smile, towards the farthest window, passing, reflected on from one grim looking-glass to another (sometimes sideways, sometimes crossing some distant room in a contrary direction to that in which she is really moving), and at last she stops in the shadowy darkness and light of the farthest casement. She can see the grey garden through its panes, the black trees and blue dull lawn, the boughs all swaying, the mists hanging from the creaking branches or heaped up at the end of the long alleys; only towards the sea the heavy clouds are rent, and a pale grey gleam lights up the silver and steel of the waters beyond the oak-tree glade. Mist and sea and land without, the familiar streaks and shadows and reflections within. It is a dozen years since she last saw it all; more than that.

My lady, whose name is Caroline, is about thirty years old, a soft happy-looking woman, with brown bright hair, with dimpled cheeks and pretty white hands, on which flash and twinkle a great many diamond rings as she unhooks the clasp of her red gipsy cloak. It slides along her black silk folds and falls in a comfortable purple red heap all round about her feet. So she stands, taking in every indication of what now is, and of what is left since the last time when she stood in this very corner: the same woman, looking out at the same sea and sky and rustling trees, so unchanged did it all seem to her, so unchanged did she feel. For in two minutes the circles have turned inversely: she has travelled back, beginning at the nearest end of her life: her return, her wanderings, her widowhood, her children, her marriage, her early troubles all whirl past. People are not only their present selves but all their old selves at the same time—sometimes one and sometimes another comes uppermost; and Caroline Rowland is one particular self of a dozen years ago at this minute, an old sad childish self with an odd prescience of the future. Other spirits are there too, dressed in their old-fashioned dresses. Some are alive, some are dead people. The spirit of poor Mr. Brandiscombe is evoked; she can see her uncle in his big chair as he sits nodding off to sleep. Mrs. Brandiscombe has cast away her front, Fanny (she is not yet married to the Archdeacon; she married a year after her cousin) is sitting at the piano singing 'Theckla's Sorrows,' set to music. How she used to sing, rolling her little fat body from side to side and winking her little pig's eyes! . . . With all this rush of old emotion more visions come, bringing a faint blush into the widow's cheek. One of them is the remembrance of a young man. It comes striding straight across the room saying goodbye in a quick impatient voice.

She remembers looking up in a bewildered incredulous way, and almost blinded by what she saw—she could not meet his parting looks, they seemed to kill her as she stood beneath them; she could not speak nor cry before them all. She remembered holding on tight by the marble table; all the rest of the room was swinging before her meanwhile in tune to Fanny Brandiscombe's screams. 'Why do people remember such things?' says poor Caroline, protesting.

Fanny Brandiscombe would have been flattered if she could have known how many years that song would go on ringing in her cousin's ears. Sometimes people quite unconsciously do something, say something, that is to last another person's lifetime. Sometimes it is, alas! their own lifetime that they put into a passing moment— a minute that never ceases for them. It goes on through life, and beyond life, perhaps, to that other life where how many of us, if the choice were ours, would not gladly carry the sorrows and remembrances of this one? It was a minute like this that Caroline was remembering. To-day, loved and trusted and independent of others, and well considered by the world, and on good terms with herself, she felt as if she could almost envy her own girlish humility and innocent helplessness. Now, her standard might be a little wider perhaps, but it was not so high; now she might be happier, perhaps, but not so happy— sorrier, but never so sorry.

The things that she hoped for of late seemed sordid and small compared to the old dreams of her youth. Men and women are not stocks and stones looking on unaltered at events as they go by; one's life must affect one in the end. One of the many voices that are in silence says to Mrs. Rowland, 'Yours is an easy life now; your old one was hard and sad and unselfish; the old one was best—the old one was the best.'

'What is the use of thinking about it?' says Mrs. Rowland, impatient even from the heights of her serene indifference, and she moves back impatiently to the fire again, glad to escape into to-day once more. 'How cold it is. I suppose aunt Brandiscombe still locks up the coal? No one should leave anything unlocked, not even the coal-cellar. It *was* a shame, wasn't it?' (the widow is appealing to her own face in the glass: it looks so sympathising that she bursts out laughing). 'How I cried that night going to bed in the moonlight, and Fanny Brandiscombe cried too. I wonder why she cried? I think if any young man ever empties the cream-jug into my little Kitty's tea, as George Hollis did into mine, I should expect him to come forward, and not to go away for ever without a word. I was civil enough when we met at Florence, and John asked him to dinner.'

I think it was to escape from spells of her own fancy, and to feel herself safe in commonplace again, that this modern Melusina rang the bell violently, pulling at a great limp worsted-work arm with a huge brazen hand.

'Will you bring me some tea, if you please?' says Mrs. Rowland to a butler, who appeared in answer to the pull, and whose calm clerical appearance dispersed the ghosts that had been disporting themselves.

The butler looks puzzled.

'Mrs Brandiscombe will be in to tea at five o'clock,' he says, doubtfully. 'She has given orders to get everything ready for five, but, of course——'

'Oh, very well,' says Mrs. Rowland, 'I'll wait. Is there anybody staying in the house?'

'The Archdeacon and Mrs. Debenham are staying till to-morrow, and Miss Ireton remains, I believe,' says the butler. 'Mr. Hollis is just gone—his luggage is to follow him to the Mount—Mr. Franks left yesterday.'

'It is very cold,' says Mrs. Rowland, with a little start and shiver; 'could you put a log on the fire,—and bring me a paper, if you please?'

'To-day's papers are only just come,' says the butler, respectfully; 'and Mrs. Brandiscombe always likes to open them herself.'

Any other time Caroline Rowland would have laughed outright at the old well-remembered cranks, that had lasted out so many better things; but to-day all this thinking and remembering have sobered her usual bright spirits; a sort of uneasy doubt has taken hold of her; a sort of self-reproach that had been waiting for her for years; lurking patiently in wait in that dim corner yonder, while other feelings and events came and passed, and time and place shifted, and sorrows changed, and melted into peace. What had she done? Could she forgive herself now? Not quite. Going back into that old corner, it had seemed to her as if her old conscience had laid hands on her—At last I hold you—at last! Why did you try to escape from me? What have you been about? Why had you so little patience? Why did you flirt with poor John when you loved George Hollis? was that why he was angry? A thought of what might have been—of a union of true hearts, a vision so far different from what its reality had been—seemed to pass before her. 'Forgive me, dear John,' she was saying in her heart all the time. And perhaps she loved her husband most at this very instant, when she told herself how little she had loved him. Caroline was a woman who, if need be, could put her conscience into another person's keeping; and in John's lifetime he had been purse-bearer and conscience-keeper for them both; and she had but to look nice, and keep within her allowance, and attend to her children, and nurse him when he had the gout, and never think of the past—that, you know, would have been wrong for a married woman; but for a widow—for a widow it was very silly.

It was odd and unexpected and uncomfortable altogether, and that odd chance mention of a name had chilled her; and if she had known she was going to feel like this, nothing would have induced her to come; but soon the widow calmed down, and the fire burnt warm, and she pulled her knitting from her pocket, and in putting the little loops together on the needles she found distraction. In 'Villette' the impetuous Emanuel desires Lucy Snow to drop every stitch of work that is not intended specially for him. Many people would have to go bare-shod if all the stitches were dropped that are not theirs by right. If the moments of distraction, of despondency, that are knitted into even rows were to be taken away from the wearers of the silken chains, and purses, and woollen socks—the hopeless regrets knitted into dumb records of grey, and red, and white wool, little Tom Rowland, for one, would have his toes through. But by degrees, as she worked on, his mother grew more quiet and more calm; her flushed face softened to its usual placid sweetness; the lights of the fire were shining on her hair; the comfortable warmth soothed and tranquillised her; and she sat at last, working much as usual, the very personification of rippling silken prosperity, installed by the fire in Mrs. Brandiscombe's own chair, the deep folds of shining black, warm in the red firelight, the needles gleaming as they crisscrossed each other on their journey.

III.

Meanwhile a grey December day is mistily spreading over the great bare plain in front of the house, across which Mrs. Brandiscombe's fat horses trot daily. It is all sandy and furze-grown, with pools gleaming black and white, and dull green prickly things growing. The roads travelling across the plain go floundering from white sand into yellow mud. Here and there in the mist some stunted slate-tiled nouse is standing. It may be warm within and dry and light; from without those lonely tenements look like little coffins lying unburied. The clouds are hanging over the plain; towards the sea they seem to break, and some of their misty veils are parting and swinging on a low gusty wind. Two figures are trudging along the road—two people, tired of sitting at home, who have come out to refresh themselves with clouds and stormy shadows, and rain-gusts, and dead furze. One of these people—the Archdeacon, who married Fanny Brandiscombe—walks regularly for a constitutional; he has an objection to getting over-stout. His companion, Miss Janet of the red petticoat, is the daughter of a less prosperous parson than himself, who married the Archdeacon's sister twenty years before. As the girl walks along her quick feet almost pass the heavy-gaitered steps; all the damp grey fogs and mist seem turning to roses on her cheeks; she has high-arched eyebrows, stiff hair, circling grey eyes. Far off in the distance comes a third person pursuing them; the gentleman in the country gaiters, who is trying to meet them at the cross-road. He had come out oppressed by a sort of day-mare of chairs and tables; and by the exhausted atmosphere of human sameness pent up for twenty-four hours in Mrs. Brandiscombe's country-house, and by the thought of a meeting that seemed to him very ill-timed, and for which he did not feel prepared just at that special moment. His is a consciousness with a strain in it, an impetuous, and yet self-doubtful nature. No one would have suspected it, seeing the tall erect figure, the firm striding step. For my own part, I believe that strain to be the saving of an overbearing character. Hollis was not quite true to himself or to his own theories—sceptical as he was by way of being, self-interested as he announced himself, hasty in conclusion as he was; this mental reservation seemed to be a chink in the wall through which the light might penetrate. The little rift may be for good as well as for bad. Mr. Hollis, seeing a red dab of colour and a black dab through the mist, hurried along as quickly as he could, with his faults and virtues, crossing stones and ruts and rucks on his way, and vaulting over a stile, and he soon approached the pair, who were proceeding together apparently, but in reality straggling off to very distant cities and thoroughfares, and talking to each other in two different languages that neither could understand.

'I am very sorry, Janet,' the Archdeacon was saying, with his nose up in the air (it was not unlike his niece's). 'You do not suppose that I have not weighed it well over in my mind? It gives me the greatest concern to refuse you, and I heartily hope that no other vacancy will ever fall to my gift. Your father, with all his good qualities, is not the man for this one. There would be a general outcry; he would be the last person to wish me to act against my CONVICTIONS.' The Archdeacon stepped out briskly, but his companion kept well up with him.

'*He* would,' she was saying; 'he never thinks of himself. But you know how good he is, uncle John, and your own convictions can't be changed by an outcry. And truth is truth, and if I were an archdeacon, and you were papa, I wouldn't mind what a few hateful, stupid, narrow-minded people said,' cried the girl, more and more excited.

'I am very sorry, my dear, but it is my duty,' began her uncle.

'Oh, uncle John, are you quite *sure* it is your duty,' implored the girl, eagerly, 'and not that you are afraid? God gives one one's relations——'

'And a conscience too,' cried the Archdeacon, with a stride, angrily, 'though you seem to have none. Enough of this, Janet. You can reserve your persuasions for Hollis; he is not a churchman, and may consult his inclinations. Ask him; Holmsdale is in his gift.'

Janet blushed up, a deep red furious blush, and jumped, with a bitter pain suddenly in her heart, right away from her uncle's side, across a great pool that was lying reflecting the cloud-heaps. How desolate it all was; some smoke was drifting from a distant factory chimney; some figure far ahead was crossing the furze; some distant cock was crowing a melancholy crow; and the wind came fluttering against her face, and the tears started from her eyes.

'There are not two rights,' she was thinking, indignantly. 'Uncle John thinks that people get on best in both worlds at once. They don't, they don't, and he doesn't love his neighbour as himself, and he *ought* to help papa. I know it. How *can* he expect me to ask Mr. Hollis for his living. I can't, I won't—now of all times. Oh, how unhappy I am! Oh, how foolish I have been! Perhaps I shall forget about it all when I get home to my poor papa. Oh, how disappointed they will be.' The grey eyes were still filling with tears, but the tears did her good, as she rubbed them away with her gauntleted fingers; she felt a hard gulping sensation in her throat, but she choked it down somehow as she hurried on.

Janet was an odd matter-of-fact young person, with a curious amount of courage in her composition. She was very young. She was not afraid of pain. She would inflict it upon herself with a remorseless determination. She was oddly defiant and mistrustful for her age, for she was very young—only eighteen, and young for eighteen. She looked upon herself as an experiment. We most of us have a vague idea of some character that we enact almost unconsciously: some of us look upon ourselves in the light of conclusions (this was the Archdeacon), others of tragedies, others of precepts. There are no end to the disguises and emblems of human nature. I have a friend who is a barometer, another a pair of slippers, another a sonata. I know a teapot (fem.), velocipedes of both genders, a harlequin, and a complete set of fire-irons. Mrs. Rowland might be looked upon as a soft hearth-rug comfortably spread out in the warmth of the blaze.

Meanwhile the experiment is hopping about in the bog, with stiff elfin locks blown by the winds, and grey eyes fixed. 'Janet, come back into the pathway,' says the Archdeacon, 'and don't be foolish.' Janet, who is used to obey, and who had spent a great part of her life under her uncle's orders, comes back, but she can't walk with him—she is too indignant for that—so she passes on in front, going on meanwhile with her self-experimentalising. While the Archdeacon, not sorry to lay hold of a grievance, continues, 'Yes, in my days young women did not set so little store by the advice of their superiors.' ('Uncles' did not sound well.) 'You think there is something specially heroic in leaving at a time when your prospects may be materially affected—I am obliged to speak plainly—in leaving when your influence may be most important. Janet, I will not have you look at me like that. *I* think it is an act of headstrong self-will.'

'Uncle John!' cried Janet, indignant. She was not afraid of pain, as I have said, and this was about the limit. She had a sort of curiosity to discover how much and how far she could bear. She had been well drilled in a school of repression and patience. Her mother was a whole course of such an education; her father's conscientious zigzags were another lesson in the art; to say nothing of money troubles without end, affairs going wrong, tempers going wrong, small store of sympathy at home, and now—now it seemed to her that her own troubles were in addition to all that had gone before. Whatever it all meant, Janet was determined not to yield weakly and meekly. What did she care for being unhappy? She could bear it as others had done before her. But she did care for this, that she should not lose one atom of the honest self-respect which was her own as yet,—the self-respect that was her right, her inheritance. Why should she put herself in a place to forfeit all of this? She was not pretty, thought Janet of the circling grey eyes, rings of grey and black under straight dark brows that were knit. A day or two ago—well, a day or two ago, she had been foolish and vain, and when her uncle, in his pompous, bungling way, said something about the reason why Mr. Hollis was staying on, she had only laughed in a delightful consciousness of power; but to-day she had heard a little word from Mr. Hollis himself that had first opened her eyes and disabused her—a little impatient word about hating the place and having no reason to like it; and as he spoke her experiments upon herself had begun that instant. The resolute Janet gave herself not one moment's thought, she shut the shutters as it were, pulled down the curtains, shut out the early dawn in her heart, tried to forget what growing sunlight gleam she had seen for an instant with dazzled eyes.

The Archdeacon, as he followed her, was also in no very pleasant state of mind. He was picking his way mentally as well as actually: on every side were pools and stones, and dangerous splashes. He was a kind-hearted man, and greatly troubled, although he would not own it to himself, and he clung to his conscience, which happened to be keeping to a moral sidepath out of the mud. He knew that for years his sister—poor Isabella, Janet's mother—had been looking forward to this living to make up to her for all her long troubles and anxieties. It was to make arid places fertile; to feed, clothe, teach the children; to steady the wavering faith of her husband; to raise them up from the depths into which their little home had been sinking, over-weighted as it was with anxieties, ill-humours, and children and debt. Once the Archdeacon himself had looked forward to this deliverance for them all and his favourite Janet in particular; but now, in these troubled and dangerous times, to set a man like Tom Ireton —who never knew his own mind, and was converted by every ranter he came across—to set such a man as that to stem the dangerous current that had lately set in at Chawhampton, it was impossible; the whole country would cry out against it. Opinion didn't matter at Merton-le-Mere (this was the name of Janet's home); the country louts had no opinions beyond their cider and their pitchforks.

Tom might preach himself black in the face, and they would be none the wiser. But at Chawhampton—it was impossible. The Archdeacon had a copy of the letter in his pocket in which he offered the living to Dr. Phillips— a man of his own mind, liberal, decided, with clear views of the future, as well as of the present; a man, like himself, fully awake to the importance of checking the dangerous advance of the tide.

Tom writes that he has always spoken his mind, that he does not know what is coming, that he looks upon change as one of the fundamental laws of the universe. A clergyman has no business to look for change, the Archdeacon says, not to Janet, but to himself; and if he does he should not say so; if he says so he cannot possibly expect that I should give him my living. And this tiresome girl is as headstrong as her father.

And so they walked on for a minute or two, splashing through a slough of despond, far away from Coombe Common.

'It won't matter much being a little more or less unhappy,' was Janet's silent monologue. 'I shan't mind very much. I don't mind things as other people do;' and the girl turned away from the almost irresistible visions that seemed to pierce even through shutters and curtains. 'Go, go, go; such things are not for me. I'm not a bit ashamed,' thinks Janet. 'There is no particular merit in being happy and successful. It's not for me, that is all. It is women like Mrs. Rowland who are made to be happy. Ah, how happy they must be.' And Janet felt that though she might not look at it, that a dawn *was* there for some —for those who were outside in the bright open, watching from their vineyards and illumined by the golden beams.

IV.

'Here is a friend,' said the Archdeacon, not sorry for the arrival of a third person, and calling Janet back with a start to the ruts, the mist, the common, as Hollis caught them up. Now that Hollis had come into the vista it seemed brighter to the girl than any sun-gilt paradise that she had been imagining. Indeed, the chances of life, unexpected and sad as they are, are also more satisfactory at times than the brightest visions of an ardent imagination. For visions partake always more or less of the visionary, and are hackneyed and incomplete just in those things where he fails himself. Reality comes with a wonder of novelty and a fresh strength of its own, with a vividness that the dearest visions fail in. Has it ever happened to any one of us to ponder over some hopeless problem, over and over, and round and about, and at last in despair to give it up as unsolvable, and suddenly one day the door opens, a living answer enters, more complete and satisfactory than any we could ever conceive? The difficulties are over, the thing we could not realise is there before us.

It may be a love that was wanted, or an intellect, or a strong will, or a friend, or a sympathy. There it is; no effort of yours has brought it, it has come; and the emptiness being there, the new power is absorbed into the vacuum.

Janet had been facing the wind; when her uncle spoke she turned with bright looks, and stood straight, with flapping grey wings, waiting for Hollis to come up to her.

Brown-legged and black-bearded, with cheerful looks of recognition, the young man arrived across the sea of rain and chalk. As he looked at Janet it struck him that there was a something about her that he had never noticed before; something simple, noble, self-reliant. He thought as he came up that he had never done her looks justice, for he had never thought her even handsome till that minute. And Janet? At that minute she felt that she was free; she might feel some pain, there might be more to come, but she was free, she was no one's bondmaid.

'If you are going through the wood,' said Mr. Hollis, cheerfully, 'I can walk with you as far as the lodge.'

'Is that on your way?' said the Archdeacon, stopping short. 'Are you going to the Merediths now, or coming back to the house?'

'I am going now,' said Hollis: 'she begged me to come early. There is a short-cut from the lodge. I said goodbye to my hostess before I came away, and told them to send on my things. I wonder what there is we could say to Miss Ireton to induce her to come over for a day or two.'

'Janet does not know her own interest,' said her uncle, testily, ' when she persists in refusing such a very pleasant and well-timed invitation.'

The Archdeacon's speech was anything but well-timed. Janet drew herself up.

'I am very sorry, I am wanted at home.' She had taught herself her lesson and could repeat it very glibly. As she spoke they had come to a gate, and George Hollis, who held it open for her as she passed, looked at her fixedly for an instant to see if this was a real reason or only an excuse. Janet saw his doubtful look, and her two eyes fell, and her bright cheeks blushed for her and then for themselves. Hollis with some temper let the gate go when she had passed. She was making an excuse,—she did not come because she would not,—she would not because . .

There was no accounting for the vagaries of girls. Miss Ireton had guessed at his displeasure; she looked up defiantly—what was it to her? Then her heart smote her, for it was not a very hard one. 'Don't think I am not very sorry,' she said. 'Who could help being sorry? I shall never forget this happy time.' The Archdeacon had waited behind a little to examine the gate; it was a curious hasp, and he wanted one of the same sort put up in his field to keep out irreverent cows.

'I am so used to come and to go,' said Hollis, in a

snappish voice, 'that I leave fewer regrets behind me than you do. I have no special reason for liking Brand House.' It was a cross speech, and only meant that he was offended. Janet thought it meant, not that he was offended, but utterly indifferent. It did not pain her much. This was what she had been expecting ever since her little talk with Mrs. Brandiscombe. The Archdeacon still lingered and the two young people walked on in silence. They had left the common behind them at last, and come into a wild green park. It seemed the last vestige of the thick woods that had once covered the country, reaching down to the sea almost. Janet, with an impatient quick step or two, had gone a-head—a bright figure against the gloom, the grey, the mist: the branches seemed heavy with it, ivy tendrils glistened in the damp, the mosses were green upon the silver trunks, and the lichens were opening wide their grey mouths. There was a faint aromatic scent in the air from the many fir-cones and spikes; from the golden drops of turpentine that were oozing from the bark; from the damp sweet decay all about, of dying leaves and spreading creepers. And then above were the bare branches, full with the buds of the coming spring; decay, and life, and change, in a sweet, subdued, silent glen, where the dim daylight came dimmer still through the crossing rustle o the beech branches. 'This is a lovely sort of Hades,' said Hollis, coming to himself again, and looking about.

'I believe it is Meredith's property,' said the Arch

deacon, who had caught them up; 'the place wants thinning, but I can quite understand a man's reluctance to cut down his own trees.'

'I shall ask him what he is about,' said Hollis. 'I know the place of old. I used to come here constantly twelve years ago, when my father lived at Portsmouth.'

Janet heard so far, and walked on faster to get out of the sound of their voices. Every word and every little event that had happened for the last hour or two, seemed to confirm her more and more in the new interpretation that Mrs. Brandiscombe's words had given to the small events that were so interesting to her. She had been played with, she had been used as a screen to conceal real feelings and interests that were unknown to her. . . . Her bright cheeks blushed with shame as she rushed along, her grey eyes had an odd misty look of anger in them, she picked up a dried stick, upon which some little lichens were clinging still, and began beating it against the stems on either side of the pathway; it soon broke; and she flung the pieces away impatiently. A word had been enough to make her happy, a word had been enough to disabuse her. And yet it was hard, she thought, that this her last walk should be so spoiled; he might have been friendly just this last time. And then she waited for them to come up and tried to make friends again, speaking of one thing and another, for she was thinking they might never meet again. Among other things she asked Hollis if he had ever met her friend, Mrs. Rowland.

'Is it a case of devoted ladies' friendship?' the young man asked, in his turn.

'Why do you laugh at women's friendships?' said Janet, gently. 'Mrs. Rowland would do anything for me.' And then she added, with a fierce look at the poor Archdeacon, 'I don't think the kindest men do things only because one asks them. I had much sooner trust a woman.'

Janet felt quite ashamed, because, instead of snubbing her, the Archdeacon interposed quite mildly—

'My dear child, that is because you are utterly unreasonable, every one of you, and never stop to think of the obstacles there may be in the way. Mrs. Rowland is charming, but she would be just as unreasonable in granting as you would be in asking.'

'I think men invent obstacles,' said Janet, mollified a little, 'for the pleasure of thinking themselves reasonable in not overcoming them.'

'I wish you would try *me* some day, Miss Ireton,' said Hollis, laughing; 'I should like to do something, reasonable or not, and prove myself as staunch a friend as Mrs. Rowland.'

He wondered why a look of pain, followed by a burning blush, came into the girl's face. Instead of answering, she looked away down the long dim avenue by which they had been coming. They had reached the little lodge by this time, where their roads divided. Janet's heart began to beat a little; she felt her uncle's mild enquiring glance fixed upon her; she felt as if she hated him almost at that instant. How could he expect it; how could he allow her to humiliate herself by asking strangers for what was his own to bestow! It was all horrid, all except Hollis's kindness. She clenched her left hand tight as she suddenly said 'Goodbye; I am tired, I want to go home. Please don't come back with me,' said the poor child. 'I had rather go back alone; I should like it best.'

She was too much in earnest to be other than cold. Hollis looked disappointed. The Archdeacon, who had been counting on this final walk to bring about some sort of explanation, looked annoyed. He offered to walk on a little way with the young man, feeling it was his part to make up to him for Janet's ungraciousness by every little attention in his power. Notwithstanding his wife's demurs and Mrs. Brandiscombe's solemn head-shakes, he had been of opinion that Hollis was very much attracted by his young niece. It was a most desirable thing in every respect; and if Dr. Phillips accepted Chawhampton, Holmesdale, his present living, would be in Hollis's gift, &c. &c. Poor Janet! She walked away for a little distance, and then she stood for an instant looking back after Hollis and her uncle. Her heart was very heavy, her steps lagged dull and wearily. She might have stayed;

Q

she might have seen him again and again; but now she was going to-morrow; it was all settled; it was goodbye! Had she done right? Alas! how could she tell; why was she all alone to work out right and wrong from this tangle? 'I should like to do something, reasonable or not.' Ah, what did he mean? Only kindness, only friendship. If she asked Hollis to help her, this was clear—she could never see him again; never, never. What, another gate? She tried to open it; it was stiff, and hurt her fingers. Janet stamped in a sort of despair. Give her a living! She might as well ask Hollis for the moon. She looked back once more: there were the two dark figures, walking away with all her best hopes, at the end of the long dark alley; then she got the gate open and trudged on. Everything seemed changed: no life, no promise, only decay; the leaves were rotting all about, a great gust of smoky mist seemed falling upon her, the little laurel-bushes alone looked green and flourishing. Janet was shivering by the time she got to the house; she was jaded and tired. Bodies are apt to be dull when the spirits are weary.

V.

Janet's was a big state-room at the end of the passage, with tall windows looking blank out upon the mist and the laurel-walks along which she had just come. There was old-fashioned furniture, in stately preparation for the guests who came to inhabit it; there were medicine-spoons of every shape and size, medicine-glasses, cap-stands, leg-rests; there was a sofa, with various-shaped cushions; there was a boot-jack. It would have all seemed more suitable to one of the dowager ladies, Mrs. Brandiscombe's contemporaries, than to Janet Ireton, who did not require any of these appliances. She threw her hat upon the great fourpost bed; she fell into the great arm-chair, and sat curled up in the seat, with her head resting on the arm and her hand hanging over—she tried to think it all out calmly for herself, but her heart beat almost too impetuously. Here was the case. She had been a goose, and had fancied that a few civil words meant a life-long devotion. She was not ashamed of herself; she had found out her mistake in time, and instantly determined to avoid any possible misunderstanding in future. But now, to do as her uncle wished,—to ask Mr. Hollis, whom of all other people in the whole world she wished to avoid, for so great a mark of favour,—ah! it was too much; she would not, she could not. Then Janet thought no more, but sat staring at the great pier-glass; then she jumped up, and began walking round and round the room. Why did everything seem to jar upon her? Her dress caught in a table-corner as she went along, she shook it free impatiently; a chair stood a little crooked, and the slanting lines worried her, but when she had put it straight she was no calmer than she had been before.

Janet of the even nerves could not understand this strange new phase. It frightened her and horrified her. She found herself asking herself, 'Why did he ask me so often to go to the Merediths? He could not know, he did not know, how hard it was to refuse. Ah, it was cruel, yes, cruel, to make such a play—if it was play.' A deep, burning blush of indignation came into her cheeks, as she felt in her deepest heart of hearts what happiness was *not*. She would not trust herself to think what it might be. Ah, if she had anyone to go to now, as other girls had,— girls who were loved and sympathised with, and comforted, and guarded from harm. Her father was no guide, dearly as she loved him. She loved her uncle, but she mistrusted him; his was too complicated a mind for a straightforward nature like Janet's. Her home was a house full of cracks and darns to be repaired, and children to be patched and borne with,—not much else; her mother's love was with the boys.

Then, of course, came a reaction, and the thought that, though Mr. Hollis's civil speeches meant nothing in one sense, they might mean something in another. He had said he would gladly help her; perhaps he meant what he said. He could not know of her father unless she told him. It was her duty to do what she could, even in a hopeless endeavour like this one. Should she ever forgive herself if, because it was horrible to speak, she was silent, and by this silence did her father an injury? It was a shame that she should have to do such a thing; she who had always held her head so high, and vowed that no poverty, no trouble, should ever bring her low. Janet stamped impatiently at the thought. Then came a ray of relief. She should not see him again. But she might write, said her officious conscience; she might send the letter by the messenger who carried over his luggage. The poor persecuted girl ran with a sort of leap across the room to the writing-table, where the old ladies were accustomed to carry on their correspondence in their delicate old-fashioned handwriting, 'hastening to reply to one another's favours of the 14th, and to announce their safe arrival,' &c. Poor Janet began writing in a desperate hurry, flying over the paper as if afraid that if she paused for one instant her courage would fail, her pen fly away, her paper slip from under her fingers.

'Dear Mr. Hollis,—I am going to take a great liberty; if you never forgive me I cannot help it. I feel I *must* say what I am going to say. Perhaps if we ever meet again you may tell me that you do forgive me, though I almost fear that this letter may make you think ill of us all.

'I am going home to-morrow to my father, who is the best father, the truest gentleman, that ever lived. He is very very anxious and suffering, and for years we had hoped that my uncle would have appointed him to Chawhampton when it fell vacant. This, he now says, he cannot do, and he has given it to Dr. Phillips, the vicar of Holmesdale. Will you give papa Holmesdale? You do not know how good he is. He speaks what he thinks. My uncle calls him impressionable and unguarded. I do not want to belong to a guarded religion, but then I am my father's daughter; a minute ago you said, " If ever I can do anything for you." I know it meant only commonplace service, not this. I know I am grasping and presumptuous. What can I do? how can I not ask you when I think of my dearest father's many many cares?

Yours truly,
' JANET IRETON.'

Janet did not trust herself even to read the blotted page. It was blotted, but she dared not write it out; she sealed it up in the envelope, and then threw the letter from her on the floor; and then, flinging her head down over her arms upon the table, she burst out crying, sobbing, as if her heart would break. Her pride seemed hurt, crushed, soiled; her maiden dignity seemed sacrificed. Anyone, anyone else in all the world she could have asked without shame, but this pang was like heart's blood given drop by drop. Had he not wounded her already, made a play and pretence of his liking for her? Before this there might have been a chance that some day they might have met again and been friends.

Now, never, never; she would never see him; she had humiliated herself before him; she would avoid him, hide out of his way. 'Oh, papa, my dear papa,' sobbed Janet, with another great burst of tears.

A noise in the passage outside reminded her that there was no time to lose, and she ran out to stop a servant and to ask if Mr. Hollis's luggage was going to the Mount.

'The luggage has gone, ma'am,' said the housemaid, placidly. 'Would you please to like your fire lighted?'

'Gone!' repeated Janet, stupidly. It seemed impossible that when all the powers of her mind and will and conscience had been brought together to write the letter, so small a thing should come to prevent the fulfilment of her scheme.

'It is an omen,' thought the girl, 'that I need not send the letter. Yes, please, light my fire,' she said to the housemaid, and a momentary thought of relief unspeakable, of a burning letter, of a mind at ease, came to beguile her.

The maid came back in a minute, saying she had been mistaken, the cart had not yet gone. Was that the letter?—(poor Janet hastily dropped her composition into the woman's hand.) The butler had desired her to say that Mrs. Rowland was in the drawing-room, and had been asking for Miss Ireton.

Caroline come! This was, indeed, a ray of comfort in all Janet's despairing troubles. What kind fate had sent her? Here was the friend, the adviser, and sympathiser for whom she had been longing.

VI.

As Janet burst into the drawing-room Mrs. Rowland looked up, with a little exclamation of delight, and held out her arms. The widow was installed by the fire. She had not moved for the last half hour or more. While Janet had been going through so much, Caroline had warmed her little feet, smoothed her soft hair, and looked at the clock a dozen times. 'My dear child,' she is saying, 'how glad I am to see you; how delightful this is; what have you been doing? Where have you been? I hoped I should find you. Come and sit down, and tell me all about yourself. Aunt Brandiscombe won't be back for half-an-hour at least.' Then they both kissed each other again, and then came that moment's silence which comes when people's liking for each other exceeds their habit of intimacy.

Mrs. Rowland, in her pleasure, laid hands upon the poker, and was on the point of stirring up the fire to a brighter welcome, when Janet, with a little cry of alarm even in her first greeting, tore it out of her friend's hand. 'Not this one, the little black one, Caroline; the bright one is *never* used.' Janet had not been so long away from schoolroom restrictions as her friend. 'Silly child!' said Mrs. Rowland, impatiently, relinquishing the shining steel, and taking Janet's soft warm hand instead into her own. Janet sat looking up with honest eyes full of admiration. She had all a young girl's enthusiasm for her friend. Miss Ireton used to think sometimes that Mrs. Rowland was like music moving on continuously from one modulation to another, never hurrying, never lagging, flowing on to a rhythm of her own. 'Now I,' thought poor Janet, 'I go on in jerks and jigs; sometimes I stop altogether, sometimes I crash out ever so many false notes.' She forgot that she was young, that Caroline had had a longer time to learn to play upon the instrument which had been granted her. Janet's tunes were very sweet and gay, if she had but known it. For her there was no cause to fear, but, alas! for those who can never master the subtle harmonies of life! It seems hard, indeed, if all the long, patient practice of years is to produce no harmonious sound, no corresponding chords in answer. Perhaps, though these sad cracked strains to our dull ears may seem to jar so painfully, they belong to a wider song and a mightier symphony than any which we can apprehend.

'Now tell me all about yourself and your people, and everything I want to know,' said Mrs. Rowland, settling herself comfortably in the blaze.

'All!' said the girl. 'That would be a melancholy

story. Papa is more out of spirits, mamma more anxious; and I—I am beginning to think that everything is disappointing, except seeing one's friends sometimes,' said Janet, as her eyes smiled and then filled up with tears.

As Janet looked at her, Caroline could not help being touched by the sad looks in the two grey eyes. The widow stooped and kissed the girl's forehead. 'I am so glad you are going to be here,' said Mrs. Rowland. 'I could not bear to think of a *tête-à-tête* with aunt Brandiscombe till Monday. But now I shall have you to support me.'

'But you won't,' said Janet, bluntly and blushing, 'for I'm going to-morrow. I have been very happy here—I'm very sorry to go, but I must.'

There was a jar in Janet's voice as she spoke which struck Mrs. Rowland, who was usually quick to hear what people didn't say, as well as what they said. She had a great many curious gifts and quicknesses of the same sort.

'You must not desert me in this unkind way,' she said. 'I want to talk over all sorts of things with you. First of all, tell me why you must go. I had hoped to persuade you to come home with me on Monday, and see my little girls.'

'How I should like it some day,' said grateful Janet; 'but I cannot stay here any longer.'

'Why cannot you stay?' said Mrs Rowland. 'You tiresome girl, what is it all about? Is there anyone you want to avoid?'

Janet pulled her hand away instinctively. 'I am wanted,' she said. 'I have had a disappointment.' Caroline looked full of sympathy, and yet a little amused. 'We have been so longing that papa might be appointed to Chawhampton, and now my uncle refuses'—(Caroline looked quite grave and much less interested)—'and you dont know what it is,' Janet went on, 'to wait and hope and wait, and fail at last. . . . '

The widow sighed. 'Waiting! I never liked waiting much,' she said.

'Oh, Caroline!' cried the girl, 'I have so longed for someone to speak to all these past days. It is so difficult to settle for oneself always, to know what is right, and when it is right to go against the wishes of people older than oneself. Of course I love papa most of all. I would do anything in the whole world for him.'

'You must marry, Janet,' said Mrs. Rowland, in a cheerful voice, drawing her big chair in a little nearer to the fire. 'That is what you must do, then you will have someone to consult with. You must come and stay with me, and I shall introduce some nice eligible young men to you.'

'Marry! Oh, Caroline!' said Janet, hurt as young people are who ask you for bread and you give them a stone. (Mrs. Rowland was twisting her own flashing guard-ring round and round upon her finger.) 'What are you saying? It is like aunt Fanny, who knows no better

—but *you*! Can people marry like that? Is there nothing more wanting?—nothing more solemn and sacred in marriage than a few dinner-parties and an eligible young man?'

Caroline coloured a little. She told herself in her heart that Janet was right, but she only said, 'Life is very matter-of-fact, my poor Janet, as you will find; and after all an eligible young man is human though eligible. And now tell me who he is, for I know now there is somebody special in the case.'

But Janet did not answer. She was still hurt. Was this the way they all felt—her uncle, her aunt, and now her friend from whom she had hoped for something more? Was this the way they spoke of feelings that seemed almost sacred to her.

'Are you vexed, Janet dear?' said Mrs. Rowland at last.

'No,' said Janet, 'only a little unhappy. I want to do right and *feel* right, and when I saw you I thought you would help me, for I had no one else to ask.'

'Dear Janet, you know I am always ready and glad to help you. Tell me what it is all about,' said Mrs. Rowland, leaning forward with a gentle little rustling, and at the same time looks of such real kindness and sympathy that Janet's shyness and stiffness melted.

'It is about papa, as I told you,' said she, colouring. 'We have so hoped that my uncle would give him Chawhampton, and—and now he wants me to ask someone else for a smaller living which will be vacant.'

'Well,' said Mrs. Rowland, 'I always detested the Archdeacon; it is just like him; and is there no chance of your getting the smaller living?'

'No; why *should* there be?' cried the girl; 'that is what is so horrible.'

'Whose gift is it in?' asked Mrs. Rowland, with a faint curiosity.

'It is Mr. Hollis's living,' said poor Janet. 'He went away just now; he has been here a week; he is gone to the Merediths now. He is very kind, *too* kind; and now, perhaps, you know all,' cried the girl, impetuously, who had in those two words said more than she had meant; 'but I know I can trust you, and that you will keep my secret. I am talking nonsense, there is no secret to keep. Dear Caroline, I was obliged to ask him. It has been so horrible. But I won't stay; I know I am right to go.'

Caroline was silent for an instant. 'What did he say?' she asked, in a low voice.

'I did not say it, I wrote it,' said Janet. 'The letter is going now. You know him better than I do,' she implored. '*Can't* I trust him? He *will* understand. He *won't* think it forward?' cried the girl, in an agony. 'Caroline, you know the world; tell me I did not do wrong; that I can trust him?' she implored.

Miss Ireton was so agitated on her own account that she did not notice her friend's odd changing looks.

'If you take my advice, Janet, you will trust nobody,' said Caroline, coldly, 'beyond a certain point. If two people were alone in the world they might trust each other, but think how many claims, memories, doubts, difficulties, there are!' Then Caroline thought for an instant, and reflected upon a past light in her old friend Mr. Hollis's character. She was trying to be true to her friendship, though sympathy she had not to give. There was a moment's struggle and an evil impulse of mischief-making to be overcome before she spoke. For my poor Caroline is no model woman, alas! only a very, very human creature; but she spoke at last, to the best of her wisdom, remembering his old impatience and fastidiousness. Had he not left her for a suspicion? 'If that letter goes, Janet,' she said, still coldly, 'I am afraid you will never see George Hollis again.'

'Do you think I ever expect to see him again?' exclaimed Janet, indignant. 'I am going away; I will never, never see him any more. There is only friendship or I *could* not ask. There is someone else he loves. It has only been liking for me. I—I was mistaken; I had never known anyone like him before.' Then she went on more fluently: 'Just now, when I came down to you, I found another note from Mrs. Meredith, on the hall table—here it is. But I shall not go.' And Janet thrust a little pink missive, with 'Dear Miss Ireton—persuade you—so disappointed all of us—a few days only—ever sincerely yours,' &c., into Caroline's hand. Then she covered her burning cheeks from the fire, and sat quite still without speaking.

Caroline, too, was silent. She could not but believe the girl's eager honesty. Once more she felt ashamed before her. She envied her, and a gentler thought of what might have been came to her mind.

As for Janet, she was shaken; her faith in her friend was not touched, but her faith in human nature had received a rude blow. Could Caroline be right? was no one to be trusted? Was this the experience of life that people spoke of mysteriously: not one, not one just man in Edom? The two sat staring at the smouldering log. Janet's foot was tapping impatiently against the fender, and the obnoxious steel poker came down with a crash. How strangely people feel round and about and under and over the things that really disquiet them. This crash disturbed Mrs. Rowland more apparently than all that had gone before.

'Do take care, my dear. Who told you about this—this old engagement of Mr. Hollis's?' she said, sharply.

'Mrs. Brandiscombe told me a little,' said Janet. 'It was someone he knew long ago; he himself said something one day. He told me that all his life for years and years he had only really loved one woman. He said it happened here, at this very house, that he saw her last, and he hated the place. He was called from her suddenly, but she deceived him in some way—never answered his letters. I don't know more of the story. I only know that he loved her.'

Mrs. Rowland didn't speak or move, but sat as if she had not listened, with the screen held up between her soft cheeks and the angry blaze; the screen trembled a little in her hand. At last, with a sudden, quick motion, she got up and walked slowly away to the end of the room where she had been standing when she first entered. Then she came back, smiling sadly. One hand was pressed against her heart. There was a bright very sweet expression on her face that Janet could not see, for she was still staring at the fire.

'Janet,' said Mrs. Rowland, in a low voice, 'I want to say that I was wrong, my dear, in what I said just now. You may trust George Hollis. I did not do him justice. He is an honourable man. Do not be unhappy. I shall see him to-morrow, and—and try to explain. We were once friends, he and I;' her voice faltered a little. She was hesitating, and looking intently at Janet, who had started up from her seat; when the clock struck five, and the butler and his assistant came in with the tea.

'Mrs. Brandiscombe begged that you would not wait for her if she was after five,' said the well-drilled butler.

Janet had blushed up, and it was her turn to look a little strangely. 'I won't have any tea, my head aches,' she said. 'Is that the sun setting? I think I will take another turn. Don't mind me; I—I will come back.'

She spoke in a nervous and agitated way, she did not know exactly what had been happening; but somehow Mrs. Rowland's words no longer comforted her; even her kindness failed to touch her. She felt there was something between them; she *almost* guessed the secret. Poor child! she did not want to know more, and meekly accepted her fate as a matter of course. But a living, breathing rival there before her was a different thing from the vague imaginations of a possibility. She could not sit quietly and hand her the milk and sugar. She felt faint for want of air. She caught up a cloak in the hall. She ran down some servants' passage, and out by some back-door into the open air. She did not see as she crossed the hall that someone was coming in at the front door.

VII.

Janet was a proud girl, as I have said. The sort of guess which she had made—the idea that Mrs. Rowland herself was the woman whom George Hollis loved—was the last drop in her cup. What had she been doing? Had she been mad, blind, dull? Had she known, she would have bitten out her tongue sooner than have spoken to Caroline as she had done. Poor Janet! She exaggerated, as young people do, the horrors of her situation; she painfully shrank from the thought. 'Oh, I wish I was at home, I wish I was at home!'—this was her one thought now. She hurried out into the garden once more, across the front lawn, round to the back of the house. The air revived her. With the evening the wind had gone down, or if it blew it came in softer and more comforting gushes. Where the clouds had parted over the sea a sunset light was breaking, turning grey waters to blue, gilding pale hills with heavenly alchemy. What was this? A quick gleam—a darting fiery stream from behind the rent cloud. Suddenly the field was in a western blaze; the donkey was browsing in a dazzling, lovely wave of rainbow light. Was this a new created world of cloud and light? Broken, glittering, rainy, divinely fresh, the clouds and the sunlight were parting, drifting, reflecting one another; a dazzling flame seemed rising from the sea. Janet's hair and clothes were on fire; she felt as if this fresh light were brightening her heavy heart. As she stood there, Janet heard the distant stable-clock striking. She began to breathe a little more quietly; a few more hours and she would be gone, she thought. Once safe home she would try never to think of this past bit of her life again.

.   .   .   .   .

By a not very extraordinary chance it was Hollis coming who had been at the front door in search of Janet.

He had met the luggage-cart about a mile from the house. having walked back part of the way with the Archdeacon to finish the discussion of some arrangements which they had been talking over. The cart stopped, the driver, knowing Hollis, touched his hat, and saying, 'I have a letter for you, sir,' put Janet's poor little scrawl into the young man's hand. Poor Janet! had she known that Hollis had come back to answer it himself, no garden end would have been distant enough for her to hide in. I do believe she would have splashed straight into the sea to avoid him.

Meanwhile Mr. Hollis had walked into the drawing-room in search of her, and found himself face to face with the very person he had wished to avoid. He thought Mrs. Rowland was not coming till six, and had calculated on a whole half-hour before her arrival. After all it was no very terrible meeting—a pretty gentlewoman, with a kind face and a friendly greeting, a good fire burning, a comfortable chair (the very one where Janet had been sitting) drawn up to it. Who shall describe the half-formed thoughts that passed through Caroline's mind as he came up to her? thoughts of herself, then of Janet, then of self again.

'How do you do?' said Mrs. Rowland. 'I hear you only left to-day. I hoped I should see you, though I was afraid I might miss you altogether.' She spoke not reproachfully, but with unaffected interest and just a little regret in her voice. Caroline could make the words she used mean anything she liked besides their natural meaning. Hollis, who, to tell the truth, had been unfeignedly sorry to see her at first, for her presence jarred upon him just then, felt mollified by her kindness, notwithstanding the implacability of his disposition. 'My aunt will be here directly,' Mrs. Rowland went on. 'Won't you sit down? We have not met since Florence.' Caroline was not kinder than she had been before, but Hollis could not help thinking there was a difference; she was more interested, more agitated, more like the Carry Russell of old days than the gentle, mature, accomplished lady he had seen of late. There was a minute's silence; and Hollis asked after the children, and then Mrs. Rowland began once more. 'I am glad to have seen you,' she said. 'I have been hearing of you from a friend of mine.' Mrs. Rowland felt her heart beat violently for a moment.

'What have you been hearing about me?' Hollis asked, with a smile. Caroline resolutely put her old self back into the corner, and then she became quite calm again, and could look up quietly into his face and try to read what was written there, as he stood with his back to the fire. 'Janet was in great trouble, poor child,' said Mrs. Rowland. 'She had some idea that it was her duty to ask you for something for her father, and that she should forfeit your good opinion for ever.' Caroline breathed a long breath as she finished this careless little speech. She had done it. Done her best to help her poor little trouble-hearted sister in her need. Had it been an effort ? It hardly seemed to her now that it was one. She blushed, and it was a self-approving little glow from her heart in her face, as she again looked up quietly to see how her speech had been taken.

'*My* good opinion!' said Hollis, uneasily.

'I advised her... not to ask you,' said the widow, going on with her knitting as quietly as she knew how. She put in her needles triumphantly and travelled on somehow, but little Tom never wore that particular stocking. 'A girl—a very young girl, I mean, like Janet—cannot know life—cannot guess how the simplest and most straightforward actions may be misread and misunderstood, and the Archdeacon is an old schemer. When Janet asked me if she could not trust *you*, I said that no one was to be trusted.'

Hollis looked at Mrs. Rowland more and more surprised. What was she talking about; what was her meaning; was she talking of the past? Surely—and the old feeling of something like scorn for the woman who had sold herself seemed to come over him—he had not been to blame or failed in trust.

'But I did not know then,' Caroline went on, 'that her instinct was right, that I had done you an injustice.' And Mrs. Rowland looked up with two bright shining orbs. 'Something Janet said made me understand it all. Do you know that uncle Brandiscombe told me you were gone, George? but they never gave me any letter. I am glad to meet you, to know how it all happened. I had thought of John before I knew you, but I was very unhappy for a time, though I am not fixed and deep like Janet: but I think my poor John would like you to think better of me than you can have done,' said Mrs. Rowland, smiling through her tears. 'And you know when I did not hear, I thought you had never . . .' She could not finish her sentence.

Caroline's tears were coming faster and faster. Hollis touched, and surprised, and embarrassed, had taken her hand and kissed it. He was still standing by the fire and looking at the gentle bent head.

'You mustn't think me better than I am,' said he, reddening. 'I guessed there had been some false play; but your cousin had told me of Mr. Rowland's admiration. I was too proud to ask for an explanation. I don't deserve, I shall never forget your goodness.'

As he spoke the sun was setting and the evening lights were shining in, and reflected from the western window with dazzling abruptness from one angle to another in the many dim glasses. For one instant the past was present again to the widow, but only for an instant. With an effort she put it all from her. No—she would be true to Janet and to her own new instincts. She would not try now to take advantage of his old feelings.

'I suppose,' said Caroline, wiping her eyes, and faltering and smiling, 'there would be no good in living on if one did not every now and then understand things that seemed strange, and learn to be just to old friends, and to guess at things unexpressed as well as expressed in life. I have been happier than I deserve, and this will make my past life dearer to me. But I like to think that I shall do you justice at last, and that you are not one of those who at any time of life, either now or twelve years ago, would willingly inflict pain on a true-hearted girl.' The next instant she was thankful that she had so spoken, for Hollis began again with some emotion.

'I don't know how to thank you,' he said, 'but I assure you I understand your real and most friendly meaning.' And then he added, 'If ever I may speak for Janet as well as for myself; for to you I will confess that I love her——'

A sound of carriage-wheels, of doors, of approaching voices in the hall, made them both stop short.

'It is my aunt come in from her drive,' said Mrs. Rowland hastily. 'I saw Janet in the garden just now,—if you like you can go out through that window.'

Hollis thanked her with a look, and hurried across the room to the western window, which he opened, and through which he stepped out into the evening gleam. Caroline went to close it after him, and stood for an instant watching him as he went striding across the grass.

Was this all? It seemed a tame conclusion to her few minutes' excitement. He had forgotten her great explanation already, and was hurrying across the field to where Janet was standing quite still in the gleam of the sudden lights. She seemed gazing seawards at the dying reflections there. Caroline could watch her old youthful visions striding away with a more tranquil spirit than in former days. He had loved her once—now he would be her friend—and so she was content. And so with sad yet gentle eyes she watched the two young people that were to live her life, feel her feelings, taking up the thread of her existence where she had left it broken.

Meanwhile out in the field the end of my story, such as it is, is being told in the bright falling radiance, which poor Janet cannot find it in her heart to enjoy very much. The donkey is browsing beside her, but it takes to its heels and scampers off when Hollis comes into the field. Janet does not even look round; she stands quite still, looking at drifting lights, and clouds, and rainbow beams with a pale, scared face, which shocks George Hollis when he gets near enough to see it. He has never seen her before without her sweet natural roses. He comes near and calls her name. As for Janet, seeing him, she stares for an instant—it is so inconceivable and unexpected. How has he come? Janet wonders where she shall escape to, and then all her strength goes away; she stands quite still like a maiden of stone or a pillar of salt; it is no use trying to speak as usual or to look unconscious,—she can only stand still.

'I came back to speak to you,' said Hollis, in his usual voice, trying to reassure her. 'I met the carrier just now, and he gave me your letter. I hope you don't regret having written it,' he said, hurriedly. 'You don't know what pleasure it gives me to do anything to serve you. I had already proposed the exchange to your uncle when I got your note. Dear Janet, don't look so overwhelmed,' Hollis continued, touched by the sudden rush of light and happiness and sweetness in her face; 'only give me a right to serve you always, and then you can ask me what you will.'

When Caroline came to the window again she saw the two walking, slowly, arm-in-arm towards the house, and then she knew what Janet's answer had been.

FROM AN ISLAND.

PART I.

I.

THE long room was full of people sitting quietly in the twilight. Only one lamp was burning at the far end. The verandah outside was dim with shadow; between each leafy arch there glimmered a line of sea and of down. It was a grey still evening, sad, with distant storms. St. Julian, the master of the house, was sitting under the verandah, smoking, with William, the eldest son. The mother and Mrs. William were on a sofa together, talking in a low voice over one thing and another. Hester was sitting at the piano with her hands in her lap, looking music, though she was not playing, with her white dress quivering in the gloom. Lord Ulleskelf, who had come over to see us, was talking to Emilia, the married daughter, and to Aileen, the youngest of the three; while I and my own little girl and the other little ones were playing at the end of the room at a sort of twilight game of beating hands and singing sing-song nursery-rhymes,—haymaking the children called it.

'Are there any letters?' said St. Julian, looking in at them all from his verandah. 'Has Emmy got hers?'

'I have sent Rogers into Tarmouth to meet the post,' said the mother; and as she spoke the door opened, and the post came in.

Poor Emmy's face, which had lighted up eagerly, fell in an instant: she saw that there was no foreign letter for her.

It was a small mail, not worth sending for, Mrs. St. Julian evidently thought as she looked at her daughter with her kind, anxious eyes. 'Here is something for you, Emmy,' she said; 'for you, Queenie' (to me). 'The other letter is from Mr. Hexham; he is coming tomorrow.'

My letter was from the grocer :—' Mrs. Campbell is respectfully informed by Mr. Tiggs that he has sent different samples of tea and coffee for her approbation, for the use of Mr. St. Julian's household and family: also a choice assortment of sperms. Mr. Tiggs regrets extremely that any delay should have arisen in the delivery of the preserved cherries and apricots. He forwards the order this day, as per invoice. Mr. T. trusts that his unremitting exertions may meet with Mrs. C.'s approval and continued recommendation and patronage.

Albert Edward House, September 21.'

This was not very interesting, except to the housekeeper (Mrs. St. Julian had set me to keep house for her down here in the country). The children, however, who generally insisted upon reading all my correspondence, were much excited by the paragraph in which Mr. Tiggs mentioned cherries and dried apricots. 'Why did Mr. Tiggs forget them?' said little Susan, the grand-daughter, solemnly. 'Oh, I wish they would come,' said my little missy. 'Greedy, greedy!' sang George, the youngest boy. Meanwhile the elders were discussing their correspondence, and the mother had been reading out Mr. Hexham's note :—

'Lyndhurst, September 21.

'Have you room for me, my dear Mrs. St. Julian, and may I come to-morrow for a few days with my van? I find it is a most delightful mode of conveyance, and I have been successful enough to take some most lovely photographic views in the New Forest. I now hope to explore your island, beginning with the "Lodges," if you are still in the same hospitable mind you were when I last saw you.

'With best remembrances to your husband and the young ladies,

'Your devoted,

'G. HEXHAM.'

'I like Mr. Hexham. I am glad he is coming,' said Mrs. St. Julian by way of postscript.

'This is an official-looking missive,' said Lord

Ulleskelf, holding out the large square envelope, with a great red seal, which had come for Emmy.

'What a handwriting!' cried Aileen. She was only fifteen, but she was taller already than her married sister, and stood reading over her shoulder. 'What a letter! Oh, Emmy, what a——'

But Mrs. St. Julian, seeing Emmy flush up, interposed again :—

'Aileen, take these newspapers to your father. What is it, my dear?' to Emilia.

'It is from my sister-in-law,' Emilia said, blushing in the light of the lamp. 'Mamma, what a trouble I am to you. . . . She says she is—may she come to stay? . . . And—and—you see she is dear Bevis's sister, and——'

'Of course, my dear,' said her mother, almost reproachfully. 'How can you ask?'

Emilia looked a little relieved, but wistful still. 'Have you room? To-morrow?' she faltered.

Mrs. St. Julian gave her a kiss, and smiled and said, 'Plenty of room, you goose.' And then she read,—

'*To the Hon. Mrs. Bevis Beverley, The Island, Tarmouth, Broadshire.*

'Scudamoro Castle, September 21.

'My dear Emilia,—Bevis told me to be sure and pay you a visit in his absence, if I had an opportunity, and so I shall come, if convenient to you, with my maid and a man, on Saturday, across country from Scudamore Castle. I hear I must cross from Helmington. I cannot imagine how people can live on an island when there is the mainland for them to choose. Yours is not even an island on the map. Things have been very pleasant here till two days ago, when it began to pour with rain, and my stepmother arrived unexpectedly with Clem, and Clem lost her temper, and Pritchard spoilt my new dress, and several pleasant people went away, and I, too, determined to take myself off. I shall only stay a couple of days with you, so pray tell Mrs. St. Julian that I shall not, I hope, be much in her way. Do not let her make any changes for me; I shall be quite willing to live exactly as you are all in the habit of doing. Any room will do for my man. The maid need only have a little room next to mine. You won't mind, I know, if I go my own gait while I stay with you, for I am an odd creature, as I dare say you may have often heard from Bevis. I expect to feel dreadfully small with all of you clever artistic people, but I shall be safe from my lady and Clem, who would never venture to come near you.

'My father is all alone at home, and I want to get back to him if I can steal a march on my lady. She is so jealous that she will not let me be alone with him for one hour if she can help it, in her absence. Before she left Castlerookham she sent for that odious sister of hers to play picquet with him, and there was a general scene when I objected. My father took part against me, so I started off in a huff, but he has managed to shake off the old wretch, I hear, and so I do not mind going back. I must say it is very pleasant to have a few halfpence that one can call one's own, and to be able to come and go one's own way. I assure you that the said halfpence do not last for ever, however. Clem took 50*l.* to pay her milliner's bill, and Bevis borrowed 100*l.* before he left, but I dare say he will pay me back.

'So good-by, my dear Emilia, for the present.

'Yours ever,

'JANE BEVERLEY.'

Mrs. St. Julian did not offer to show Lady Jane's letter to St. Julian, but folded it up with a little suppressed smile. 'I think she must be a character, Emmy,' she said. 'I dare say she will be very happy with us. Queenie' (to me), 'will you see what can be done to make Lady Jane comfortable?' and there was an end of the matter. Lord Ulleskelf went and sat out in the verandah with the others until the storm burst which had been gathering, through which he insisted on hurrying home, notwithstanding all they could say to detain him.

We had expected Lady Jane by the boat which brought our other guest the next day, but only Mr. Hexham's dark close-cropped head appeared out of the carriage which had been sent to meet them. The coachman declared there was no lady alone on board. Emilia wondered why her sister-in-law had failed: the others took Lady Jane's absence very calmly, and after some five o'clock tea St. Julian proposed a walk.

'Perhaps I had better stay at home,' Mrs. Beverley said to her mother.

'No, my dear, your father will be disappointed. She cannot come now,' said Mrs. St. Julian, decidedly; 'and if she does, I am here to receive her. Mr. Hexham, you did not see her on board? A lady alone? . . .'

No. Hexham had not seen any lone lady on board. There was a good-looking person who might have answered the description, but she had a gentleman with her. He lost sight of them at Tarmouth, as he was looking after his man, and his van, and his photographic apparatus. It was settled Lady Jane could not possibly come till next day.

II.

Lady Jane Beverley had always declared that she hated three things—islands, clever people, and interference. She knew she was clever, but she did not encourage this disposition. It made people bores and radical in her own class of life, and forward if they were low. She was not pretty. No; she didn't care for beauty, though she confessed she should be very sorry if she was not able to afford

to dress in the last fashion. It was all very well for
artists and such people to say the contrary, but she knew
that a plain woman well dressed would look better than
the loveliest dowdy that ever tied her bonnet-strings
crooked. It was true her brother Bevis had thought
otherwise. He had married Emilia, who was not in his
own rank of life; but Lady Jane supposed he had taught
her to dress properly after her marriage. She had done
her very best to dissuade him from that crazy step: once
it was over she made the best of it, though none of them
would listen to her; and indeed she had twice had to lend
him sums of money when his father stopped his allowance
It is true he paid her back, otherwise she really did not
know how she could have paid her bills that quarter. If
she had not had her own independence she scarcely could
have got on at all or borne with all Lady Mountmore's
whims. However, thanks to old aunt Adelaide, she need
not think of anybody but herself, and that was a very
great comfort to her in her many vexations. As it was,
Clem was for ever riding Bazook, and laming her ponies,
and borrowing money. Beverley and Bevis, of course,
being her own brothers, had a right to expect she would
be ready to lend them a little now and then; but really
Clem was only her step-sister, and considering the terms
she and Lady Mountmore were on . . . Lady Jane had a
way of rambling on, though she was a young woman still,
not more than six or seven and twenty. It was quite true

that she had had to fight her own battles at home, or she would have been utterly fleeced and set aside. Lord Beverley, her eldest brother, never quite forgave her for being the old aunt's heiress, and did not help her as he should have done. Bevis was always away on his missions or in disgrace. Old Lord Mountmore was feeble and almost childish. Lady Mountmore was not a pleasant person to deal with, and such heart as she possessed was naturally given to Lady Clem, her own child.

Lady Jane was fortunately not of a sensitive disposition. She took life calmly, and did not yearn for the affection that was not there to get, but she made the best of things, and when Bevis was sent to South America on a mission, she it was who brought about a sort of general reconciliation. She was very much pleased with herself on this occasion. Everybody looked to her, and consulted her. 'You will go and see Emmy sometimes, won't you, Jane?' said poor Bevis, who was a kind and handsome young fellow. Lady Jane said, 'Most likely,' and congratulated herself on her own tact and success on this occasion, as well as on her general ways, looks, style, and position in life. She thought poor Emmy was not certainly worth all this fuss, but determined to look after her. Lady Jane was rather Low Church, slightly suspicious, but good-natured and not unamenable to reason. She cultivated an abrupt frankness and independence of manner. Her frankness was almost bewildering at times, as Lady Jane expected her dictums to be received in silence and humility by the unlucky victims of her penetration. But still, as I have said, being a true-hearted woman, if she was once convinced that she was in the wrong, she would always own to it. Marriage was rather a sore subject with this lady. She had once notified to a young evangelical rector that although his prospects were not brilliant, yet she was not indisposed to share them, if he liked to come forward. To her utter amazement, the young man got up in a confused manner, walked across the room, talked to Lady Clem for the rest of his visit, and never called again. Lady Jane was much surprised; but, as her heart was not deeply concerned in the matter, she forgave him on deliberation. The one softness in this strange woman's nature lay in her love for children. Little Bevis, her brother's baby, would coo at her, and beat her high cheek-bones with his soft little fat hand; she let him pull her hair, the curls, and frills, and plaits of an hour's erection, poke his fingers into her eyes, swing her watch violently round and round. She was still too young to have crystallised into a regular old maid. She had never known any love in her life except from Bevis, but Bevis had been a little afraid of her. Beverley was utterly indifferent to anybody but himself.

Lady Jane had fifteen hundred a year of her own. She was not at all bad-looking. Her thick reddish hair was of the fashionable colour. She was a better woman than some people gave her credit for being, seeing this tall over-dressed and overbearing young person going about the world with her two startled attendants and her hunters. Lady Jane had not the smallest sense of humour or feeling for art: at least, this latter faculty had never been cultivated, though she had furnished her boudoir with bran new damask and sprawling gilt legs, and dressed herself in the same style; and had had her picture taken by some travelling artist—a pastille all frame and rose-coloured chalk—which hung up over her chimney, smirking at a rose, to the amusement of some of her visitors. Lady Jane's notion of artists and art was mainly formed upon this trophy, and by what she had seen of the artist who had produced it. Lady Clem used to say that Jane was a born old maid, and would never marry; but everybody was not of that opinion. Lady Jane had been made a great deal of at Scudamore Castle, especially by a certain Captain Sigourney, who had been staying there, a nephew of Lady Scudamore's,—tall, dark, interesting, in want of money, notwithstanding his many accomplishments. Poor Tom Sigourney had been for many years a hanger-on at Scudamore. They were extremely tired of him, knew his words, looks, tones by heart. Handsome as he undoubtedly was, there was something indescribably wearisome about him after the first introduction—a certain gentle drawl and prose that irritated some people. But Lady Jane was immensely taken by him. His deference pleased her. She was not insensible to the respectful flattery with which he listened to every word she spoke. Tom Sigourney said she was a fine spirited girl, and Lady Scudamore seized the happy occasion—urged Tom forward, made much of Lady Jane. 'Poor girl! she needs a protector,' said Lady Scudamore gravely to her daughters. At which the young ladies burst out laughing. 'Can you fancy Tom Sigourney taking care of anybody?' they cried.

Lady Mountmore arrived unexpectedly, and the whole little fabric was destroyed. Sigourney, who had not much impudence, was driven off the field by the elder lady's impertinences. Lady Jane was indignant, and declared she should not stay any longer under the same roof as her step-mother. Lady Scudamore did not press her to remain. She had not time to attend to her any longer or to family dissensions; but she did write a few words to Tom, telling him of Lady Jane's movements, and then made it up with Lady Mountmore all the more cordially that she felt she had not been quite loyal to her in sending off this little missive.

The little steamer starts for Tarmouth in a crowd and excitement of rolling barrels and oxen driven and plunging sheep in barges. The people come and look over the side of the wooden pier and talk to the captain at his wheel. Afternoon rays stream slant, and the island glistens across the straits, and the rocks stand out in the water; limpid waters beat against the rocks, and toss the buoys and splash against the busy little tug; one or two coal-barges make way. Idlers and a child or two in the way of the half-dozen passengers are called upon by name to stand aside on this occasion. There are two country dames returning from market; friend Hexham in an excitement about his van, which is to follow in a barge; and there is a languid dark handsome gentleman talking to a grandly dressed lady whose attendants have been piling up wraps and 'Times' and dressing-cases and umbrellas.

'Let me hold this for you, it will tire you,' said the gentleman, tenderly taking 'The Times' out of her hand; 'are you resting? I thought I would try and meet you, and see if I could save you from fatigue. My aunt Scudamore told me you were coming this way. There, that is where my people live; that white house among the trees.'

'It is a nice place,' said Lady Jane.

The rocks were coming nearer, and the island was brightening to life and colour, and the quaint old bricks and terraces of Tarmouth were beginning to show. There was a great ship in the distance sliding out to sea, and a couple of gulls flew overhead.

'Before I retired from the service,' said Sigourney, 'I was quartered at Portsmouth. I knew this coast well; that is Tarmouth opposite, and that is—ah, 'm—a pretty place, and an uncommon pretty girl at the hotel.'

'How am I to get to these people if they have not sent to meet me, I wonder?' interrupted Lady Jane, rather absently.

'Leave that to me,' said Captain Sigourney; 'I am perfectly at home here, and I will order a fly. They all know me, and if they are not engaged they will always come for *me*. You go to the inn. I order you a cup of tea, and one for your maid. I see a fast horse put up into a trap, and start you straight off.'

'Oh, Captain Sigourney, I am very much obliged,' said Lady Jane; and so the artless conversation went on.

At Tarmouth the ingenious captain would not let her ask whose was a carriage she saw standing there, nor take one of the two usual flys in waiting, but he made her turn into the inn until a special fast horse, with whose paces he was well acquainted, could be harnessed. This took a long time; but Lady Jane, excited by the novelty of the adventure, calmly enjoyed her afternoon tea and devotion, and sat on the horse-hair sofa of the little inn, admiring the stuffed carp and cuttle-fish on the walls, and listening with a charmed ear to Tom's reminiscences of the time when he was quartered at Portsmouth.

The fast horse did not go much quicker than his predecessors, and Lady Jane arrived at the Lodges about an hour after Hexham, and at the same time as his great photographic van.

III.

They were all strolling along the cliffs towards the beacon. It stood upon the summit of High Down, a long way off as yet, though it seemed close at hand, so clearly did it stand out in the still atmosphere of the sunset. It stood there stiff and black upon its knoll, an old weather-beaten stick with a creaking coop for a crown, the pivot round which most of this little story turns. For when these holiday people travelled away out of its reach, they also passed out of my ken. We could see the beacon from most of our windows, through all the autumnal clematis and ivy sprays falling and drifting about. The children loved the beacon, and their little lives were one perpetual struggle to reach it, in despite of winds, of time of meals, of tutors and lessons. The elders, too, loved it after their fashion. Had they not come and established themselves under the shadow of High Down, where it had stood as long as the oldest inhabitant could remember! Lord Ulleskelf, in his yacht out at sea, was always glad to see the familiar old stubby finger rising up out of the mist. My cousin, St. Julian the R.A., had made a strange rough sketch of it, and of his wife and her eldest daughter sitting beneath it; and a sea, and a cloud horizon, grey, green, mysterious beyond. He had painted a drapery over their heads, and young Emilia's arms round the stem. It was a terrible little picture

Emilia the mother thought when she saw it, and she begged her husband to turn its face to the wall in his studio.

'Don't you see how limpid the water is, and how the mist is transparent and drifting before the wind?' St. Julian said. 'Why do you object, you perverse woman?'

The wife didn't answer, but her soft cheeks flushed. Emilia the daughter spoke, a little frightened.

'They are like mourners, papa,' she whispered.

St. Julian shrugged his shoulders at them. 'And this is a painter's wife!' he cried; 'and a painter's daughter!' But he put the picture away, for he was too tender to pain them, and it lay now forgotten in a closet. This was two years ago, before Emilia was married, or had come home with her little son during her husband's absence. She was carrying the child in her arms as she toiled up the hill in company with the others, a tender bright flush in her face. Her little Bevis thinks it is he who is carrying 'Mozzer,' as he clutches her tight round the neck with his two little arms.

I suppose nobody ever reached the top of a high cliff without some momentary feeling of elation,—so much left behind, so much achieved. There you stand at peace, glowing with exertion, raised far above the din of the world. They were gazing as they came along (for it is only of an island that I am writing) at the great sight of shining waters, of smiling fertile fields and country; and of distant waters again, that separated them from the pale glimmering coast of the mainland. The straits, which lie between the island and Broadshire, are not deserted as is the horizon on the other side (it lies calm, and tossing, and self-sufficing); but the straits are crowded and alive with boats and white sails: ships go sliding past, yachts drift, and great brigs slowly travel in tow of the tiny steamer that crosses and recrosses the water with letters and provisions, and comers and goers and guests to Ulles Hall and to the Lodges, where St. Julian and his family live all through the summer-time; and where some of us indeed remain the whole year round.

The little procession comes winding up the down, Lord Ulleskelf and the painter walking first, in broad-brimmed hats and coats fashioned in the island, of a somewhat looser and more comfortable cut than London coats. The tutor is with them. Mr. Hexham, too, is with them; as I can see, a little puzzled by the ways of us islanders.

As St. Julian talks his eyes flash, and he puts out one hand to emphasize what he is saying. He is not calm and self-contained as one might imagine so great a painter, but a man of strong convictions, alive to every life about him and to every event. His cordial heart and bright artistic nature are quickly touched and moved. He believes in his own genius, grasps at life as it passes, and translates it into a strange quaint revelation of his own, and brings others into his way of seeing things almost by magic. But his charm is almost irresistible, and he knows it, and likes to know it. The time that he is best himself is when he is at his painting; his brown eyes are alight in his pale face, his thick grey hair stands on end; he is a middle-aged man, broad, firmly-knit with a curly grey beard, active, mighty in his kingdom. He lets people in to his sacred temple; but he makes them put their shoes off, so to speak, and will allow no word of criticism except from one or two. In a moment his thick brows knit, and the master turns upon the unlucky victim.

The old tutor had a special and unlucky knack of exciting St. Julian's ire. He teaches the boys as he taught St. Julian in bygone days, but he cannot forget that he is not always St. Julian's tutor, and constantly stings and irritates him with his caustic disappointed old wits. But St. Julian bears it all with admirable impatience for the sake of old days and of age and misfortune.

As they all climb the hill together on this special day, the fathers go walking first, then comes a pretty rout of maidens and children, and Hexham's tall dark head among them. Little Missie goes wandering by the edge of the cliff, with her long gleaming locks hanging in ripples not unlike those of the sea. The two elder girls had come out with some bright-coloured scarves tied round their necks; but finding them oppressive, they had pulled them off, and given them to the boys to carry. These scarves were now banners streaming in the air as the boys attacked a tumulus, where the peaceful bones of the bygone Danish invaders were lying buried. The gay young voices echo across the heather calling to each other.

Hester comes last with Mrs. William—Hester with the mysterious sweet eyes and crown of soft hair. It is not very thick, but like a dark yet gleaming cloud about her pretty head. She is quite pale, but her lips are bright carnation red, and when she smiles she blushes. Hester is tall, as are all her sisters. Aileen is walking a little ahead with Mrs. William's children, and driving them away from the edge of the cliff, towards which these little moths seem perpetually buzzing.

The sun begins to set in a strange wild glory, and the light to flow along the heights; all these people look to one another like beatified men and women. Ulleskelf and St. Julian cease their discussion at last, and stand looking seawards.

'Look at that band of fire on the sea,' said Lord Ulleskelf.

'What a wonderful evening,' said St. Julian. 'Hester, are you there?'

Hester was there, with sweet, wondering, sunset eyes. Her father put his hand fondly on her shoulder. There was a sympathy between the two which was very touching; they liked to admire together, to praise together. In sorrow or trouble St. Julian looked for his wife, in happiness he instinctively seemed to turn to his favourite daughter.

Hester's charm did not always strike people at first sight. She was like some of those sweet simple tunes which haunt you after you have heard them, or like some of those flowers of which the faint delicate scent only comes to you when you have waited for an instant.

Hexham, for instance, until now had admired Mrs. Beverley infinitely more than he did her sister. He thought Miss St Julian handsome certainly, but charmless; whereas the sweet, gentle young mother, whose wistful eyes seemed looking beyond the sunset, and trying in vain to reach the distant world where her husband would presently see it rise, appealed to every manly feeling in his nature. But as the father and daughter turned to each other, something in the girl's face—a dim reflex light from the pure bright soul within—seemed to touch him, to disclose a something, I cannot tell you what. It seemed to Hexham as if the scales had fallen suddenly from his eyes, and as if in that instant Hester was revealed to him. She moved on a little way with two of the children who had joined her. The young man followed her with his eyes, and almost started when some one spoke to him. . .

As St. Julian walked on, he began mechanically to turn over possible effects and combinations in his mind. The great colourist understood better than any other, how to lay his colours, luminous, harmonious, shining with the real light of nature, for they were in conformity to her laws; and suddenly he spoke, turning to Hexham, who was a photographer, as I have said, and who indeed was now travelling gipsy fashion, in search of subjects for his camera. . .

'In many things,' he said, 'my art can equal yours, but how helpless we both are when we look at such scenes as these. It makes me sometimes mad to think that I am only a man with oil-pots attempting to reproduce such wonders.'

'Fortunately they will reproduce themselves whether you succeed or not,' said the tutor. St. Julian looked at him with his bright eyes. The old man had spoken quite simply, he did not mean to be rude,—and the painter was silent.

'My art is "a game half of skill, half of chance,"' said Hexham. 'When both these divinities favour me I shall begin to think myself repaid for the time and the money and the chemicals I have wasted.'

'Have you ever tried to photograph figures in a full blaze of light?' Lord Ulleskelf asked, looking at Aileen, who was standing with some of the children by Hester. They were shading their eyes from a bright stream that was playing like a halo about their heads. There was something unconscious and lovely in the little group, with their white draperies and flowing locks. A bunch of illumined berries and trailing creepers hung from little Susan's hair: the light of youth and of life, the sweet wondering eyes, all went to make a more beautiful picture than graces or models could ever attain to. St. Julian ooked and smiled with Lord Ulleskelf.

Hexham answered, a little distractedly, that he should like to show Lord Ulleskelf the attempt he had once made. 'Nature is a very uncertain sort of assistant,' he added; 'and I, too, might exclaim, " Oh, that I am but a man, with a bit of yellow paper across my window, and a row of bottles on a shelf, trying to evoke life from the film upon my glasses!"'

'I think you are all of you talking very profanely,' said Lord Ulleskelf, 'before all these children, and in such a sight as this. But I shall be very glad to come down and look at your photographs, Mr. Hexham, to-morrow morning,' he added, fearing the young man might be hurt by his tone.

The firebrand in the still rippled sea turned from flame to silver as the light changed and ebbed. The light on the sea seemed dimmer, but then the land caught fire in turn, and trees and downs and distant roof-tops blazed in this great illumination, and the shadows fell black upon the turf.

Here Mrs. William began complaining in a plaintive tone of voice that she was tired, and I offered to go back with her. Everybody indeed was on the move, but we two took a shorter cut, while the others went home with Lord Ulleskelf, turning down by a turn of the down towards the lane that leads to Ulles Hall.

And so, having climbed up with some toil and effort to that beautiful height, we all began to descend once more into the everyday of life, and turn from glowing seas and calm sailing clouds to the thought of cutlets and chickens. The girls had taken back their scarves and were running down hill. Aileen was carrying one of Mrs. William's children, Emilia had her little Bevis in her arms, Hester was holding by her father's arm as they came back rather silent, but satisfied and happy. The sounds from the village below began to reach us, and the lights in the cottages and houses to twinkle; the cliffs rose higher and higher as we descended our different ways. The old beacon stood out black against the ruddy sky: a moon began to hang in the high faint heaven, and a bright star to pierce through the daylight.

Ulles Hall stands on the way from Tarmouth to the Lodges: it is a lovely old house standing among woods in a hollow, and blown by sea-breezes that come through pine-stems and sweet green glades, starred with primroses in spring, and sprinkled with russet leaves in autumn. The Lodges where St. Julian lives are built a mile nearer to the sea. Houses built on the roadside, but inclosed by tall banks and hedges, and with long green gardens running to the down. They have been built piece

T

by piece. It would be difficult to describe them: a gable here, a wooden gallery thatched, a window twinkling in a bed of ivy, hanging creepers, clematis and loveliest Virginian sprays reddening and drinking in the western light and reflecting it undimmed in their beautiful scarlet veins—scarlet gold melting into green: one of the rooms streams with light like light through stained windows of a church.[1]

IV.

As I reached the door with Mrs. William, I saw a bustle of some sort, a fly, some boxes, a man, a maid, a tall lady of about seven or eight and twenty, dressed in the very height of fashion, with a very tall hat and feather, whom I guessed at once to be Lady Jane. Mrs. William, who has not the good manners of the rest of the family, shrunk back a little, saying,—'I really cannot face her: it's that Lady Jane;' but at that moment Lady Jane, who was talking in a loud querulous tone, suddenly ceased, and turned round.

[1] A little child passing by in the road looked up one day at the Lodges, and said, 'Oh, what pretty leaf houses! Oh, mother, do let us live there. I think the robins must have made them.' 'I think that is where we are going to, Missie,' said the mother. She was a poor young widowed cousin of St. Julian's. She came for a time, but they took her in and never let her go again out of the leaf house. She stayed and became a sort of friend, chaperone, governess, and housekeeper to these kind and tender friends and relations; if she were to attempt to set down here all that she owes to them, to their warm, cordial hearts, and bright, sweet natures, it would make a story apart from the one she has in her mind to write to-day.

'Here is Mrs. St. Julian,' said the fly-man; 'she always give somethin' for the driver;' and my dear mistress came out into the garden to receive her guest.

'I am so glad you have come,' I heard her say quietly, 'we had given you up—are you tired? Come in. Let the servant see to your luggage.' She put out her white gentle hand, and I was amused to see Lady Jane's undisguised look of surprise: she had expected to meet with some bustling, good-humoured housekeeper. Beevis had always praised his mother-in-law to her, but Lady Jane had a way of not always listening to what people said, as she rambled on in her own fashion: and now, having fully made up her mind as to the sort of person Mrs. St. Julian would be, Lady Jane felt slightly aggrieved at her utter dissimilarity to her preconceptions. She followed her into the house, with her high hat stuck upon the top of her tall head, walking in a slightly defiant manner.

'I thought Emilia would have been here to receive me,' said Lady Jane, not over pleased.

'I sent her out,' the mother said. 'I thought you would let me be your hostess for an hour. Will you come up into my room?'

Mrs. St. Julian led the way into the drawing-room, where Lady Jane sank down into a chair, crossing her top-boots and shaking out her skirts.

'I am afraid there was a mistake about meeting you,' said the hostess; 'the carriage went but only brought back Mr. Hexham and a message that you were not there.'

'I fortunately met a friend on board,' said Lady Jane, hurriedly. 'He got me a fly; thank you, it did not signify.'

Lady Jane was not anxious to enter into particulars, and when Mrs. St. Julian went on to ask how it was she had had to wait so long, the young lady abruptly said something about afternoon tea, asked to see her room and to speak to her maid.

'Will you come back to me when you have given your orders?' said Mrs. St. Julian. 'My cousin, Mrs. Campbell, will show you the way.'

Lady Jane, with a haughty nod to poor Mrs. Campbell, followed with her high head up the quaint wooden stairs along the gallery, with its odd windows and slits, and china, and ornaments.

'This is your room; I hope you will find it comfortable,' said the housekeeper, opening a door, through which came a flood of light.

'Is that for my maid?' asked Lady Jane, pointing to a large and very comfortably furnished room just opposite to her own door.

'That room is Mr. Hexham's,' said Mrs. Campbell; 'your maid's room leads out of your dressing-room.' The arrangement seemed obvious, but Lady Jane was not quite in a temper to be pleased.

'Is it comfortable, Pritchard? Shall you be able to work there? I must speak about it if you are not comfortable.'

Pritchard was a person who did not like to commit herself. Not that she wished to complain, but she should prefer her ladyship to judge; it was not for her to say. She looked so mysterious that Lady Jane ran up the little winding stair that led to the turret, and found a little white curtained chamber, with a pleasant, bright look-out over land and sea.

'Why, this is a delightful room, Pritchard,' said Lady Jane. 'I should like it myself; it is most comfortable.'

'Yes, my lady, I thought it was highly comfortable,' said Pritchard; 'but it was not for me to venture to say so.'

Lady Jane was a little afraid of Mrs. St. Julian's questionings. To tell the truth, she felt that she had been somewhat imprudent; and though she was a person of mature age and independence, yet she was not willing to resign entirely all pretensions to youthful dependence, and she was determined if possible not to mention Sigourney's name to her entertainers. Having frizzed up her curling red locks, with Mrs. Pritchard's assistance, shaken out her short skirts, added a few more bracelets, tied on a coroneted locket, and girded in her tight silver waistband, she prepared to return to her hostess and her tea. She felt excessively ill-used by Emilia's absence but, as I have said, dared not complain for fear of more questions as to the cause of her delay.

All along the passage were more odds and ends, paintings, pictures, sketches framed, a cabinet or two full of china. Lady Jane was too much used to the ways of the world to mistake the real merit of this heterogeneous collection ; but she supposed that the artists made the things up, or perhaps sold them again to advantage, and that there was some meaning which would be presently explained for it all. What most impressed Lady Jane with a feeling of respect for the inhabitants of the house was a huge Scotch sheep-dog, who came slowly down the gallery to meet her, and then passed on with a snuff and a wag of his tail.

The door of the mistress's room, as it was called, was open ; and as Lady Jane followed her conductress in, she found a second five-o'clock tea and a table spread with rolls and country butter and home-made cake. A stream of western light was flowing through the room and out into the gallery beyond, where the old majolica plates flashed in the glitter of its sparkle. The mistress herself was standing with her back turned, looking out through the window across the sea, and trying to compose herself before she asked a question she had very near at heart.

Lady Jane remained waiting, feeling for once a little shy, and not knowing exactly what to do next, for Mrs. Campbell, who was not without a certain amount of feminine malice, stood meekly until Lady Jane should take the lead. The young lady was not accustomed to deal with inferiors who did not exactly behave as such, and though inwardly indignant, she did not quite know how to resent the indifference with which she considered she was treated. She tossed her head, and at last said, not in the most conciliatory voice, 'I suppose I may take some tea, Mrs. St. Julian?' The sight of the sweet pale face turning round at her question softened her tone. Mrs. St. Julian came slowly forward, and began to push a chair with her white feeble hands, evidently so unfit for such work that Jane, who was kind-hearted, sprang forward, lockets, top boots, and all, to prevent her. 'You had much better sit down yourself,' said she, goodnaturedly. 'I thought you looked ill just now, though I had never seen you in my life before. Let me pour out the tea.'

Mrs. St. Julian softened, too, in the other's unexpected heartiness and kindness. 'I had something to say to you. I think it upset me a little. I heard—I feared'—she said, nervously hesitating. 'Lady Jane, did you hear from your brother—from Bevis—by the last mail? . . . Emmy does not know the mail is in. . . . I have been a little anxious for her,' and Mrs. St. Julian changed colour.

'Certainly I heard,' said Lady Jane; 'or at least my father did. Bevis wanted some money raised. Why were you so anxious, Mrs. St. Julian?' asked Lady Jane, with a slightly amused look in her face. It was really too absurd to have these people making scenes and alarms when she was perfectly at her ease.

'I am thankful you have heard,' said Mrs. St. Julian, with a sudden flush and brightness in her wan face, which made Lady Jane open her eyes in wonder.

'Do you care so much?' said she, a little puzzled. 'I am glad that I do not belong to an anxious family. I am very like Bevis, they say; and I know there is nothing that he dislikes so much as a fuss about nothing.'

'I know it,' said Mrs. St. Julian. 'He is very good and kind to bear with my foolish alarms, and I wonder,— could you,—would you too,—forgive me for my foolishness, Lady Jane, if I were to ask you a great favour? Do you think I might see that letter to your father? I cannot tell you what a relief it would be to me. I told you Emilia does not know that the mail is in; and if—if she might learn it by seeing in his own handwriting that Bevis was well, I think it would make all the difference to her, poor child.'

There was something in the elder lady's gentle persistence which struck the young one as odd, and yet touching; and although she was much inclined to refuse, from a usual habit of contradiction, she did not know how to do so when it came to the point.

'I'll write to my father,' said Lady Jane, with a little laugh. 'I have no doubt he will let you see the letter since you wish it so much.'

'Thank you, my dear,' said Mrs. St. Julian, 'and for the good news you have given me; and I will now confess to you,' she added, smiling, 'that I sent Emmy out on purpose that I might have this little talk. Are you rested? Will you come into the garden with me for a little?'

Lady Jane was touched by the sweet maternal manner of the elder woman, and followed quite meekly and kindly. As the two ladies were pacing the garden-walk they were joined by the housekeeper and by Mrs. William, with her little dribble of small talk.

Many of the windows of the Lodges were alight. The light from without still painted the creepers, the lights from within were coming and going, and the gleams were falling upon the ivy-leaves here and there. One-half of the place was in shadow, and the western side in daylight still. There was a sweet rush of scent from the sweetbriars and clematis. It seemed to hang in the still evening air. Underneath the hedges, bright-coloured flowers seemed suddenly starting out of the twilight, while above, in the lingering daylight, the red berries sparkled and caught the stray limpid rays. There was a sound of sea-waves washing the not distant beach; a fisherman or two, and soldiers from the little fort, were strolling along the road, and peering in as they passed the bright little homes. The doors were wide open, and now and then a figure passed, a servant, Mrs. Campbell, who was always coming and going; William, the eldest son, leaving the house; he had been at work all day.

The walking-party came up so silently that they were there in the garden almost before the others had heard them: a beloved crowd, exclaiming, dispersing again. It was a pretty sight to see the meetings: little Susan running straight to her father, William St. Julian. He adored his little round-eyed daughter, and immediately carried her off in his arms. Little Missie, too, had got hold of her mother's hand, while Lady Jane was admiring Bevis, and being greeted by the rest of the party, and introduced to those whom she did not already know.

'We had quite given you up, dear Jane,' said Emilia, wistfully gazing and trying to see some look of big Bevis in his sister's face. 'How I wish I had stayed; but you had mamma.'

'We gave you up,' said Hester, 'when Mr. Hexham came without you . . .'

'I now find I had the honour of travelling with Lady Jane,' said Hexham, looking amused, and making a little bow.

Lady Jane turned her back upon Mr. Hexham. She had taken a great dislike to him on board the boat; she had noticed him looking at her once or twice, and at Captain Sigourney. She found it a very good plan and always turned her back upon people she did not like. It checked any familiarity. It was much better to do so at once, and let them see what their proper place was. If people of a certain position in the world did not keep others in their proper places, there was no knowing what familiarity might not ensue. And then she ran back to little Bevis again, and lifted him up, struggling. Bevis would gladly have turned his back if he could.

'Lady Jane Beverley has something military about her,' said Hexham to Mrs. Campbell.

As he spoke a great loud bell began to ring, and with a gentle chorus of exclamations, the ladies began to disperse to dress for dinner.

'You know your way, Mr. Hexham,' said Mrs. Campbell, pointing. 'Go through that side-door, and straight up and along the gallery.'

Mrs. St. Julian had put her arm into her husband's, and walked a little way with him towards the house.

'Henry,' she said, 'thank heaven, all is well. Lord Mountmore heard from his son by this mail. Lady Jane has promised to show me the letter: she had heard nothing of that dreadful report.'

'It was not likely,' St. Julian said; 'Ulleskelf only saw the paper by chance. I am glad you were so discreet, my dear.'

'I should like to make a picture of them,' said Hexham to the housekeeper, looking back once more before he hurried into the house.

The two were standing at the threshold of their home,

Mrs. St. Julian leaning upon her husband's arm: the strong keen-faced man with his bright gallant bearing, and the wife with her soft and feminine looks fixed upon him as she bent anxiously to catch his glance. She was as tall as he was: for St. Julian was a middle-sized man, and Mrs. St. Julian was tall for a woman.

Meanwhile Hexham, who was not familiar with the ways of the house, and who took time at his toilet, ran upstairs, hastily passed his own door, went along a passage, up a staircase, down a staircase... He found himself in the dusky garden again, where the lights were almost put out by this time, though all the flowers were glimmering, and scenting, and awake still. There was a red streak in the sky; all the people had vanished, but turning round he saw —he blinked his eyes at the sight—a white figure standing, visionary, mystical, in the very centre of a bed of tall lilies, in a soft gloom of evening light. Was it a vision? For the first time in his life Hexham felt a little strangely; and as if he could believe in the super-nature which he sometimes had scoffed at, the young man made one step forward and stopped again. 'It is I, Mr. Hexham,' said a shy clear voice. 'I came to find some flowers for Emilia.' It was Hester's voice. Surely some kindly providence sets true lovers' way in pleasant places; and all they do and say has a grace of its own which they impart to all inanimate things. The evening, the sweet stillness, the trembling garden hedges, the fields beyond, the sweet girlish *tinkle* of Hester's voice, made Hexham feel for the first time in his life as if he was standing in a living shrine, and as if he ought to fall down on his knees and worship.

'Can I help you?' he said. 'Miss Hester, may I have a flower for my button-hole?'

'There are nothing but big lilies,' said the voice.

PART II.

V.

In writing this little episode I have tried to put together one thing and another—to describe some scenes that I saw myself, and some that were described to me. My window looks out upon the garden, and is just over the great bed of lilies. I shut it down, and began to dress for dinner, with a dim feeling already of what the future might have in store, and a half-conscious consciousness of what was passing in the minds of the people all about.

For some days past Mrs. St. Julian's anxious face had seemed to follow me about the room. Emilia, Hexham, Hester, even Lady Jane, each seemed to strike a note, in my present excited and receptive state of mind. It is one for which there is no name, but which few people have not experienced. I dressed quickly, the dark corners of my room seemed looming at me, and it was with an odd anxious conviction of disturbance at hand that I hurried down along the gallery to the drawing-room, where we assembled before dinner. On my way I met Emilia on the stairs, in her white dinner dress, with a soft white knitted shawl drawn closely round her. She slid her little chill hand through my arm, and asked me why I looked so pale. Dear soft little woman, she seemed of us all the most tender and disarming. Even sorrow and desolation, I thought, should be vanquished by her sweetness. And perhaps I was right when I thought so.

We were not the last. Hester followed us. She was dressed in a floating gauze dress, and she had one great white lily in her dark hair. 'It is a great deal too big, Hester,' cried Mrs. William; but I thought I had never seen her more charming.

'How much better mamma is looking,' Hester said that evening at dinner, and as she spoke she glanced at her mother sitting at the head of the long table in the tall carved chair.

When the party was large, and the sons of the house at home, we dined in an old disused studio of St. Julian's: a great wooden room, unpapered and raftered, with a tressel-table of the painter's designing, and half-finished frescos and sketches hanging upon the walls. There was a high wooden chimney and an old-fashioned glass reflecting the scene, the table, the people, the crimson drugget, of which a square covered the boards. In everything St. Julian touched there was a broad quaint stamp of his own, and his room had been inhabited and altered by him. Two rough hanging lamps from the rafter lit up the long white table, and the cups of red berries and green leaves with which I had attempted to dress it. There was something almost patriarchal in this little assembly: the father at the end of the table, the sons and daughters all round. William and his wife by Mrs. St. Julian, and pretty Hester sitting by her father. Lady Jane was established at her other hand. St. Julian had taken her in. He had asked her a few questions at first, specially about the letter she had received from Bevis, but carefully, so that Emilia should not overhear them.

'He seemed to be enjoying himself,' said Lady Jane. 'He was talking of going on a shooting-party a little way up the river if he could get through his work in time.'

She did not notice St. Julian's grave look as she spoke, and went on in her usual fashion. I remember she was giving him one person's views on art and another's, and her own, and describing the pastille she had had done. St. Julian looked graver and graver, and more impatient as she went on. Patience was not his strong point.

'How long does it take you to paint a picture, Mr. St. Julian?' Lady Jane asked. 'I wish I could paint, and I'm sure I wish Beverley could, for he cannot manage upon his allowance at all. How nice it must be to take up a brush and—paint cheques, in fact, as you do. Clem can sketch wonderfully quickly; she took off Lord Scudamore capitally. Of course she would not choose to sketch for money, but artists have said they would gladly offer large sums for her paintings. Do your daughters help you?' enquired poor Lady Jane, affably feeling that she was suiting her conversation to her company. 'Do you ever do caricatures?'

'We will talk about painting, Lady Jane, when you have been here some days longer,' said St. Julian. 'You had better ask the girls any questions you may wish to have answered, and get them, if possible, to give you some idea of the world we live in.'

To poor Lady Jane's utter amazement, St. Julian then began talking to Hexham across the table, and signed to his wife to move immediately after dinner was over. We all went back walking across the garden to the drawing-room, for the night was fine, and the little covered way was for bad weather.

Some of us sat in the verandah. It was a bright starry evening. A great bright planet was rising from behind the sweeping down. The lights from the wooden room were shining too. Lady Jane presently seemed to get tired of listening to poor Mrs. William's nursery retrospections—Mary Annes, and Sarahs, and tea and sugar, and what Mrs. Mickleman had said when she parted from her nursery-maid; and what Mrs. William herself meant to say to the girl when she got home on Monday; not that Mrs. William was disposed to rely entirely upon Mrs. Mickleman, who was certainly given to exaggerate, &c The girls were in the garden. Emilia had gone up to little Bevis. Lady Jane jumped up from her place,

U

with the usual rattle of bracelets and necklaces, and said she should take a turn too, and join the young ladies in the garden.

Mrs. William confessed, as Lady Jane left the verandah, that she was glad she was not *her* sister-in-law.

'She has such a strange abrupt manner,' said the poor lady. 'Don't you find it very awkward, Queenie? I never know whether she likes me to talk to her or not—do you?'

'I have no doubt about it,' I said, laughing.

The evening was irresistible: starlit, moonlit, soft-winded.

A few minutes later I, too, went out into the garden, and walked along the dark alley towards the knoll, from whence there is a pretty view of the sea by night, and over the hedge and along the lane. From where I stood I saw that the garden-gate was open, for the moon was shining in a broad silver stream along the lane that led to the farm. The farm was not really ours, but all our supplies came from there, and we felt as if it belonged to us. Missie knew the cows and the horses, and the very sheep enclosed in their pen for the night. As I was standing peaceful and resting under the starlit dome, something a little strange and inexplicable happened, which I could not at all understand at the time. I saw some one moving in the lane beyond the hedge. I certainly recognised Lady Jane walking away in the shadow that lay along the banks of that moonlight stream; but what was curious to me was this: it seemed to me that she was not alone, that a dark tall figure of a man was beside her. It was not one of our men, though I could not see the face —of this I felt quite sure. The two went on a little way, then she turned; and I could have declared that I saw the gleam of his face in the distance through the shadow. Lady Jane's hand was hanging in the moonlight, and her trinkets glistening. Of her identity I had no doubt. There is a big tree which hangs over the road, and when they, or when she, reached it, she stopped for a moment, as if to look about her, and then, only Lady Jane appeared from its shadow—the other figure had vanished. I could not understand it at all. I have confessed that I am a foolish person, and superstitious at times. I had never seen poor Bevis. Had anything happened? Could it be a vision of him that I had seen? I got a little frightened, and my heart began to beat. It was only for an instant that I was so absurd. I walked hastily towards the garden-door, and met Lady Jane only a few steps off, coming up very coolly.

'How lovely this moonlight is, Mrs. Campbell!' she cried, more affably than usual.

'Who was that with you? Didn't I see someone with you, Lady Jane?' I asked hurriedly.

Lady Jane looked me full in the face.

'What do you mean?' said she. 'I went out for a stroll by myself. I am quite alone, as you see.'

Something in her tone reassured me. I felt sure she was not speaking the truth. It was no apparition I had seen, but a real tangible person. It was no affair of mine, though it struck me as a singular proceeding. We both walked back to the house together. The girls' white dresses were gleaming here and there upon the lawn. Hexham passed us hastily and went on and joined them. William was taking a turn with his cigar. As we passed the dining-room window I happened to look in. St. Julian was sitting at the table, with his head resting on his hands, and beside him Mrs. St. Julian, who must have gone back to the room after dinner. A paper was before them, over which the two were bending.

We found no one in the drawing-room, and only a lamp spluttering and a tea-table simmering in one corner, and Mrs. William, who was half asleep on the sofa. 'Don't let us stay indoors. Let us go back to the others,' said Lady Jane.

What a night it was! Still, dark, sweet, fragrant shadows quivering upon the moon-stream; a sudden, glowing, summer's night, coming like a gem set in the midst of grey days, of storms, swift gales, of falling autumnal leaves and seasons

The clear three-quarter moon was hanging over the gables and roofs of the Lodges; the high stars streamed light; a distant sea burnt with pale radiance; the young folks chattered in the trembling gleams.

'Look at that great planet rising over the down,' said Hexham. 'Should you like that to be your star, Miss St. Julian?'

'I should like a fixed star,' Hester answered, gravely. 'I should like it to be quite still and unchanging, and to shine with an even light.'

'That is not a bit like you, Hester,' said William, who had come up, and who still had a schoolboy trick of teasing his sisters; 'it is much more like Emilia, or my wife. You describe them, and take all the credit to yourself.'

'Oh, William! Emilia is anything but a fixed star,' cried Aileen. 'She would like to jump out of her orbit to-morrow, and go off to Bevis, if she could. Margaret is certainly more like.'

'You shall have the whole earth for your planet, Miss Hester,' said Hexham. Then he added less seriously, 'They say it looks very bright a little way off.'

Moonlight gives a strange, intensified meaning to voices as well as to shadows. No one spoke for a minute, until Lady Jane, who was easily bored, jumped up, and said that people ought to be ashamed to talk about stars now-a-days, so much had been said already; and that, after all, she should go back for some tea.

I left her stirring her cup, with Mrs. William still

half asleep in her corner, and I myself went up to my room. Mrs. St. Julian was sitting with her husband in the studio, the parlour-maid told me. Outside was the great burning night, inside a silent house, dark, with empty chambers and doors wide open on the dim staircase and passages. I would gladly have stayed out with the others, but I had a week's accounts to overlook on this Saturday night. The odd anxiety I had felt before dinner came back to me again now that I was alone. I tried to shake off the feeling which oppressed me, and I went in and stood for a moment by my little girl's bedside. Her sweet face, her quiet breath, and peaceful dreams seemed to me to belong to the stars outside. As I looked at the child, I found myself once more thinking over my odd little adventure with Lady Jane, and wondering whether it would be well to speak of it, and to whom? I had lived long enough to feel some of the troubles and complications both of speech and of silence. Once more my heart sank, as it used to do when difficulties seemed to grow on every side before I had come to this kind house of refuge. I pulled my table and my lamp to the window: the figures were still wandering in the garden; I saw Hester's white dress flit by more than once. Such nights count in the sum of one's life.

VI.

Missie was standing ready dressed in her Sunday frills and ribbons by my bedside when I awoke next morning.

'It is raining, mamma,' she said. 'We had wanted to go up to the beacon before breakfast.'

It seemed difficult to believe that this was the same world that I had closed my eyes upon. The silent, brilliant, mysterious world of stars and sentiment was now grey, and mist-wreathed, and rain-drenched. The practical result of my observations was to say, 'Missie, go and tell them to light a fire in the dining-room.'

St. Julian, who is possessed by a horrible stray demon of punctuality, likes all his family to assemble to the sound of a certain clanging bell, that is poor Emilia's special aversion. Mrs. St. Julian never comes down to breakfast. I was only just in time this morning to fulfil my duties and make the tea and the coffee. Hester came out of her room as I passed the door. She, too, had come back to every-day life again, and had put away her white robes and lilies for a stuff dress,—a quaint blue dress, with puffed sleeves, and a pretty fanciful trimming of her mother's devising, gold braid and velvet round the wrists and neck. Her pretty gloom of dark hair was pinned up with golden pins. As I looked at her admiringly, I began to think to myself that, after all, rainy mornings were perhaps as compatible with sentiment as purple starry skies. I could not help thinking that there was something a little shy and conscious in her manner: she seemed to tread gently, as if she were afraid of waking someone, as if she were thinking of other things. She waited for me, and would not go into the dining-room until she had made sure that I was following. Only Hexham was there, reading his letters by the burning fire of wood, when we first came in. He turned round and smiled :—had the stars left their imprint upon him too ? He carried his selection of eggs and cutlets and toasted bread from the side-table, and put himself quietly down by Hester's side : all the others dropped in by degrees.

'Here is another French newspaper for you, papa,' said Emilia, turning over her letters with a sigh. St. Julian took it from her quickly, and put it in his pocket.

Breakfast was over. The rain was still pouring in a fitful, gusty way, green ivy-leaves were dripping, creepers hanging dully glistening about the windows, against which the great fresh drops came tumbling. The children stood curiously watching, and making a play of the falling drops. There was Susy's raindrop, and George's on the window-ledge, and Mr. Hexham's.

'Oh, Mr. Hexham's has won!' cried Susy, clasping her little fat hands in an agony of interest.

I looked out and saw the great gusts of rain beating

and drifting against the hedgerows, wind-blown mists crossing the fields and the downs. It was a stormy Sunday, coming after that night of wonders. But the wind was high; the clouds might break. The church was two miles off, and we could not get there then; later we hoped we might have a calmer hour to walk to it.

The afternoon brightened as we had expected, and most of us went to afternoon service snugly wrapped in cloaks, and stoutly shod, walking up hill and down hill between the bright and dripping hedges to the little white-washed building where we Islanders are exhorted, buried, christened, married by turns. It is always to me a touching sight to see the country folks gathering to the sound of the jangling village bells, as they ring their pleasant calls from among the ivy and birds'-nests in the steeple, and summon—what a strange, toil-worn, weather-beaten company!—to prayer and praise. Furrowed faces bent, hymn-books grasped in hard crooked fingers, the honest red smiling cheeks of the lads and lasses trudging along side by side, the ancient garments from lavender drawers, the brown old women from their kitchen corners, the babies toddling hand-in-hand. Does one not know the kindly Sunday throng, as it assembles, across fields and downs, from nestling farm and village byways? Mrs. William's children came trotting behind her, exchanging cautious glances with the Sunday-school, and trying to imitate a certain business-like, church-going air which their mother affected. Hexham and the others were following at some little distance. Emilia never spoke much, and to-day 1 e was very silent; but though she was silent I could feel her depression, and knew, as well as if she had put it all into words, what was passing in her mind. Once during the service, I heard a low shivering sigh by my side, but when I glanced at her, her face looked placid, and as we came away the light of the setting sun came shining full upon it. A row of boys were sitting on the low churchyard wall in this western light, which lit up the fields and streamed across the homeward paths of the little congregation. I must not forget to say that, as we passed out, it seemed to me that, in the crowd waiting about the door, I recognised a tall and bending figure that I had seen somewhere before. Somewhere—by moonlight. I remembered presently where and when it was.

'Who was that?' asked Emilia, seeing me glance curiously.

'That is what I should like to know,' said I. 'Shall we wait for Lady Jane? I have a notion she could tell us.'

We waited, but no Lady Jane appeared.

'She must have gone on,' said Emilia. 'It is getting cold; let us follow them, dear Queenie.'

I was still undecided as to what I had better do. It seemed that it would be better to speak to Lady Jane herself than to relate my vague suspicions to anybody else.

Little Emilia of all people was so innocent and unsuspecting that I hesitated before I told her what I had seen. I was hesitating still, when Emmy took my arm again.

'Come!' she said; and so we went on together through the darkening village street, past the cottages where the pans were shining against the walls as the kitchen fires flamed. The people began to disperse once more: some were at home, stooping as they crossed their low cottage thresholds; others were walking away along the paths and the hills that slope from the village church to cottages by the sea. We saw Hester and Aileen and Hexham going off by the long way over the downs; but no Lady Jane was with them. We were not far from home when Emilia stopped before a little rising mound by the roadside, on which a tufted holly-tree was standing, already reddening against the winter.

'That is the tree my husband likes,' said she. 'It was bright red with holly-berries the morning we were married. Little Bevvy watches the berries beginning to burn, as he calls it. I often bring him here.'

Some people cannot put themselves into words, and they say, not the actual thing they are feeling, but something quite unlike, and yet which means all they would say. Some other people, it is true, have words enough, but no selves to put to them. Emilia never said a striking thing, rarely a pathetic one, but her commonplaces came often more near to me than the most passionate expressions of love or devotion. Something in the way she looked, in the tone with which she spoke of the holly-tree, touched me more than there seemed any occasion for. I cannot tell what it was; but this I do know, that silence, dulness, everything utters at times, the very stones cry out, and, in one way or another, love finds a language that we all can understand.

We stood for a few minutes under the holly-tree, and then walked quickly home. I let Emilia go in. I waited outside in the dim grey garden, pacing up and down in the twilight. Lady Jane, as I expected, arrived some ten minutes after we did; but I missed the opportunity I had wished for, for Hexham and the two girls appeared almost at the same minute, with bright eyes and fresh rosy faces, from their walk, and we all went up to tea in the mistress's room.

This was the Williams' last evening. Only one little incident somewhat spoilt its harmony.

'Who was that Captain Sigourney, who called just after we had gone to church?' Mrs. William asked, innocently, during a pause in the talk at dinner.

This simple question caused some of us to look up curiously.

'Captain Sigourney,' said Lady Jane, in a loud, trumpet-like tone, 'is a friend of mine. I asked him to call upon me.'

St. Julian gave one of his flashes, a look half-amused,

half-angry. He glanced at his wife, and then at Lady Jane, who was cutting up her mutton into long strips, calmly excited, and prepared for battle. St. Julian was silent, however, and the engagement, if engagement there was to be, did not take place until later in the evening. I felt very glad the matter was taking this turn and that the absurd mystery, whatever it might be, should come to an end without my being implicated in it. It was no affair of mine if Lady Jane liked to have a dozen Captains in attendance upon her, but it seemed to me a foolish proceeding. I had reason to conclude that St. Julian had said something to Lady Jane that evening. I was not in the drawing-room after dinner. One of the servants was ill, and I was obliged to attend to her; but as I was coming down to say good-night to them all I met Lady Jane— I met a whirlwind in the passage. She gave me one look. Her whole aspect was terrible; her chains and many trinkets seemed rattling with indignation. She looked quite handsome in her fury; her red hair and false plaits seemed to stand on end, her eyes to pierce me through and through, and if I had been guilty I think I must have run away from this irate apparition. Do I dream it, or did I hear the two words, 'impertinent interference,' as she turned round with the air of an empress, and shut her door loud in my face? Mrs. St. Julian happened to be in her room, and the noise brought her kind head out into the passage, and, not I am afraid very calmly or coherently, I told her what had happened.

'I must try and appease her. I suppose my husband has spoken to her,' said Mrs. St. Julian; and she boldly went and knocked at the door of Lady Jane's room, and, after an instant's hesitation, walked quietly in. I do not know what charm she used, but somewhat to my dismay, a messenger came to me in the drawing-room presently to beg that I would speak to Lady Jane. I saw malicious Aileen with a gleam of fun in her eyes at my unfeigned alarm. I found Lady Jane standing in the middle of the room, in a majestic sort of dressing-gown, with all her long tawny locks about her shoulders. Mrs. St. Julian was sitting in an arm-chair near the toilet-table, which was all glittering with little bottles and ivory handles. This scarlet apparition came straight up to me as I entered, with three brisk strides. 'I find I did you an injustice,' she said, loftily relenting, though indignant still. 'Mrs. St. Julian has explained matters to me. I thought you would be glad to know at once that I was aware of the mistake I had made. I beg your pardon. Good evening, Mrs. Campbell,' said Lady Jane, dismissing me all of a breath. I found myself outside in the dark passage again, with a curious dazzle of the brilliantly lighted room, with its odd perfume of ottar of roses, of that weird apparition with its flaming robe and red hair and burning cheeks.

I was too busy next morning helping Mrs. William and

her children and boxes to get off by the early boat, to have much time to think of apparitions or my own wounded feelings. Dear little Georgy and Susy peeped out of the carriage-window with many farewell kisses. The three girls stood waving their hands as the carriage drove past the garden. The usual breakfast-bell rang and we all assembled, and Lady Jane, whose anger was never long-lived, came down in pretty good-humour. To me she was most friendly. There was a shade of displeasure in her manner to St. Julian. To Hexham she said that she had quite determined upon an expedition to Warren Bay that afternoon, and to the castle next day, and she hoped he would come too. Lady Jane bustled off after breakfast to order a carriage.

VII.

From 'the mistress's' room, with its corner windows looking out every way, we could see downs, and sea, and fields, and the busy road down to the shore. Mrs. St. Julian was able to be out so little that she liked life at second-hand, and the sight of people passing, and of her children swinging at the gate, and of St. Julian as he came and went from his studio sometimes, with his pipe and his broad-brimmed hat—all this was a never-failing delight to her. Hester sat writing for her mother this morning. It was the Monday after Lady Jane's arrival, and I established myself with my work in the window. Suddenly the mother asked, 'Where is Emilia?'

'Emilia is in the garden with Bevis,' said Hester; 'they were picking red berries off the hedge when I came up.'

'And were is Lady Jane?' said Mrs. St. Julian.

'She is gone to look at a pony-carriage, with her maid,' said Hester.

'Poor Lady Jane was very indignant last night. You will be amused to hear that I am supposed to be encouraging a young man at this moment, for purposes of my own, to carry her off,' said Mrs. St. Julian. 'I am afraid Henry is vexed about it. Look here.' As she spoke she gave me a satiny, flowingly-written note to read.

'Castle Scudamore, Saturday.

'Dear Mrs. St. Julian,—I have been made aware that my stepdaughter has been followed to your house by a person with whom I and her father are most anxious that she should have no communication *whatever*. Whether this has happened with your cognizance I cannot tell, but I shall naturally consider you responsible while she is under your roof, and I must beg you will be so good as not to continue to admit Captain Sigourney's visits. He is a person totally unsuitable in *every* respect to my step-daughter, and it is a marriage her father could not sanction.

'I hope Emilia is well, and that she has had satisfactory accounts by this last mail. We received a few lines only, on business, from Bevis.

'Believe me, Yours truly,
'E. MOUNTMORE.'

'The whole thing is almost too absurd to be vexed about,' said Mrs. St. Julian, smiling.

'Why was Lady Jane so angry with you, Queenie?' Hester asked; and then it was I confessed what I had seen that evening on the Knoll.

'Lady Jane told me all about it,' my mistress continued. 'She says Captain Sigourney's only object in life is to see her pass by. To tell you the truth, I do not think she cares in the least for him. She found him at the gate that evening, she says.' Mrs. St. Julian hesitated, and then went on. 'She must be very attractive. She tells me that she believes Mr. Hexham admires her very much, and that, on the whole, she thinks he is more the sort of person to suit her.' Mrs. St. Julian spoke with a little gentle malice; and yet I could see she half believed, and that there was prudence, too, in what she was saying.

There was a pause. Hester looked straight before her, and I stitched on. At last the mother spoke again,—

'I wish you would go to Emilia, my Hester,' she said, a little anxiously. 'I am afraid she is fretting sometimes when she is by herself.'

'You poor mamma,' cried Hester, jumping up and running to her, and kissing her again and again: 'you have all our pain and none of our fun.'

'Don't you think so, my dear,' said the mother; 'I think I have both.' Then she called Hester back to her, held her hand, and looked into her face tenderly for a minute. 'Go, darling!—but—but take care,' she said, as she let her go.

'Take care of what, mamma?' the girl asked, a little consciously; and then Hester ran off, as all young girls will do, nothing loth to get out into the sunshine.

I stitched on at my work, but presently looking up I saw that Hester and Emilia were not alone; Mr. Hexham, who had, I suppose, been smoking his cigar in the garden, had joined them. He was lifting Bevis high up over head, to pick the berries that were shining in the hedge. The Lodges seemed built for pretty live pictures; and the mistress's room, most specially of all the rooms in the house, is a peep-show to see them from. Through this window, with its illuminated border of clematis and ivy and Virginian creeper, I could see the bit of garden lawn, green still and sunlit; the two pretty sisters, in their flowing dresses, straight and slim, smiling at little Bevis; the high sweetbriar hedge, branching like a bower over their heads; and the swallows skimming across the distant down. This was the most romantic window of the three which lighted her room, and I asked my cousin to come and see a pretty group. She smiled, and then sighed as she looked. Poor troubled mother!

'I cannot feel one moment's ease about Bevis,' she said. 'My poor Emmy! And yet Lady Jane was very positive.'

'We shall know to-morrow. You are too anxious, I think,' I answered cheerfully; and then I could not help asking her if she thought she should ever be as anxious about George Hexham.

She did not answer except by a soft little smile. Then she sighed again.

Lady Jane's expected letter had not come that Monday evening, but Mrs. St. Julian hoped on. Emilia was daily growing more anxious; she said very little, but every opening door startled her, every word seemed to her to have a meaning. She began to have a clear, ill-defined feeling that they were hiding something from her, and yet, poor little thing, she did not dare ask, for fear of getting bad news. Her soft, wan, appealing looks went to the very hearts of the people looking on. Lady Jane was the only person who could resist her. She was, or seemed to be, ruffled and annoyed, that anyone should be anxious when she had said there was no occasion for fear. Mrs. St. Julian would have quietly put off a certain expedition which had been arranged some time before for the next day; but Lady Jane, out of very opposition, was most eager and decided that it should take place. An invitation came for the girls to a ball; this the parents decidedly refused, though Hexham, and Hester too, looked sorely disappointed. Of course Lady Jane knew no reason for any special anxiety, any more than Emilia, and perhaps her confidence and cheerfulness were the best medicine for the poor young wife; who, seeing the sister so bright, began to think that she had over-estimated dangers which she only dimly felt and guessed at. So the carriages were ordered after luncheon; but the sun was shining bright in the morning, and Hexham asked Hester and Aileen (shyly, and hesitating as he spoke), if they would mind being photographed directly.

'Why should you not try a group?' said St. Julian. 'Here are Hester, Lady Jane, Missie and Emilia, all wanting to be done at once.'

Emilia shrank back, and said she only wanted baby done, not herself.

'I was longing to try a group,' said Hexham, 'and only waiting for leave. How will you sit?' And he began placing them in a sort of row, two up and one down, with a property-table in the middle. He then began focussing, and presently emerged, pale and breathless and excited, from the little black hood into which he had dived. 'Will you look?' said he to St. Julian.

'I think it might be improved upon,' said S. Julian, getting interested. 'Look up, Missie—up, up. That is better. And cannot you take the ribbon out of your hair?'

'Yes, uncle St. Julian,' said Missie ; ' but it will all tumble down.'

'Never mind that,' said he ; and with one hand Missie pulled away the snood, and then the beautiful stream came flowing and rippling and falling all about her shoulders.

'That is excellent,' said the painter. 'You, too, Hester, shake out your locks.' Then he began sending one for one thing and one for another. I was despatched for some lilies into the garden, and Lady Jane came too, carrying little Bevis in her arms. When we got back we found one of the prettiest sights I have ever yet seen,—a dream of fair ladies against an ivy wall, flowers and flowing locks, and sweeping garments. It is impossible to describe the peculiar charm of this living, breathing picture. Emilia, after all, had been made to come into it: little Bevis clapped his hands, and said, 'Pooty mamma,' when he saw her.

'I don't mind being done in the group,' said Lady Jane, ' if you will promise not to put any of those absurd white pinafores on me.'

Neither of the gentlemen answered, they were both too busy. As for me, I shall never forget the sweet child wonder in my little girl's face, Hester's bright deep eyes, or my poor Emilia's patient and most affecting expression, as they all stood there motionless; while Hexham held his watch, and St. Julian looked on, almost as excited as the photographer. As Hexham rushed away into his van, with the glass under his arm, we all began talking again.

'It takes one's breath away,' said St. Julian, quite excited, 'to have the picture there, breathing on the glass, and to feel every instant that it may vanish or dissolve with a word, with a breath. I should never have nerve for photography.'

'I believe the great objection is that it blackens one's fingers so,' said Lady Jane. 'I should have tried it myself, but I did not care to soil my hands.'

As for the picture, Hexham came out wildly exclaiming from his little dark room: never had he done anything so strangely beautiful,—he could not believe it; it was magical. The self-controlled young man was quite wild with delight and excitement. Lord Ulleskelf walked up, just as we were all clustering round, and he, too, admired immensely.

Hexham rushed up to St. Julian. 'It is your doing,' he said. 'It is wonderful. My fortune is made.' He all but embraced his precious glass.

St. Julian was to be the next subject. What a noble wild head it was! There was something human and yet almost mysterious to me in the flash of those pale circling eyes with the black brows and shaggy grey hair. But Hexham's luck failed him, perhaps from over-excitement and inexperience in success. Three or four attempts failed, and we were still at it when the luncheon-bell rang.

Hexham was for going on all day; but St. Julian laughed and said it should be another time. This sentiment was particularly approved by Lady Jane, who had a childish liking for expeditions and picnickings, and who had set her heart upon carrying out her drive that afternoon.

VIII.

Hexham had known scarcely anything before this of home life or home peace. He had carefully treasured his liberty, and vowed to himself that he would keep that liberty always. But now that he had seen Hester, fair and maidenly, and serene, he could not tell what mysterious sympathy had attracted him. To speak of her, to hear her shy tender voice, affected him strangely. George Hexham did not care to give way to sentimental emotion; he felt that his hour had come. He had shared the common lot of men. It was a pity, perhaps, to give up independence and freedom and peace of mind, but no sacrifice was too great to win so dear a prize. So said the photographer to himself as he looked at the glass upon which her image was printed, that image with the wondering eyes. He must get one more picture, he thought, eating his luncheon thoughtfully, but with a good appetite,—one more of Hester alone. He determined to try and keep her at home that afternoon.

He followed her as she left the room

'You are not going? Do stay,' said Hexham, imploringly: 'I want you; I want a picture of you all to myself. I told my man we should come back after luncheon.'

Hester coloured up. Her mother's warning was still in her ears.

'I—I am afraid I must go,' she said shyly.

'What nonsense!' cried Hexham, who was perfectly unused to contradiction, and excited by his success. 'I shall go and tell your mother that it is horrible tyranny to send you off with that *corvée* of children and women, and that you want to stay behind. Lady Jane would stay if I asked her.'

Hester did not quite approve of this familiar way of speaking. She drew herself up more and more shyly and coldly.

'No, thank you,' she said; 'mamma lets me do just as I like. I had rather go with the others.'

'In that case,' said Hexham, offended, 'I shall not presume to interfere.' And he turned and walked away.

What is a difference? A word that means nothing,— a look a little to the right or to the left of an appealing glance. I think that people who quarrel are often as fond of one another as people who embrace. They speak a different language, that is all. Affection and agreement are things quite apart. To agree with the people you love is a blessing unspeakable. But people who differ may also be travelling along the same road on opposite sides. And there are two sides to every road that both lead the same way.

Hexham was so unused to being opposed that his indignation knew no bounds. He first thought of remaining behind, and showing his displeasure by a haughty seclusion. But Lady Jane happened to drive up with Aileen in the pony-carriage she had hired, feathers flying, gauntleted, all prepared to conquer.

'Won't you come with us, Mr. Hexham?' she said, in her most gracious tone.

After a moment's hesitation, Hexham jumped in, for he saw Hester standing not far off, and he began immediately to make himself as agreeable as he possibly could to his companion. It was not much that happened this afternoon, but trifles show which way the wind is blowing. Lady Jane and her cavalier went first, the rest of us followed in Mrs. St. Julian's carriage. We were bound for a certain pretty bay some two miles off. The way there led across a wide and desolate warren, where sand and gorse spread on either side to meet a sky whose reflections always seemed to me saddened by the dark growth of this arid place. A broad stony military road led to a building on the edge of the cliff—a hotel, where the carriages put up. Then we began clambering down the side of the cliff, out of this somewhat dreary region, into a world brighter and more lovely than I have words to put to it—a smiling plain of glassy blue sea, a vast firmament of heaven; and close at hand bright sandy banks, shining with streams of colour reflected from the crystals upheaved in shining strands; and farther off the boats drifting towards the opal Broadshire Hills.

I do not suppose that anybody seeing us strolling along these lovely cliffs would have guessed the odd and depressing influence that was at work upon most of us. As far as Lady Jane and Hexham and Aileen were concerned, the expedition seemed successful enough; they laughed and chattered, and laughed again. Emilia and her sister followed, listening to their shrieks, in silence, with little Bevis between them. Missie and I brought up the rear. Lady Jane seemed quite well pleased with her companion, and evidently expected his homage all to herself. I could have shaken her for being so stupid. Could she not see that not one single word he spoke was intended for her. Every one of Hexham's arrows flew straight to the gentle heart for which they were intended. It was not a very long walk—perhaps half an hour in duration—but half an hour is long enough to change a lifetime, to put a new meaning to all that has passed, and to all that is yet to come. People may laugh at such a thing as *désillusionnement*, but it is a very real and very bitter thing, for all that people may say. To some constant natures certainty and unchangeableness are the great charm, the whole meaning of love. Hester, suddenly bewildered and made to doubt, would freeze and change, and fly at a shadow where Hester, once certain, would endure all things, bear, and hope- and forgive. I could see that Hexham did not dislike a little excitement; *l'imprévu* had an immense charm for him. He was rapid, determined; so sure of himself that he could afford not to be sure of others. Hexham's tactics were very simple. He loved Hester.[1] Of this he had no doubt, but he had no

---

[1] (Fragment of a letter found in Mr. Hexham's room after his departure :—)

. . . . A little bit of the island is shining through my open glass-pane. I see a green field with a low hedge, a thatched farm, woods, flecks of shade, a line of down rising from the frill of the muslin blind to the straggling branch of clematis that has been put to grow round my window. It is all a nothing compared to really beautiful scenery, and yet it is everything when one has once been conquered by the charm of the place,—the still, sweet influence of its tender lights, its charming *humility* and unpretension, if one can so speak of anything inanimate. It is six o'clock; the sky is patched and streaked with grey and yellowish clouds upon a faint sunset aquamarine; a wind from the sea is moving through the clematis and making the light tendrils dance and swing; a sudden unexpected gleam of light has worked enchantment with the field and the farmstead, the straw is a-flame, the thatch is golden, the dry stubble is gleaming. A sense of peace and evening and rest comes over me as I write and look from my window. This sort of family-life suits me. I do not find time heavy on my hands. St. Julian is a lucky fellow to be the ruler of such a pleasant dominion. I never saw anything more charmingly pretty than its boundaries studded with scarlet berries, and twisted twigs, with birds starting and flying across the road, almost under our horse's feet, as we came along. I am glad I came. Old St. Julian is as ever capital company, and the most hospitable of hosts. Mrs. St. Julian is an old love of mine: she is a sweet and gracious creature. This is more than I can say of my fellow-guest Lady Jane Beverley, who is the most overpowering of women. I carefully keep out of her way, but I cannot always escape her. Hester St. Julian is very like her mother, but with something of St. Julian's strength

idea of loving a woman as Shakspeare, for instance, was content to love, or at least to write of it—'Being your slave, what should I do but wait?' This was not in Hexham's philosophy. Hester had offended him, and he had been snubbed; he would show her his indifference, and punish her for his punishment.

We were all on our way back to the carriages when Hester stopped suddenly at a little zigzag path leading down to the sands, down which Missie and I had been scrambling. 'Do you think Bevvy could get down here?' she asked. 'Do let us go down, Emilia. I think we have time; the carriages are not yet ready.'

Emilia, although frightened out of her wits, instantly assented, and Missie and I watched Hester springing from rock to rock, and from step to step. She lifted Bevis safe down the steep side; little falling stones, and shells, and

---

of character—she has almost too much. She was angry with me to-day. Perhaps I deserved it. I hope she has forgiven me by this time, for I, to tell the truth, cannot afford to quarrel with her.

Lord Ulleskelf is here a good deal; his long white hair is more silvery than ever; he came up this morning to see my photography; I wish you had been standing by to see our general eagerness and excitement; the fact is, that here in this island, the simplest emotions seem intensified and magnified. Its very stillness and isolation keep us and our energies from overpassing its boundaries. I have been here two days,—I feel as if I had spent a lifetime in the place, and were never going away any more, and as if the world all about was as visionary as the grey Broadshire Hills that we see from High Down. As for certain old loves and interests that you may have known of, I do not believe they ever existed, except upon paper. If I mistake not, I have found an interest here more deep than any passing fancy. . . .

sands went showering on to the shingle below: a seagull came out of a hole in the sand, and flew out to sea. Bevvy screamed with delight. Hester's quick light step seemed everywhere: she put him safe down below, and then sprang up again to her sister's help. The little excitement acted like a tonic: 'How pretty it is here,' she said.

We had sat for some ten minutes under the wing of the great cliff, in an arch or hollow, lined with a slender tracery of granite lines close following one another. The arching ridge of the cliff cut the high line of blue sea sharply into a curve.

'It was like a desert island,' Hester said, looking at the little cove enclosed in its mighty walls, with the smooth unfurrowed crescent of shingle gleaming and shining, and the white light little waves rushing against the stones; 'an island upon which we had been wrecked.'

'An island,' I thought to myself, 'that no Hexham had as yet discovered.' I wondered how long it would be deserted.

Missie, tired of sitting still, soon wandered off, and disappeared beyond the side of the cliff. I do not know how long we should have stayed there if little Bevis, who had never yet heard of a desert island, and who thought people always all lived together, and that it was naughty to be shy, and that he was getting very hungry, and that he had better cry a little, had not suddenly set up a shrill and imperious demand for his dinner, his 'ome,' as he called it, Tarah his nurse, and his rocking-horse. Emilia jumped up, and Hester too.

'It must be time for us to go,' said Mrs. Beverley

It is generally easier to climb up than to descend, and so it would have been now for Hester alone. I do not know why the sun-beaten path seemed so hard, the blocks of stone so loose and crumbling. Hester went first, with Bevis in her arms, and at first got on pretty well; but for some reason or other—perhaps that in coming down we had disturbed the stones—certainly as she went on her footsteps seemed less rapid and lucky than they usually were. She stumbled, righted herself, took another step, Bevis clinging tight to her neck. Emilia cried out, frightened. Hester, a little nervous, put Bevvy on a big stone, and stood breathless for an instant. 'Come up, Emmy,' she said; 'this way—there, to that next big step. Emmy did her best, but before she could catch at Hester's extended hand her foot slipped again, and she gave another little scream.

'Hester, help me!'

I was at some little distance. I had tried a little independent track of my own, which proved more impracticable than I had expected. It was in vain I tried to get to Emilia's assistance. There was no real danger for Emilia, clinging to a big granite boulder fixed in the sand, but it was absurd and not pleasant. The sun baked upon the sandy paths. Hester told Bevvy to sit still while she went to help mamma. 'No, no, no,' cried little Bevis when his aunt attempted to leave him, clutching at her with a sudden spring, which nearly overset her. It was at this instant that I saw, to my inexpressible relief, two keen eyes peering over the edge of the cliff, and Hexham coming down the little path to our relief.

'I could not think where you had got to,' he said; 'I came back to see. Will you take hold of my stick, Mrs. Beverley; I will come back for the boy, Miss St. Julian.' Hexham would have returned a third time for Hester, but she was close behind him, and silently rejected his proffered help. George Hexham turned away in silence. Hester was already scarcely grateful to him for coming back at all. He had spoken to her, but her manner had been so cold, his voice so hard, that it seemed as if indeed all was over between them. Hester was no gentle Griselda, but a tender and yet imperious princess, accustomed to confer favours and to receive gratitude from her subjects. Here was one who had revolted from his allegiance.

IX.

The day had begun well and brightly, but there was a jar in the music that evening which was evident enough to most of us. We had all been highly wrought from

one cause and another, and this may have accounted for
some natural reaction. For one thing, we missed William
and his family; tiresome as Mrs. William undoubtedly
was, her placid monotone harmonised with the rest of the
performance, for though she was prosy, she was certainly
sweet-tempered, and the children were charming. It
had seemed like the beginning of the summer's end to see
them drive off; little hands waving and rosy faces
smiling good-by. Poor Missie was in despair, and went
to bed early. Lady Jane sat in her corner, looking black
and still offended with her host; something had
occasioned a renewed access of indignation. Mrs. St.
Julian did her very best to propitiate her indignant guest,
but the poor lady gave up trying at last, and leant back
in her chair wearily, and closed her eyes. I myself was
haunted by the ill-defined feeling of something amiss,—of
trouble present or at hand. Hester, too, was out of
spirits. It was evident that she and Mr. Hexham had
not quite forgiven each other for the morning's discussion.
Altogether it was a dismal disjointed evening, during
which a new phase of Hexham's character was revealed
to us, and it was not the best or the kindest. There was a
hard look in his handsome face and sceptical tone in his
voice. He seemed possessed by what the French call
l'esprit moqueur. Hester, pained and silenced at last,
would scarcely answer him when he spoke. Her father
with an effort got up and took a book and began to read

something out of one of Wordsworth's sonnets. It is always delightful to me to hear St. Julian read. His voice rolled and thrilled through the room, and we were all silent for a moment:

> Thy soul was like a star, and dwelt apart.
> Thou hadst a voice whose sound was like the sea

'I hate Wordsworth. He is always preaching,' said Hexham, as St. Julian ceased reading. 'I never feel so wicked as when I am being preached at.'

'I am sorry for you,' said St. Julian drily. 'I have never been able to read this passage of Wordsworth without emotion since I was a boy, and first found it in my school-books.'

Hester had jumped up and slipped out of the room while this discussion was going on; I followed presently, for I remembered a little bit of work which St. Julian had asked us to see to that evening.

He used sometimes to give me work to do for him, although I was not so clever as Hester in fashioning and fitting the things he wanted for his models; but I did my best, and between us we had produced some very respectable coiffes, wimples, slashed bodices, and other bygone elegancies. We had also concocted an Italian peasant, and a mediæval princess, and a dear little Dutch girl—our triumph. I found I had not my materials at hand, and I went to the studio to look for them. I was looking for a certain piece of silken stuff which I thought I had seen in the outer studio, and which my cousin had asked me to stitch together so as to make a cloak. I turned the things over and over, but I could not discover what I was in quest of among the piles and heaped-up properties that were kept there. I supposed it must be in the inner room, and I lifted the curtain and went in. I had expected to find the place dark, and silent, and empty. But the room was not dark. The wood-fire was burning; the tall candles were lighted; the pictures on the walls were vivid with the light, and looking almost alive, with those strange living eyes that St. Julian knew so well how to paint; there was the statesman in his robe; the musician leaning against the wall, drawing his bow across the strings of his violin. As I looked at him in the stream of the fire-flame, I almost expected to hear the conquering sound of the melody. But he did not play; he seemed to be waiting, and looking out, and listening to other music than his own. All these pictures were so familiar to us all as we came and went, that we often scarcely paused to look at them. But to-night in the firelight, they impressed me anew with a sense of admiration for the wonderful power of the man who had produced them. Over the chimney hung a poet, noble and simple and kingly, as St. Julian had painted him. Next to the poet was the head of a calm and beautiful woman, bending in a stream of light. It was either Emilia or her mother in her youth. . . An evangelist, with a grand, quiet brow and a white flood of silver beard, came next; and then warriors, and nobles, and maidens with flowing hair. There was someone in the room. Hester was standing underneath the picture of the evangelist, a real living picture. Her head was leaning wearily against the wall. She had come in before me, and seemed standing in a dreary way, and lost in thought. The silk stuffs she had collected were on the ground at her feet and the pattern cloak was hanging from a chair; but she had thrown her work away. I don't know why, unless it was that her eyes were full of great tired tears that she was trying vainly to keep back.

'My dear,' I said, frightened; 'my dear, what is it? What has happened? Has he vexed you?' I hated myself next instant. I had spoken hastily and without reflection. My question upset her; she struggled for a minute, and then burst out crying, though she was a brave girl—courageous and not given to useless complaints. Then she looked up, flushing crimson reproach at me. 'It is not what you seem to think,' she said. 'Don't you know me better? It is something—I don't know what. How foolish I am.' And this time, with an effort, she conquered her tears. 'Oh, Queenie!' she said, 'I know there is something wrong; some terrible news. I don't dare ask, for they have not told me; and I don't, don't dare ask,' she repeated. I was silent, for she was speaking the thought which had been in my own heart of late.

At last I said, 'One has foolish, nervous frights at times. What makes you so afraid, Hester?'

Hester smiled, with her tear-dimmed face.

'There has been another absurd and provoking scene,' she said, 'with Lady Jane. Something she said of anxiety, and a letter, and—and—I don't know what frightened me,' said Hester, faltering. 'She said she would go immediately, that she should marry, meet, write, invite anybody she chose, and that if it were not for this anxiety for Emilia—some letter she expected—she would leave us that instant; and then my mother stopped her, and that is all I know,' said Hester, with a great sigh. 'It is not worth crying for, is it, Queenie?'

As she spoke the door opened and St. Julian and Hexham came in to smoke their evening pipes. Hester drew herself up with bright flushed cheeks and said a haughty good-night to Hexham as she passed him. But in my heart I thought more than one doubt had caused Hester's tears to flow that night.

Hexham seemed unconscious enough. 'I shall be quite ready for sitters to-morrow morning, Miss Hester,' said the provoking young man cheerfully. 'You won't disappoint me again?'

Hester did not answer, and walked out of the room.

Hexham tried to persuade himself next day that he had made it all right with Hester over-night. He had come down late and had missed her at breakfast, but he made sure she would not fail him, and he got ready his chemicals and kept telling himself that she would come. The glasses were polished bright, and in their places. Everything was as it should be, he thought; the sun was shining as photographers wish it to shine. Once hearing steps Hexham turned hastily, but it was only St. Julian on his way to his studio; Lady Jane went by presently; then Lord Ulleskelf passed by; and each time Hexham felt more aggrieved and disappointed. Hexham came to me twice as I sat at work in the drawing-room window, but I did not know where Hester had gone, or if she meant to sit to him. Little Missie went by last of all. The child had her hands full of grasses that I had sent her to gather. She went wandering on between the garden beds with a little busy brain full of pretty fancies, strange fairy dreams and stories of a world in which she was living apart from us all. The tall pampas grasses waved over my little maiden's head and bowed their yellow flowers in the wind. The myrtles glimmered mysteriously, the tamarisks drooped their fringed stems, wind-blown shrubs shivered and shook, while a woodpecker from the outer world who had ventured into fairy realms was laboriously climbing the stem of a slender elm-tree. Hexham asked Missie if she knew where Hester was, and the child, waking up, pointed to the house: 'She was there, at work for uncle Henry, in the housekeeper's room, as I passed,' said she.

Hexham was, as I have said, a young man of an impatient humour. He was a little hard as young men are apt to be. But there was something reassuring in his very hardness and faith in himself and his own doings. It was reassuring because it was a genuine expression of youthful strength and power. No bad man could have had that perfect confidence which marked most of George Hexham's sayings and doings. His was, after all, the complacency of good intentions.

He had taken it as a matter of course, not only that Hester would come, but that she would come with a feeling not unlike the feeling with which he was expecting her. He could not understand her absence, her continued coldness. What did it mean? did it, could it mean that she was unconscious of his admiration? It had suddenly become a matter of utter consequence to the young man that he should find her now, reproach her, read her face, and discover why she had thwarted him. He might see her all day and at any hour, and yet this was the hour he had set apart as his own—when he wanted her—the hour he had looked forward to and counted on and longed for. He came to me a third time, and asked me if I would take a message for him. I was a little sorry for him, although I thought he deserved this gentle punishment.

'If you will come with me we will go and look for her,' I said.

' You are doing me an immense kindness,' cried Hexham, gratefully.

The housekeeper's room could be entered by the courtyard: it was next to the outer studio, into which it led by a door. It was used for models and had been taken from the servants. As Missie had said, Hester was sitting in the window at work when we came in; the door into the studio was open, and I heard voices of people talking within.

Hester's needle flew along in a sort of rhythmic measure. She knew Hexham had come in with me, but she did not look up, only worked on. Poor Hester! her heart was too heavy for blushes or passing agitations. Hexham had wounded her and disappointed her, but, young as she was, the girl had a sense of the fitness of things which kept her from betraying all she felt; and, indeed, this great unaccountable feeling of anxiety now occupied most thoughts and feelings, except those to which she would not own. George Hexham stood with a curious face, full of anger and sympathy and compunction, watching her stitches as they flew. One, two, three, he counted, and the quaint little garment turned and twisted in her pale hands. Once she looked up at him. It would have been better if she had looked reproachful; but no, it was a grave cold glance she gave, and then her head bent down once more over her work. I left them to their own explanations, and went back to my drawing-room window.

Afterwards Hester told me how angry she was with me for bringing him.

'Have you nearly done? May I talk to you when you have finished that stitching?' he said to her presently.

'I can listen while I work,' said Hester, still sewing, and if she paused it was only to measure the seams upon the little model for whom they were intended.

That needle flying seemed to poor Hexham an impassable barrier—a weapon wielded by this Amazon that he could not overcome. It kept him at arms' length; it absorbed her attention; she scarcely listened to what he said as she stuck and threaded and travelled along the strange little garment. He found himself counting the stitches—one, two, three, four, five, six, seven, eight,—it was absurd; it was like an enchantment.

'Hester,' cried Hexham, 'you won't understand me!' Hester worked on and did not answer. His voice was quick, passionate, and agitated. 'You are so calm,' he cried. 'I do not believe the common weaknesses of life touch you in the least, or that you ever know how to make any allowance for others.'

'I can make allowance,' faltered Hester, as with trembling hands she stooped and began tying on the child's little garment.

To Hexham's annoyance, at that moment St. Julian appeared.

'You here, Hexham? Come and see Lord Ulleskelf.

Is the child ready?' he asked. 'That is right;' and he led off the little girl, in her funny Velasquez dress, trotting along to his long quick strides. Hexham followed them to the door, and then turned back slowly.

Hester had sunk wearily in the chair in which she had been sitting, leaning her head upon her hand. She thought it was all over; Hexham was gone. 'She did not care,' she said to herself; as people say they do not care, when they know in their heart of hearts that they have but to speak to call a welcome answering voice, to put out their hand for another hand to grasp. They do not say so when all is really gone, and there is no answer anywhere. Sometimes she softened, but Hester was indignant to think of the possibility of having been laughed at and made a play of when she herself had come with a heart trusting and true and tender. He could not care for Lady Jane, but he had ventured to say more than he really felt to Hester herself. Now it seemed to her that the whole aim and object of her behaviour should be to prevent Hexham from guessing what she had foolishly fancied —Hexham, who had come back, and who was standing looking with keen doubtful glances into her face. She turned her two clear inscrutable eyes upon him once more, and tried to meet his gaze quietly, but her eyes fell beneath his.

'Hester,' he said once again, and stopped short, hearing a step at the door. Poor Hester blushed up crimson with blushes that she blushed for again. Had she betrayed herself? Ah, no, no! She started up. 'I must go,' she said. Ah! she would go to her father. There was love, tender and generous love, to shield, to protect, to help her; not love like this, that was but a play, false, cruel, ready to wound.

'Dear Hester, don't go! Stay!' Hexham entreated, as she began to move towards the door leading to her father's studio. He had not chosen his time well, poor fellow, for Lady Jane, who was still in the outer studio, hearing his voice, came to the door, looked in for one instant, and turned away with an odd expression in her face and a brisk shrug of the shoulders. They both saw her. Hester looked up once again, with doubtful, questioning eyes, and then there was a minute's silence. Hexham understood her: a minute ago he had been gentle, now her doubts angered him.

'Why are you so hard to me?' he burst out at last, a little indignantly, and thoroughly in earnest. 'How can you suppose I have ever fancied that odious woman? Will you believe me, or not, when I tell you how truly and devotedly I love and admire you? You are the only woman I have ever seen whom I would make my wife. If you send me away you will crush all that is best and truest in my nature, and destroy my only chance of salvation.'

'This is not the way to speak,' said Hester, gravely,

with a beating heart. His hardness frightened her, as her coldness and self-control angered him; and yet he could not quite forget her sudden emotion of a moment before. It was a curious reluctant attraction that seemed to unite these two people, who loved each other, and yet were cold; and who were playing with their best chance of happiness, and wilfully putting it away. They stood looking at each other, doubtful still, excited, at once angry and gentle.

'How can I trust you,' said proud Hester, 'after yesterday?—after—— No, you do not really care for me, or——'

It was, I think, at that moment that they heard a sort of low stifled scream from outside, and then hasty footsteps. Hester started. 'Was that Lady Jane?' she said. 'Oh, what is it? Oh, has it come?' Unnerved, excited, she put up her two hands nervously, and instinctively turning to Hexham for help.

'My dearest,' said Hexham, melting, utterly forgetting all her coldness, thinking only of her—'what is it—wnat do you fear?' and as he spoke he kept her back for one instant by the two trembling hands, grasping them firmly in his own. . . .

No other word was spoken, but from that moment they felt that they belonged to each other.

'I don't know what I fear,' she said. 'Oh, come, come!'

PART III.

X.

LADY JANE had walked angrily out through the studio door into the garden. Her temper had not been improved by a disagreeable scolding letter from Lady Mountmore which had just been put into her hand. It contained the long-looked-for scrap from Bevis, which his father had forwarded. Lady Jane was venting a certain inward indignation in a brisk walk up and down the front of the house, when Lord Ulleskelf came towards her.

'Are you coming this afternoon to explore the castle with us?' she asked. 'I believe we are all going—that is, most of us. Aileen and Missie have gone off with my maid in the coach.'

He shook his head. 'No,' he said. 'And I think if it were not for the children's sake you none of you would much care to go. But I suppose it is better to live on as usual and make no change to express the hidden anxieties which trouble us all at times.'

'Well, I must say I think it is very ridiculous,' said Lady Jane, who was thoroughly out of temper. 'These young wives seem to think that they and their husbands are of so much consequence, that every convulsion of life and nature must combine to injure them and keep them apart.'

Lord Ulleskelf had spoken forgetting that Lady Jane was quite ignorant of their present cause for alarm. He was half indignant at what he thought utter want of feeling, half convinced by Lady Jane's logic. He had first known St. Julian at Rome, years before, and had been his friend all his life. He admired his genius, loved the girls, and was devoted to the mother: any trouble which befell them came home to him almost as a personal matter. . . .

'It is perfectly absurd,' the young lady went on. 'We have heard at home all was well! and I cannot sympathise with this mawkish sentimentality. I hate humbug. I'm a peculiar character, and I always disliked much ado about nothing. I am something of a stoic.'

'You heard by this mail?' said Lord Ulleskelf, anxiously.

'Of course we did,' said Lady Jane. 'I had written to my father to send me the letter. Here it is.' And she put it into his hand.

They had walked on side by side, and come almost in front of the house, with its open windows. Lady Jane was utterly vexed and put out. Hexham's look of annoyance when she had burst in a minute before was the last drop in her cup, and she now went on, in her jerky way,—

'Emilia is all very well; but really I do pity poor Bevis if this is the future in store for him—an anxious wife taking fright at every shadow. Mrs. St. Julian only encourages her in her want of self-control. It is absurd.'

Lord Ulleskelf, who had been examining the letter with some anxiety, folded it up. He was shocked and overcome. He confessed to me afterwards that he thought there was no necessity for sparing the feelings of a young lady so well able as Lady Jane to bear anxiety and to blame the over-sensitiveness of others. The letter was short, and about money affairs. In a postscript to the letter, Bevis said,—' Da Costa and Dubois want me to join a shooting expedition; but I shall not be able to get away.' This was some slight comfort, though to Lord Ulleskelf it only seemed a confirmation of his worst fears.

'It is not a shadow,' he said, gravely. 'If you like to look at this'—and he took a folded newspaper out of his pocket—'you will see why we have been so anxious for poor Emmy. Someone sent me a French paper, in which a paragraph had been copied from the Rio paper, containing an account of an accident to some young Englishman there. I have now, with some difficulty, obtained the original paper itself, with fuller particulars. You will see that this translation is added. I need not ask you to spare Mrs. Bevis a little longer, while the news is uncertain. The accident happened on the 2nd, four days before the steamer left. This letter is dated the 30th August, and must have been written before the accident happened.'

He turned away as he spoke, and left her standing there, poor woman, in the blaze of sunshine. Lady Jane never forgot that minute. The sea washed in the distance, a flight of birds flew overhead, the sun poured down. She stamped upon the crumbling gravel, and then, with an odd, choked sort of cry—hearing some of them coming—fairly ran into the house and upstairs and along the passage into the mistress's room, of which the door happened to be open.

This was the cry which brought Hester and Hexham out into the yard. I was in the drawing-room, when Lord Ulleskelf came in hurriedly, looking very much disturbed.

'Mrs. Campbell, for heaven's sake go to Lady Jane!' he cried. 'Do not let her alarm Emilia. I have been most indiscreet—much to blame. Pray go.'

I put down my work and hurried upstairs as he told me. As I went I could hear poor Lady Jane's sobs. I had reached the end of the gallery when I saw a door open, and a figure running towards the mistress's room. Then I knew I was too late, for it was Emmy, who from her mother's bedroom had also heard the cry.

'Mamma, something is wrong,' said Emilia, 'hold Bevvy for me!' And before her mother could prevent her she had put the child in her arms and run along the passage to see what was the matter.

How shall I tell the cruel pang which was waiting for her, running up unconscious to meet the stab. Lady Jane was sitting crying on Mrs. St. Julian's little sofa. When she saw Emmy she lost all presence of mind: she cried out, 'Don't, don't come, Emmy!—not you—not you!' Then jumping up she seized the newspaper and ran out of the room; but the translation Lord Ulleskelf had written out fell on the floor as she left, and poor frightened Emilia fearing everything took it up eagerly.

I did not see this—at least I only remembered it afterwards, for poor Lady Jane, meeting me at the door, seized hold of my arm, saying, 'Go back, go back! Oh take me to St. Julian!' The poor thing was quite distraught for some minutes. I took her to her room and tried to quiet her, and then I went, as she asked me, to look for my cousin. I ran down by the back way and the little staircase to the studio. It was empty, except that the little model and her mother were getting ready to go. The gentleman was gone, the child said: he had told her to come back next day. She was putting off her little quaint cloak, with her mother's help, in a corner of the big room. I hurried back to the house. On the stairs I found Hester, with her companion, and my mistress at the head of the stairs. Hester and Hexham both turned to me, and my mistress eagerly asked whether I had found St. Julian. I do not know how it was—certainly at the time I could not have described what was happening before my eyes;

but afterwards, thinking things over, I seemed to see a phantasmagoria of the events of the day passing before my eyes. I seemed to see the look of motherly sympathy and benediction with which, in all her pain for Emilia, Mrs. St. Julian turned to her Hester. I don't know if the two young folks had spoken to her. They were standing side by side, as people who had a right to one another's help; and afterwards, when I was alone, Hester's face came before me, sad, troubled, and yet illumined by the radiance of a new-found light.

I suppose excitement is a mood which stamps events clearly-marked and well-defined upon our minds. I think for the most part our lives are more wonderful, sadder, and brighter, more beautiful and picturesque, than we have eyes to see or ears to understand, except at certain moments when a crisis comes to stir slow hearts, to brighten dim eyes to sight, and dull ears to the sounds that vibrate all about. So it is with happy people, and lookers-on at the history of others: for those who are in pain a merciful shadow falls at first, hiding, and covering, and tempering the cruel pangs of fear and passionate regret.

XI

Emmy read the paper quite quietly, in a sort of dream. this old crumpled paper, lying on the table, in which she saw her husband's name printed. Her first thought was why had they kept it from her? Here was news, and they had not given it. Bevis Beverley! She even stopped for an instant to think what a pretty, strange name it was: stopped wilfully, with that sort of instinct we all have when we will not realise to ourselves that something of ill to those we love is at hand. Then she began to read, and at first she did not quite understand. A shooting-party had gone up the Paranà River; the boat was supposed to have overturned. The names, as well as they could gather, were as follows:—Don Manuel da Costa, Mr. P. Dubois, Mr. Bevis Beverley of the English Embassy, Mr. Stanmore, and Señor Antonio de Caita,— of whom not one had been saved. Emilia read it once quietly, only her heart suddenly began to beat, and the room to swing round and round; but even in the bewildering circles she clutched the paper and forced herself to read the dizzy words again. At first she did not feel very much, and even for an instant her mind glanced off to something else—to her mother waiting down below with little Bevis in her lap—then a great dark cloud began to descend quietly and settle upon the poor little woman, blotting out sunlight and landscape and colour. Emilia lost mental consciousness as the darkness closed in upon her, not bodily consciousness. She had a dim feeling as if someone had drawn a curtain across the window, so she told me afterwards. She was sitting in her mother's room, this she knew; but a terrible, terrible trouble was all about her, all around, everywhere, echoing in the darkness, and cold at her heart. Bevis, she wanted Bevis or her mother: they could send it away; and with a great effort she cried out, 'Mamma! mamma!' And at that instant somebody who had been talking to her, but whom she had not heeded, seemed to say, 'Here she is,' and in a minute more her mother's tender arms were round her, and Emilia coming to herself again looked up into that tender, familiar face.

'My darling,' said the mother, 'you must hope, and trust, and be brave. Nothing is confirmed; and we must pray and love one another, and have faith in a heavenly mercy. If it had been certain, do you think I should have kept it from you all this time?'

'How long?' said the parched lips; and Emilia turned in a dazed way from Mrs. St. Julian to Lady Jane, who had come back, and who was standing by with an odd, startled face, looking as pale almost as Emmy herself.

'Oh, Emmy, dear, dear Emmy, don't believe it, we have had a letter since. I shall never forgive myself as long as I live—never! I left it out; that hateful paper. Oh, dear! oh, dear! oh, dear!' sobbed poor Lady Jane, once more completely overcome, as she sank into a chair and hid her face in her hands.

Little Emilia made a great effort. She got up from

her seat with a piteous look; she went up to her sister-in-law and put her hand on her shoulder. 'Don't cry, Jane,' she said, trembling very much. 'Mamma says there is hope; and Bevis said I was to try and make the best of things. I had rather know,' said poor Emilia, turning sick and pale again. 'May I see your letter?'

Lady Jane was almost overawed by the gentle sweetness of these two women.

'How can you think of me just now? Oh, Emilia! I—I don't deserve it!' And she got up and a second time rushed out of the room.

Emmy's wonderful gentleness and self-control touched me more than I can express. She did not say much more, but went back to her mother, and knelt down and buried her face in her knees in a childish attitude, kneeling there still and motionless, while all the bright light came trembling and shining upon the two bent heads, and the sound of birds and of bleating sheep and shouting children came in at the open windows. I thought they were best alone, and left them, shutting the door. The house was silent and empty of the life which belonged to it, only it seemed to me crowded to suffocation by this great trouble and anxiety. This uncertainty was horrible. How would the time pass until the next mail came due? I was thankful from my heart to think that half the time had passed. Only I felt now at this moment that I must breathe, get out upon the downs, shake off the overpowering sense of sorrow, I could not but feel when those so dear and so near to me were in so much pain; but on my way, as I passed Lady Jane's door, some compunction made me pause for a moment, and knock and go in. Poor Lady Jane! She was standing at the toilette-table. She had opened her dressing-case to get out the letter which she had hidden away there only a few minutes before, and in so doing she seemed to have caught sight of her own face in the glass, frightened and strange, and unlike anything she had ever seen before. And so she stood looking in a curious stupid way at the tears slowly coursing down her cheeks. She started as I came in, and turned round.

'I—I am not used to this sort of thing,' said she. 'I have been feeling as if I was somebody else, Mrs. Campbell. I don't know what I ought to do. What do you think? Shall I take this in? Will it be of any comfort?'

'It will be of no comfort, I fear. It was written before—before that happened. But I fear it is of no use trying to keep anything from her now,' I said, and then together we went back to the door of the mistress's little room. Mrs. St. Julian put out her hand for the letter, and signed to us to go. Only as we walked away along the passage I heard a great burst of sobbing, and I guessed that it was occasioned by the sight of poor Bevis's well-known handwriting. Poor Lady Jane began to cry too, and then jerked her tears impatiently away, beginning to look like herself again.

'It's too absurd,' she said. 'All about nothing. Dear old Bevis! I am sure he will come back all safe. I have no patience with such silly frights. I am frightened too now; but there is no more danger than there was yesterday.'

I could not help thinking there was some sense in Lady Jane's cheerful view of things: after all it was the barest uncertainty and hint of evil, when all round, on every side, dangers of every sort were about each one of those whom we loved, from which no loving cares or prayers could shield them: a foot slips, a stone falls, and a heart breaks, or a life is ended, and what then? . . . A horrible vision of my own child—close, close to the edge of the dreadful cliff, came before me. I was nervous and infected too, with sad terrors and presentiments which the sight of the poor sweet young wife's misery had suggested.

Lady Jane, in her odd, decided way, said she must come out too. She could not bear the house, she could not bear to see the others.

She walked beside me with firm, even footsteps, occasionally telling me one thing and another of her favourite brother. Her flow of talk was interrupted: the real true heart within her seemed stirred by an unaffected sympathy for the trouble of the people with whom she was living. Her face seemed kindled, the hard look had gone out of it; for the first time I could imagine a likeness between her and her brother, and I began to feel a certain trust and reliance in this strange, wayward woman. After a little she was quite silent. We had a dreary little walk, pacing on together along the lane: how long the way seemed, how dull the hedges looked, how dreary the road! It seemed as if our walk had lasted for hours, but we had been out only a very little time. When we came in there was a three-cornered note addressed to Lady Jane lying on the hall table. 'A gentleman brought it,' said the parlour-maid; and I left Lady Jane to her correspondence, while I ran up to see how my two dear women were going on.

The day lagged on slowly: Emmy had got her little Bevis with her, and was lying-down in her own room while he played about. Mrs. St. Julian came and went, doing too much for her own strength; but I could not prevent her. She put me in mind of some bird hovering about her nest, as I met her again and again standing wistful and tender by her daughter's door, listening, and thinking what she could do more to ease her pain.

In the course of the afternoon St. Julian, who had been out when all this happened—having suddenly dismissed his model, and gone off for one of the long solitary tramps to which he was sometimes accustomed— came home to find the house in sad confusion. I think his presence was better medicine for Emmy than her mother's tender, wistful sympathy.

'I don't wonder at your being very uncomfortable,' he said; 'but I myself think there is a strong probability that your fears are unfounded. Bevis says most distinctly that he has refused to join the expedition. His name has been talked of: that is enough to give rise to a report that he is one of the party. . . . I would give you more sympathy if I did not think that it won't be wanted, my dear.' He pulled her little hand through his arm as he spoke, and patted it gently. He looked so tender, so encouraging, so well able to take care of the poor little thing, she clung to him closer and closer.

'Oh, my dearest papa,' she said, 'I will try, indeed I will!' And she hid her face, and tried to choke down her sobs.

I had prepared a beautiful tea for them, but neither Mrs. St. Julian nor Emilia appeared. Lady Jane came down, somewhat subdued, trying to keep up a desultory conversation, as if nothing had happened, which vexed me at the moment. Even little Bevis soon found out that something was wrong, and his little voice seemed hushed in the big wooden room.

And then the next day dawned, and another long day lagged on. St. Julian would allow no change to be made in the ways of the house. He was right, for any change would but have impressed us all more strongly with the certainty of misfortune. On Thursday we should hear our fate. It was but one day more to wait, and one long, dark, interminable night. Hexham did not mean to leave us: on the contrary, when St. Julian made some proposal of the sort, he said, in true heart-tones, 'Let me stay; do not send me away. Oh! St. Julian, don't I belong to you? I don't think I need tell you now that the one great interest of my life is here among you all.' The words touched St. Julian very much, and there could be no doubt of their loyalty. 'Let him stay, papa,' said Hester, gently. In his emotion the young man spoke out quite openly before us all. It was a time which constrained us all to be simple, from the very strength of our sympathy for the dear, and gentle, and stricken young wife above.

Little Bevis came down before dinner, and played about as usual. I was touched to see the tenderness which they all showed to him. His grandfather let him run into his studio, upset his colour-pots, turn over his canvasses—one of them came down with a great sound upon the floor. It was the picture of the two women at the foot of the beacon waiting together in suspense. Bevis went to bed as usual, and we dined as usual, but I shall never forget that evening, how endless and interminable it seemed. After dinner St. Julian, who had been up to see Emmy in her room, paced up and down the drawing-room, quite unnerved for once. 'My poor child,' he kept repeating; 'my poor child!'

The wind had arisen: we could hear the low roar of the

sea moaning against the shingle; the rain suddenly began to pour in the darkness outside, and the fire burnt low, for the great drops came down the chimney. Hexham did his best to cheer us. He was charming in his kindness and thoughtfulness. His manner to Hester was so tender, so gentle, at once humble and protecting, that I could only wonder that she held out as she did against its charm. She scarcely answered him, scarcely looked at him. She sat growing paler and paler. Was it that it seemed to her wrong, when her sister was in such sorrow and anxiety, to think of her own happiness, or concerns? It was something of this, for once in the course of the evening I heard her say to him,—

'I cannot talk to you yet. Will you wait?

'A lifetime,' said Hexham, in a low moved voice.

Hexham went away to smoke with St. Julian. I crossed the room and sat down by Hester, and put my arms round her. The poor child leant her head upon my shoulder. Lady Jane was with Emilia, who had sent for her. Long after they had all gone up sad and wearily to their rooms, I sat by the fire watching the embers burn out, one by one, listening to the sudden gusts of wind against the window-pane, to the dull rush of the sea breaking with loud cries and sobs.

All the events of the day were passing before me, over and over again: first one troubled face, then another; voice after voice echoing in my ears. Was there any hope anywhere in Hester's eyes? I thought; and they seemed looking up out of the fire into my own, as I sat there drowsily and sadly.

It was about two o'clock, I think, when I started; for I heard a sound of footsteps coming. A tall white-robed woman, carrying a lamp, came into the room, and advanced and sat down beside me. It was poor Lady Jane. All her cheerfulness was gone, and I saw now what injustice I had done her, and how she must have struggled to maintain it; she looked old and haggard suddenly.

'I could not rest,' she said. 'I came down—I thought you might be here. I couldn't stay in my room listening to that dreadful wind.' Poor thing, I felt for her. I made up the fire once more, and we two kept a dreary watch for an hour and more, till the wind went down and the sea calmed, and Lady Jane began to nod in her arm-chair.

XII.

I awoke on the Thursday morning, more hopeful than I had gone to bed. I don't know why, for there was no more reason to hope either more or less than there had been the night before. On Thursday or on Friday the French mail would come with news: that was our one thought. We still tried to go on as usual, as if nothing was the matter. The bells rang, the servants came and went with stolid faces. It is horrible to say, but already at the end of these few interminable hours it seemed as if we were getting used to this new state of things. Emilia still kept upstairs. Lady Jane paced about in her restless way: from one room to another, from one person to another, she went. Sometimes she would burst out into indignation against Lady Mountmore, who had driven poor Bevis to go. She had influenced his father, Lady Jane declared, and prevented him from advancing a certain sum which he had distinctly promised to Bevis before his marriage. 'A promise is a promise,' said Lady Jane, 'The poor boy was too proud to ask for his rights. He only went, I do believe, to escape that horrid Ephraim. We behaved like brutes, every one of us. I am just as bad as the rest,' said the poor lady.

It was as she said. One day in June, when the Minister had sent to Mr. F., of the Foreign Office, to ask who was next on the list of Queen's messengers, it was found that the gentleman first in order had been taken ill only the day before; the second after him was making up his book for the Derby next year.

Poor Bevis—who was sitting disconsolately wondering how it would be possible to him to take up that bill of Ephraim's, which was daily appearing more terrible and impossible to meet—had heard St. Gervois and De Barty, the two other men in his room, discussing the matter, and announcing in very decided language their intention of remaining in London for the rest of the season, instead of starting off at a moment's notice with despatches to some unknown President in some unknown part of South America.

Bevis said nothing, but got up and left the room. A few minutes after he came back looking very pale. 'You fellows,' he said, 'I shall want you to do a few things for me. I start for Rio to-morrow.'

'Mr. St. Gervois told me all about it,' poor Lady Jane said, with a grunt, as she told me the story.

This sudden determination took the Mountmores and Mr. Ephraim by surprise, and as I have said, it was on this occasion that Lady Jane spoke up on her brother's behalf, and that Emilia, after his departure, was formally recognised by his family. 'If he,—when he comes back,' cried Lady Jane, in a fume, ' my father, in common decency, must increase his allowance.' A sudden light came into her face as she spoke. The thought of anything to do or to say for Bevis was a gleam of comfort to the poor sister.

All that day was a feverish looking for news. St. Julian had already started off to London that morning in search of it. Once I saw the telegraph-boy from Tarmouth coming along the lane. I ran down eagerly, but Lady Jane was beforehand, and had pocketed the despatch which the servant had brought her. 'It is nothing,' she said, ' and only concerns me.' A certain conscious look seemed to indicate Sigourney. But I asked no questions. I went on in my usual plodding way, putting by candles and soap, serving out sugar. Sometimes now when I stand in the store-closet I remember the odd double feeling with which I stood there that Thursday afternoon, with my heart full of sympathy, and then would come a sudden hardness of long use to me, looking back at the storms of life through which I had passed. A hard, cruel feeling, of the inevitable laws of fate came over me. What great matter was it: one more life struck down, one more innocent happiness blasted, one more parting; were we not all of us used to it, was anyone spared ever? . . . One by one we are sent forth into the storm, alone to struggle through its fierce battlings till we find another shelter, another home, where we may rest for a little while, until the hour comes when once more we are driven out. It was an evil frame of mind, and a thankless one, for one who had found friends, a shelter, and help when most in need of them. As I was still standing among my stores that afternoon, Aileen came to the door, looking a little scared. 'Queenie,' she said, 'Emilia is not in her room. Lady Jane, too, has been out for ever so long. Her maid tells me that she had a telegraphic message from that Captain Sigourney. Is it not odious of her now, at such a time? Oh, she can't have—can't have——'

'Eloped?' I said, smiling. 'No, Aileen, I do not think there is much fear.'

As time went on, however, and neither of them reappeared, I became a little uneasy. Lady Jane's maid when questioned knew nothing of her mistress's intentions. Bevis was alone with his nurse, contentedly stocking a shop in his nursery out of her work-box. But it was not for Lady Jane that I was anxious—she could take care of herself; it was Emilia I was looking for. I put on my bonnet, and set off to try and find her. Hester and Hexham said they would go towards Ulleshall, and see if she was there.

I walked up the down, looking on every side. I thought each clump of furze was Emilia; but at last, high up by the beacon, I saw a dark figure against the sky.

Yes, it was Emilia up there, with beaten garments and with wind-blown hair. She had unconsciously crouched down to escape the fierce blast. She was looking out seawards, at the dull tossing horizon. It seemed to me such an image of desolation that it went to my heart to see her so. I called her by her name, and ran up and put my hand upon her shoulder.

'My dear,' I said, 'we have been looking for you everywhere.'

Emilia gave a little start. She had not heard me call.

'I could not rest at home,' she said. 'I don't know what brought me here. I think I ran almost all the way.'

She spoke with a trembling desperateness that frightened me. Two nights of sleeplessness, and these long maddening hours, were enough to daze the poor child. If she were to break down? But gentle things like Emilia bend and rise again.

'Come home now, dear Emilia,' I said; 'it is growing dark. Your mother will be frightened about you.'

'Ah! people are often frightened when there is nothing to fear,' said Emilia, a little strangely.

I could see that she was in a fever. Her cheeks were burning, while I was shivering: for the cold winds came eddying from the valley, and sweeping round and round us, making the beacon creak as they passed. The wind was so chill, the sky so grey, and the green murky sea so dull at our feet, that I longed to get her away. It seemed to me much later than it really was. The solitude oppressed me. There was no life anywhere—no boats about. Perhaps they were lost in the mist that was writhing along from the land, and spreading out to sea. I cannot say why it was so great a relief to me at last to see one little dark speck coming across the straits where the mist was not drifting. The sight of life—for boats are life to people looking out with lonely eyes—this little dark grey speck upon the waters seemed to me to make the blast less dreary, and the lonely heights less lonesome.

We began our walk back in silence. Emilia's long blue cloak flapped in the wind, but I pulled it close about her. She let me do as I liked. She didn't speak. Once I said to her,—' Emilia, do you know, when I came up just now, I thought you looked like the picture your father painted. Do you remember it?'

' I—I forget,' said poor Emilia, turning away her face suddenly. All her strength seemed to have left her; her limbs seemed scarcely able to drag along; her poor little feet slipped and stumbled on the turf and against the white chalk-stones. I put my arm round her waist and helped her along as best I could, as we crept down the side of the hill.

' I think I cannot walk because my heart is so heavy,' said Emilia once in her childish way, and her head dropped on my shoulder. I hardly can tell what I feared for her, or what I hoped. Sleeplessness and anxiety were enemies too mighty for this helpless little frame to encounter.

I was confused and frightened, and I took a wrong turning. It brought us to the end of a field where a gate had once stood, which was now done away with. We could not force through the hedges and the palings: there was nothing to do but to turn back. It seems childish to record, but when I found that we must retrace so many of our weary steps, stumbling back all the way, in one of those biting gusts of wind, I burst out crying from fatigue, and sympathy, and excitement. It seemed all so dreary and so hopeless. Emilia roused herself, seeing me give way. Poor child, her sweet natural instincts did not desert her, even in her own bewildered pain. She took hope suddenly, trying to find strength to help me.

'Oh, Queenie,' she said. 'Think if we find, to-morrow, that all is well, and that all this anxiety has been for nothing. But it could not be for nothing, could it?' she said.

It is only another name for something greater and holier than anxiety, I thought; but I could not speak, for I was choking, and I had not yet regained command of my own voice. Our walk was nearly over; we got out on to the lane, and so approached our home. At the turn of the road I saw a figure standing looking for us. A little figure, with hair flying on the gale, who, as we appeared, stumbling and weary, sprang forward to meet us; then suddenly stopped, turned, and fled, with fluttering skirts and arms outstretched, like a spirit of the wind. I could not understand it, nor why my little Missie (for it was her) should have run away. Even this moment's sight of her, in the twilight, did me good and cheered me. How well I remember it all. The dark rustling hedges, a pale streak of yellow light in the west shining beyond the hedge, and beyond the stem of the hawthorn-tree. It gleamed sadly and weirdly in the sky, among clouds of darkness and vaporous shadows; the earth reflected the light faintly at our feet, more brightly in the garden, which was higher than the road. Emilia put out her hand, and pulled herself wearily up the steps which led to the garden. It was very dark, but in the light from the stormy gleam she saw something which made her cry out. I myself pulled Emilia back, with some exclamation, being still confused and not knowing what dark figure it was standing before me in the gloaming; but Emilia burst away from me with a cry, with a low passionate sob. She flew from me straight into two arms that caught her. My heart was beating, my eyes were full of tears, so that I could scarcely see what had happened.

But I heard a low 'Bevis! Oh, Bevis!' For a moment I stood looking at the two standing clinging together. The cold wind still came in shrill gusts, the grey clouds still drifted, the sun-streak was dying: but peace, light, love unspeakable were theirs, and the radiance from their grateful hearts seemed to overflow into ours.

XIII.

'Where is Lady Jane?' interrupted Hexham, coming home in the twilight, from a fruitless search with Hester, to hear the great news. It was so great, so complete, so unexpected, that we none of us quite realised it yet. We were strangely silent; we looked at each other: some sat still; the younger ones went vaguely rushing about the house, from one end to the other. Aileen and Missie were like a pair of mad kittens, dancing and springing from side to side. It was pretty to see Hester rush in, tremulous, tender, almost frightened by the very depth of her sympathy. The mother was holding Emilia's hand, and turning from her to Bevis.

'Oh, Bevis, if you knew what three days we have spent,' said Hester, flinging her arms round him.

'Don't let us talk about it any more,' said he, kissing her blooming cheek, and then he bent over the soft mother's hand that trembled out to meet his own.

It was not at first that we any of us heard very clearly what had happened, for Emilia turned so pale at first when her husband began speaking of that fatal expedition in the boat up the Paraná River, that he abruptly changed the subject, and began describing the road from London to Tarmouth, instead of dwelling on his escape from the accident, or the wonders of that country from whence he had come—an unknown land to us all, of mighty streams and waving verdure; of great flowers, and constellations, and mysterious splashings and stirrings along the waters: Emmy turned pale, and Bevis suddenly began to describe his journey from Waterloo to Tarmouth, and his companion from London.

'A fellow gets suspicious,' said honest Bevis, recounting his adventure. 'But I can't understand the fellow now. He seemed dodging me about, and I only got away from him by a chance. I don't mind so much now that I have seen you, little woman. Ephraim may have a dozen writs out against me, for all I know. I thought there was something uncomfortable about the man the moment I saw him; and I asked the porter at the Foreign Office not to tell him anything about me. I may have been mistaken,' Bevis ended, shrugging his shoulders, ' since here I am. But if not to-day, that confounded old Ephraim will have me to-morrow. I only put off the evil day by running away. Well, I've brought back Jane's hundred pounds, and I have seen my little woman again, and the boy, and all of you, and now I don't care what happens.'

'Hush,' said Mrs. St. Julian: ' my husband must help you. Your father has written to him. You should have come to us.'

'I believe I acted like a fool,' said Beverley, penitently. ' Perhaps I fancied things worse than they were. I couldn't bear to come sponging on St. Julian, and I was indignant at the things they said at home, and—is Jane here, do you say?'

We were all getting seriously uneasy? Lady Jane had disappeared. Her maid brought in a telegram she had found in her room, which seemed to throw some vague light upon her movements.

' *Captain Sigourney, Waterloo Station, to Lady Jane Beverley, Tarmouth, Broadshire.*

'I implore you to meet me at Tarmouth. I come by the four o'clock boat. I have news of your brother.

('Signed) SIGOURNEY.'

'Sigourney!' cried Bevis, 'who the devil is Sigourney?'

There was a dead silence, and nobody knew exactly what to say next. All our anxiety and speculation were allayed before dinner by the return of the pony-carriage with a hasty note from Lady Jane herself:

'Dearest Mrs. St. Julian,—Kind Captain Sigourney has been to London enquiring for us. He has heard confidentially, from a person at the Foreign Office, that my brother *has been heard of* by this mail. He thought it best to come to me straight, and I have decided to go off to London immediately. I shall probably find my father at home in Bruton Street. I will write to-morrow. Fond love to dearest Emilia.

'Your affectionate, anxious

'JANE BEVERLEY.'

'But what does it all mean?' cried Bevis, in a fume. 'What business has Captain Sigourney with my safety?' And it was only by degrees that he could be appeased at all.

'This fire won't burn!' cried Missie.

There is a little pine-wood growing not far from the Lodges, where Aileen and Missie sometimes boil a kettle and light a fire of dry sticks, twigs, and fir-cones. The pine-wood runs up the side of a steep hill that leads to the down.

In the hollow below lie bright pools glistening among wet mosses and fallen leaves and pine-twigs; but the abrupt sides of the little wood are dry and sandy, and laced and overrun by a network of slender roots that go spreading in every direction. In between the clefts and jagged fissures of the ground the sea shines, blue and gleaming, while the white ships, like birds, seem to slide in between the branches. The tea-party was in honour of Bevis's return, the little maidens said. They had transported cups and cloths, pats of butter and brown loaves, all of which good things were set out on a narrow ledge; while a little higher, the flames were sparkling, and a kettle hanging in the pretty thread of smoke. Missie, on her knees, was piling sticks and cones upon the fire; Aileen was busy spreading her table; and little Bevis was trotting about picking up various little shreds and stones that took his fancy, and bringing them to poke into the bright little flame that was crackling and sparkling and growing every moment more bright.

Bevis and Emilia were the hero and heroine of the entertainment. Hexham was fine, Aileen said, and would not take an interest, and so he was left with Hester pasting photographs in the dining-room, while the rest of us came off this bright autumnal afternoon to camp in the copse. The sun still poured unwearied over the country, and the long delightful summer seemed unending. It was during this picnic tea-drinking that I heard more than I had hitherto done of Mr. Beverley's adventures.

'This kettle *won't* boil!' said Missie.

And while Bevis was good-naturedly poking and stirring the flames, Emilia began in a low, frightened voice: —'Oh, Queenie, even now I can hardly believe it. He has been telling me all about it. He finished his work sooner than he expected. The poor General was shot with whom he was negotiating: he found that there was nothing more for him to do, and that he might as well take his passage by the very next ship. And then, to pass the time, he went off with those other poor men for a couple of days' shooting, and then they met a drove of angry cattle swimming across the stream, and they could not get out of the way in time, and two were drowned,' faltered Emilia; 'but when dear Bevis came to himself, he had floated a long way down the stream. He had been unconscious, but bravely clinging to an oar all the time . . . and then he scrambled on shore and wandered on till he got to a wooden house belonging to two young men, who took him in,—but he had had a blow on the head, and he was very ill for three days, and the steamer was gone when he got back to Rio—and that was how it was.'

As she ceased she caught hold of little Bevis, who was trotting past her, and suddenly clutched him to her heart. How happy she was! a little frightened still, even in her great joy, but with smiles and lights in her radiant face,—

her very hair seemed shining as she sat under the pine-trees, sometimes looking up at her husband, or with proud eyes following Bevvy's little dumpling figure as he busily came and went.

'Here is Hexham, after all,' cried big Bevis from the heights, looking down as he spoke, and Hexham's head appeared from behind a bank of moss and twigs.

'Why, what a capital gipsy photograph you would all make,' cried the enthusiastic Hexham as he came up. 'I have brought you some letters. Hester is coming directly with William St. Julian, who has just arrived.'

'I really don't think we can give you all cups,' said Aileen, busily pouring from her boiling kettle into her teapot. 'You know I didn't expect you.'

Bevis took all the letters and began to read them out :—

I.

'*Lord Mountmore to the Hon. Bevis Beverley.*

'Friday.

'My dear Boy,—The news of your safe return from Rio has relieved us all from a most anxious state of mind. You have had a providential escape, upon which we most warmly and heartily congratulate you. With regard to the subject of your letter, I am willing to accede to your request, and to allow you once more the same sum that you have always had hitherto. I will also assist you to take up the bill, if you will give me your solemn promise never to have anything more to do with the Jews. Jane has pleaded your cause so well that I cannot refuse her. My lady desires her love.

' Your affectionate father,
' M——.

' Jane is writing, so I send no message from her. She arrived, poor girl, on Thursday in a most distressed state of mind. I hope we shall see you here with your wife before long.'

II.

Unknown Friend, Ch. Coll., Cambridge, to George Hexham, Esq., The Island, Tarmouth.

'My dear George,—I have been expecting this letter ever since I received your last, from which, by the bye, one page was missing. Farewell, O friend of my bachelorhood. Seriously, I long to see you, and to hear all about it. I must also beg to congratulate the future Mrs. Hexham upon having secured the affections of one of the best and truest-hearted of men. I have no doubt she fully deserves her good fortune.

' Ever, my dear fellow, affectionately yours,
'—— ——.'

III.

*Mrs. William St. Julian, Kensington Square,
to Mrs. St. Julian, Tarmouth.*

'My dearest Mrs. St. Julian,—I send this by William, who cannot rest until he has seen you all and told you how heartfelt are our sympathies and congratulations. How little we thought, as we drove off on Monday morning, of all that was at hand. It seems very *unfeeling* as I look back now. I shall feel quite nervous until William comes back, but he has promised to take a return-ticket to reassure me. I am quite surprised by the news you send me this morning of Hester's engagement. I always had my own ideas, though I did not speak of them (we quiet people often see a good deal more than people imagine), and I quite expected that Lady Jane would have been the lady. However, it is much better as it is, and Mr. Hexham is, I have no doubt, all you could wish for dear Hester Do give my best and kindest congratulations to dear Emilia. How delighted she must have been to get the good news of her husband's safety. I hope it was not too much for her,—excitement is very apt to knock one up. The children send a hundred loves and kisses.

'Believe me,

'Your affectionate daughter,

'Margaret St. Julian.'

'P.S.—I have had a visit from a very delightful Captain Sigourney. He called upon me to ask for news of you all. It seems he escorted Lady Jane to town, and that in consequence of information he had received at the Foreign Office he was able to be of great service to her, although the information afterwards turned out incorrect. A person there had assured him that Mr. Beverley had been in town some time, and had returned to South America for good. What strange reports get about! One should be very careful never to believe anybody.'